SERVICES FOR DEVELOPMENTALLY DISABLED ADULTS

SERVICES FOR DEVELOPMENTALLY DISABLED ADULTS
Development, Implementation, and Evaluation

by
Robert L. Schalock, Ph.D.
Chairman, Department of Psychology
Hastings College;
Program Consultant
Mid-Nebraska Mental Retardation Services;
Adjunct Research Professor of
Medical Psychology
The University of Nebraska Medical Center

University Park Press
Baltimore

UNIVERSITY PARK PRESS
International Publishers in Medicine and Human Services
300 North Charles Street
Baltimore, Maryland 21201

Typeset by Brushwood Graphics
Manufactured in the United States of America
by The Maple Press Company

Library of Congress Cataloging in Publication Data

Schalock, Robert L.
Services for developmentally disabled adults.

Includes bibliography references and index.
1. Developmentally disabled—Services for—Management. 2. Social work administration. I. Title. [DNLM: 1. Community mental health services—Organization and administration. 2. Handicapped. 3.Mental retardation—In adulthood. 4. Rehabilitation. HV 3004 S298s]
HV3004.S3 1983 362.1'968 82-246798
ISBN 0-8391-1819-8

CONTENTS

PREFACE

Many administrators of programs for developmentally disabled individuals that I know are frustrated because of what they refer to as their "journey into incompetence." Few have had formal training in program management; yet all are expected to be financial wizards, public relations experts, program specialists, personnel directors, creative writers, standards setters, and evaluation experts. This book is directed and dedicated to those administrators. It is also intended for use within Human Service Administration training programs, with which I have been associated for the last 5 years. These training programs have developed in response to the growing need to train program administrators in administrative skills and to help them acquire an understanding of the economic, political, social, and psychological aspects of human needs and services. It is hoped that this book will give these students the necessary competencies so that their involvement is not a "journey into incompetence." Simply put, we can no longer afford either incompetence or the phenomenal burnout rate we now see in human service programs. The 1980s will be a decade of tight financial resources, in which only accountable programs will survive. To be accountable, a program must be well managed and have measurability and reportability—two recurrent themes of this book.

The book focuses on the major problems an administrator must overcome in planning, implementing, monitoring, and evaluating services for developmentally disabled adults. Although the emphasis is on services for developmentally disabled citizens, the author's experience with education, mental health, aging, and alcohol programs suggests that problems and solutions are common across categorical groupings. Section I deals first with understanding an organization and why agencies frequently act like a rat in a Skinner Box—sometimes pressing the bar, sometimes backing off in distrust or ignorance, and at other times remaining inactive. Chapter 2 sensitizes the reader to the needs and environmental demands of developmentally disabled persons and to community attitudes. With that knowledge in hand, strategic planning (Chapter 3) can begin, resulting in the formulation of an organization's philosophy, goals, objectives, and anticipated products. Chapter 4 moves the reader from strategic to process planning and discusses how administrators can direct available resources, technology, and staff toward implementing the specific programmatic services necessary to meet the organization's goals and desired outputs.

Section II focuses on specific implementation strategies. Chapter 5 begins with the words, "Becoming operational is easier said than done," but this should not prevent us from trying. Accordingly, the chapter outlines steps required to become operational, including fulfilling legal requirements, becoming financially solvent, providing for comprehensive services, and developing a data base. Chapter 6 concentrates on identifying potential barriers and suggests specific problem-solving strategies to help overcome the frequent and multi-faceted problems administrators encounter. Staff development and retention, and prevention of burnout are the themes of Chapter 7. Staff-related issues are the biggest frustration encountered by any program administrator.

Section III emphasizes managing, monitoring, and evaluating services. Chapter 8 stresses the distinction between the administrator as a developer or implementor, and the administrator as manager, and discusses a number of management skills that should generalize across an organization's planning, implementing, monitoring, and evaluating phases. Monitoring programs and processes for the purposes of improving their effectiveness and efficiency is the subject of Chapter 9. Chapter 10 elaborates on the importance of monitoring as a permanent management tool and outlines the major steps involved in client and program evaluation. In this regard, administrators are currently confronted with seemingly overwhelming but, in the author's opinion, not unexpected, demands. Not only are administrators required increasingly to account for and evaluate (re)habilitative services, which has forced them to become educated in performance audits, weighted closure systems, and cost-benefit analysis, but they are also expected to be experts in program evaluation so that they can know, for example, whether to focus on formative or summative evaluation, which specific outcome measures to use, and which program evaluation research designs are feasible. That administrators have to date been hard pressed to satisfy the above demands helps explain why even though we know something about the quantity of (re)habilitation services being provided, and the approximate cost of those services, we still do not have a precise understanding of the outcome of the large investment made. The specific evaluation strategies outlined in Chapter 10 will help resolve this administrative dilemma.

The book concludes with a look in Chapter 11 at the decades ahead and suggests that the future will be brighter both for developmentally disabled persons and for the programs that serve them if we move toward a comprehensive service delivery system. Integral to such a system is the application of sound management principles that will improve the measurability, reportability, and accountability of programs.

The essence of "handicapism," in the author's opinion, is a person's lack of independence, productivity, and social acceptance. If sound rehabilitation, economic, and management principles are not incorporated into human service programs, we may well find ourselves in the position of fostering in our clientele personal and economic dependence rather than growth and economic independence. I hope this book helps prevent that calamity.

Robert L. Schalock

ACKNOWLEDGMENTS

A book and its author evolve in ways analogous to the Piagetian concepts of assimilation and accommodation. Input to the author has come primarily from the training needs of the Mid-Nebraska Mental Retardation Services clientele, the programmatic needs of the Mid-Nebraska staff, and the accountability needs of a number of program administrators with whom I have worked. The author is indebted to all the persons involved in the above endeavors, and especially to Roger Harper, who has been both a colleague and mentor. In addition, a number of professional colleagues have been instrumental in the author's growth and development. Appreciation and respect are directed to Drs. John Copenhaver, Orv Karan, Frank Menolascino, and Jack Stark for their stimulation, support, and friendship.

To my students and the Mid-Nebraska staff who made me think; to the clients who kept me humble; to my wife who made me laugh; and to my parents who made the above possible.

SERVICES FOR DEVELOPMENTALLY DISABLED ADULTS

Section I

DEVELOPING SERVICES

Developing programmatic services for the developmentally disabled adult can be confusing, frustrating, and nonproductive, especially if you do not know where to begin or what to do. The first five chapters of this book provide a starting point for answering both of these questions by introducing you to characteristics of organizations, the needs of developmentally disabled persons, strategic and process planning activities, and the development of training programs aimed at increasing your clientele's independence, productivity, and social acceptance. Simply reading these chapters will not make you an organization or program expert; you will, however, be initiated into the complex world of the developmentally disabled person and provided suggestions on how to plan programs that will meet these persons' needs for growth and development, and your organization's requirements for measurability, reportability, and accountability. Do not be surprised if the principles presented apply to other clinical populations and service delivery programs. All persons need to feel independent, productive, and socially acceptable; similarly, all organizations should be accountable to their heterogeneous constituency.

1
ORGANIZATIONAL BEHAVIOR

> *. . . client-serving organizations may well be quite far along the road to becoming voluntary associations in the sense that the needs and expectations of the clients become the goals of the organization staff and the determinants of the pattern of work which develops.*
>
> *(Perrow, 1970)*

Welcome to the world of organizational behavior! Organizations are like people: they vary in complexity, flexibility, friendliness, effectiveness, and efficiency. While this book is not designed to treat organizational behavior in-depth, it will explore some important insights on general organizational characteristics gleaned from my experiences with human service programs. While not exhaustive, these characteristics are intended to encourage an appreciation of the dynamics and potential present in your organization so that you may become a more competent administrator and your organization a more effective and efficient service-provider.

ORGANIZATIONAL CHARACTERISTICS

Among the most significant organizational characteristics in terms of the quality of services provided include the organization's philosophy and resources, the approach it takes to people, how it responds to its heterogeneous constituency, the information systems it employs, how its design relates to staff behavior, its use of a supplemental management resource team, and its key players. Each of these characteristics is discussed in some detail below.

Philosophy and Technology

Organizational development and operation can usually be reduced to the two basic issues of philosophy and technology. Philosophically, the organization will find itself somewhere along a continuum regarding such issues as normalization, dehumanization, least restrictive environment, deinstitutionalization, dignity of risk, developmental model and domains, adaptive behavior, individual program plans, interdisciplinary teams, and advocacy. Our society has made significant progress over the last two decades toward overcoming such philosophical "isms" as racism, sexism, handicapism, and ageism; however, value clarification is still necessary to discourage discrimination in all its forms and, in regard to severely and profoundly handicapped persons specifically, to encourage their participation to the maximum extent possible in the "normal" environment.

Modern technology related to instrumentation, sophisticated programming techniques, and prosthetic devices is frequently overlooked in programs for developmentally disabled persons. There is increasing recognition, however, that a handicapped person's inability is often environmentally-based, and that the "mismatch" between a person and his or her environment can be reduced through behavioral skill training, prosthetic usage, and/or environmental modification. For example, alternate communication systems, prosthetic sensorimotor systems, and prosthetic cognitive systems such as calculators and cue-response memory techniques can reduce appreciably the extent of a person's handicapping condition. Unfortunately, human service organizations have been slow to implement these approaches, partly because of orientation, training, and the cost of a highly labor-intensive profession. Finances can be a crucial problem, especially as increasing numbers of organizations compete for scarcer resources. But, as an administrator once told me, "if you don't shoot for the moon, you won't hit the top of the bank."

Upstream or Downstream Approach

Many human service organizations have focused to date more on the care, custody, or maintenance of the status quo of handicapped persons than on rehabilitation. For example, in 1977, 15.5 billion federal dollars were spent on income maintenance and support of handicapped individuals, whereas only 2.8 billion federal dollars were spent on rehabilitation training and employment (Whitehead, 1981). This trend, which is consistent with mental health center funding that typically allocates 87% for direct services and only 13% for prevention (Egan and Cowan, 1979), reflects our "downstream" service delivery model for curing sick people rather than an "upstream" preventive and skill development model.

The downstream or "curing" approach has its origin in a number of phenomena, including over-reliance on the medical model, emphasis on individualistic or "person psychology," and insensitivity to the social-ecological context within which people live and behave (Egan and Cowan, 1979). Increasingly, however, organizations are providing services to developmentally disabled persons that stress an "upstream" approach, which is characterized by an emphasis on skill development and the interfacing of persons with their environments.

The Heterogeneous Constituency

One of the primary reasons some administrators have become an endangered species is their failure to acknowledge or appreciate the conflicting expectations of their organization's constituency. As shown in Figure 1.1, the basic constituents of

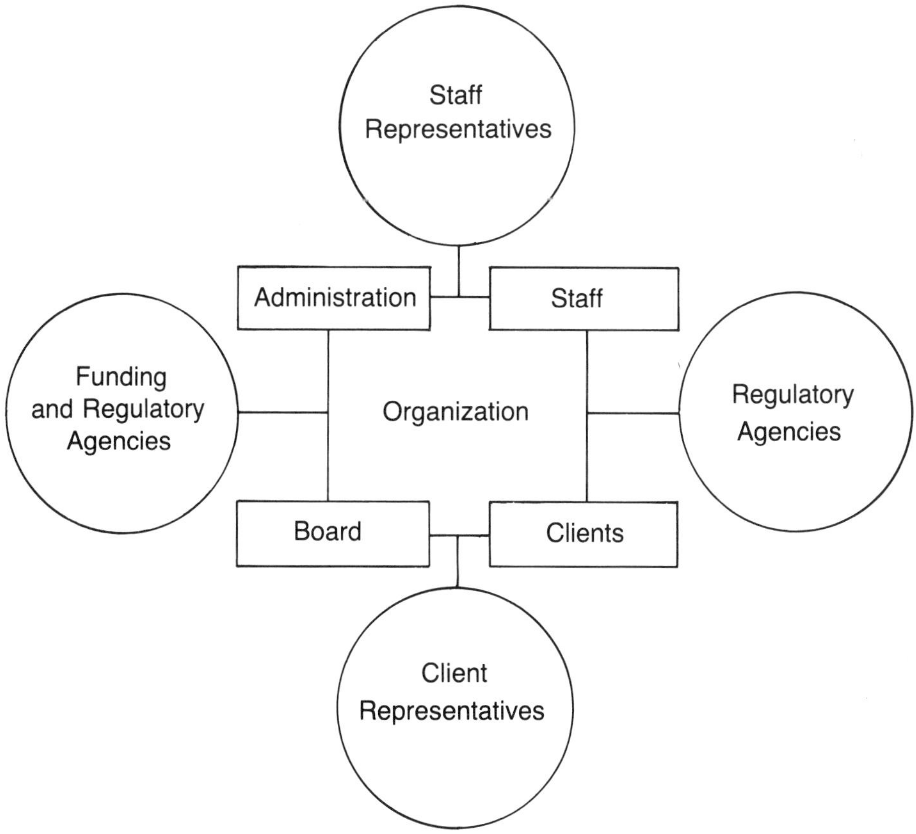

Figure 1.1. An organization's heterogeneous constituency.

most agencies include clients, staff, administrators, and the board of directors. Each has its own needs, demands, and accountability requirements. But that is only part of the picture; in addition, there are ancillary constituents such as funding and regulatory agencies, community supporters, and client-staff representatives, all of whom have their own demands and accountability requirements that frequently conflict with those of the basic constituents. For example: the fire marshal may require red exit markers and fire extinguishers that the staff regard as "non-normalizing"; city health officials may require plastic garbage cans, whereas state health departments require metal; parents may demand protection and safety, whereas advocates stress independence and the dignity of risk; staff may stress behavior modification, while advocates stress humanism; and staff or professional representatives may focus on working conditions and professional service standards, while the administrator asks "How can I fund or deal with that?" Probably, no one forewarned the administrator of the organization's heterogeneous constituents or "alligators," to use a well-worn aphorism; all organizations have them and each administrator must deal with them. It is hoped that the techniques and procedures suggested throughout this book will help to remove successful administrators from the endangered species list.

The Information System

Despite the reams of forms and paperwork that human service organizations must process, they are often still criticized for lack of measurability, reportability, and accountability. If appropriate documentation is the problem, perhaps what is needed is a more functional, easy-to-access information system rather than more file cabinets. The major purpose of any information system is to improve the *management* of the organization; a corollary is that sound management requires good, valid information.

The management information system proposed in this book stems from systems analysis that relates the systems variables of input, process, and output to program management. This relationship is depicted in Figure 1.2 which illustrates that an organization needs feedback in order to improve its service delivery. Organizations should not be afraid of evaluation. As reflected in both the management information system and the program evaluation strategies presented in Chapter 10, data can be your best friend. However, to retrieve the data, the system has to be up and running long enough to generate meaningful, longitudinal feedback. Too frequently, I find that an organization reacts to a crisis or new situation by "changing the system" in a *reactive* fashion rather than in a systematic, data-based *proactive* manner.

Organizational Design and Staff Behavior

Human service organizations are usually characterized by low salaries and high attrition. There is increasing sensitivity to the fact that staff motivation and performance are directly affected by the organization's power and normative

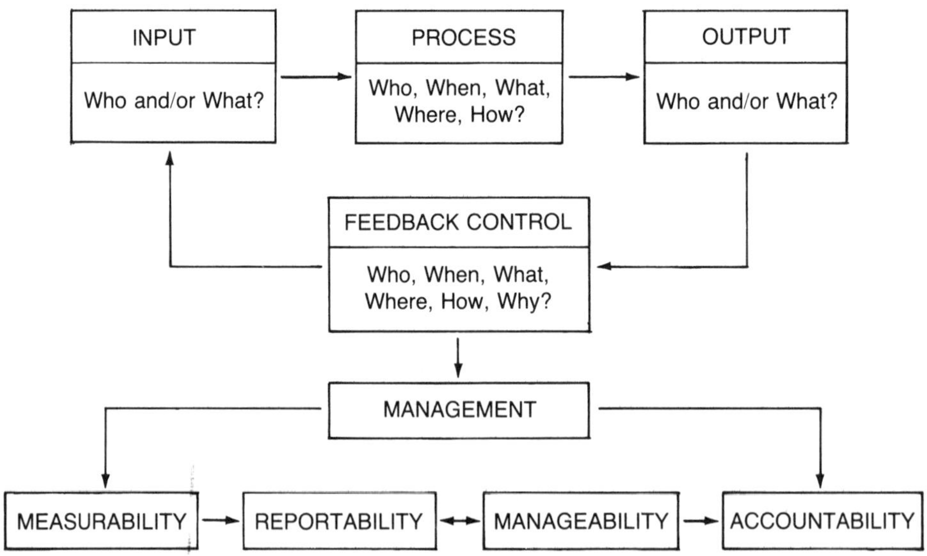

Figure 1.2. Systems variables related to program management.

structures (Cherniss, 1980a). For example, job satisfaction and motivation are directly related to the presence of job satisfiers such as variety, autonomy, feedback, challenge, responsibility, achievement, and recognition. Staff may also be influenced by job ''hygiene'' or maintenance factors such as supervisor attitudes, salary, work load, working conditions, and organizational policy—all of which can become dissatisfiers if they are inadequate (Herzberg, Mausner, and Snyderman, 1959).

It has been my experience (and I am sure yours) that high staff ''burnout'' and turnover cause considerable instability, generating phenomenal costs in productivity, staff training needs, program stability, and client behavior. Sometimes it is necessary for an organization to alter its style and philosophy in order to accommodate the staff's need to be involved, to feel a part of the management team, and to be challenged. This requires that the organization change some of its role and power structure, as well as work to ensure that staff espouse similar attitudes about the values, goals, and beliefs of the organization. More about this later in Chapter 7, ''Staff Development.'' The point to remember is: An organization can change.

Supplemental Management Resource Team

Organizations are highly complex and, therefore, program administrators must be competent (or at least knowledgeable) as to legal, financial, and programmatic issues. Recall, however, the ''journey to incompetence'' concept discussed in this book's Preface. The sign of a good administrator, and the distinguishing characteristic of a functional organization, is the use of what I call a ''supplemental management resource team.'' Such a team functions at the analysis level of organizational behavior, and contributes directly to management decisions. As shown in Figure 1.3, management can take this input and transform it into specific policies and procedures implemented at the detail level by a bookkeeper, case manager, data processor, or diagnostic-programmer. As emphasized throughout this book, the supplemental management team is critical in all phases of organizational life, including planning, implementing, monitoring, and evaluation.

The Key Players and the *Zeitgeist*

Have you ever wondered why some organizations move forward, some stagnate, and still others regress? The key factor in progress may depend on what Anderson (1975) refers to as a latent division of labor that all social movements need—including a theoretician, a promoter, an organizer, and a core action group. The *theoretician* is the visionary or idea person. The *promoter* is one who gets people excited, involved, and active. The *organizer* takes over at this point and channels the core action group into service planning and delivery. The recent social movement involving deinstitutionalization and mainstreaming of handicapped individuals reflects just such a division of labor (Stark, 1978).

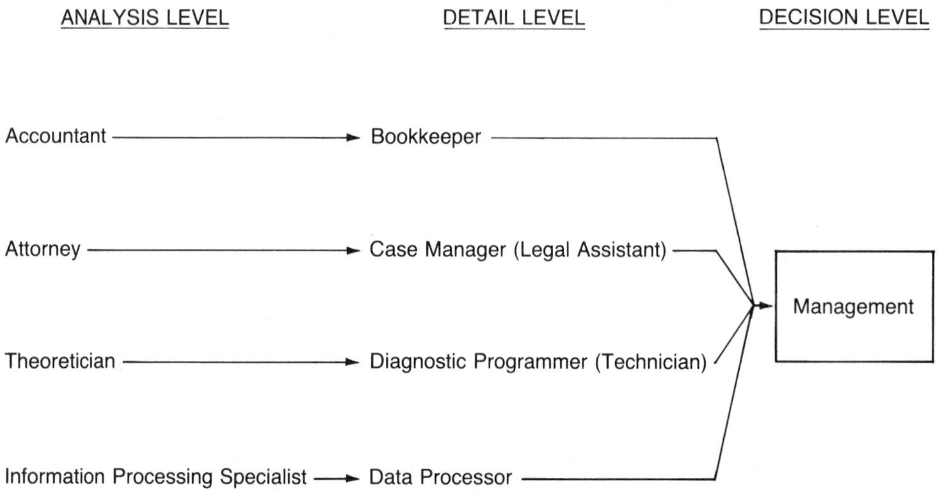

Figure 1.3. Supplemental management resource team.

One must not forget, however, the *Zeitgeist* or "mood of the time." As Anderson (1975) further points out, a social movement and its resulting organizations are on the right track if the organizing concept is sound, if people believe and support the movement, and if leadership is adequate. Conversely, the movement and its organizations will fail if the concept is unsound, behind, or ahead of its time, and if support and good leadership are lacking. It appears that the key concepts and players in the 1980s will center on the major issues of an organization's effectiveness and efficiency. Organizations that survive will be those that respond appropriately to these two vital issues.

SUMMARY

Effective organizations do not just happen, but are the product of good planning, implementation, and evaluation. As a prerequisite, an administrator should be familiar with a number of organizational principles that frequently make the difference between a functional and dysfunctional organization. These principles relate to the organization's philosophy and technology, the approach it takes to people, how it responds to its heterogeneous constituency, the information systems it employs, how its design and operation affect staff behavior, its use of a supplemental management resource team, and its key players. In addition, the health of an organization is directly related to its responsiveness to the *Zeitgeist* or "mood of the time." The author hypothesizes that organizations that survive the current decade will be those that demonstrate effectiveness and efficiency.

DISCUSSION QUESTIONS

1. Analyze your organization (or any organization with which you are familiar) in reference to its philosophy and approach to people. On the basis of your analysis, would you characterize the organization as using an "upstream or downstream" approach? Also, is there congruence between the organization's philosophy and programmatic approach? What are the discrepancies?
2. List your organization's constituency. Beside each, indicate the constituent's most vocal need or demand and most pressing accountability requirement. Look for areas of congruence, conflict, and needed conflict resolution.
3. Outline the management information system employed by your organization and the uses you make of that information. A recent survey (*Time* magazine, November 13, 1978) suggests that 80% of a manager's time is spent in 150 to 300 "management transactions" daily. What information do you use and have readily available in your transactions; what information do you need and do not have readily available?
4. The following types of survey questions (from Cherniss, 1980a) can be used to assess an organization's design and, by implication, how the design affects client and staff behavior. Use these and similar questions to evaluate each design dimension of your organization.
   a. Role structure—"What tasks or duties must be routinely performed by staff in this program?"
   b. Power structure—"What are the rules and procedures that clients and staff must follow in this program?"
   c. Normative structure—"Three types of programs have been identified: custodial, therapeutic, and maintaining. What type does this program most resemble?"
   d. Role strain—"To what extent do the different things you have to do on your job conflict with each other?"
   e. Motivation—"To what extent have you reached your maximum growth potential on this job?"
   f. Job satisfaction—"If you won a lottery tomorrow and could retire for the rest of your life, would you continue working? If so, would you continue working here?"
5. Use any organization or social movement with which you are familiar. Within the organization or movement, identify the theoretician, promoter, organizer, and core action group. Do the people or the roles they play change over time? If so, in what ways?

2

INPUT

Managers are responsible for directing vision and resources toward achieving greatest results.

(Drucker, 1977)

Good planning requires good information. This chapter focuses on three important input variables—client needs, mandated services, and community attitudes—regarding developmentally disabled persons that an organization must be sensitive to in order to complete the strategic and program planning outlined in Chapters 3 and 4. Developmentally disabled persons require a wide array of services to adequately meet their needs. A wide variety of organizations and agencies must be involved in a comprehensive service system. A broad-based planning effort, built on a coordinated data system in which the various service agencies agree upon and integrate services, will produce the required diversity of services. Planning in a vacuum or planning for planning's sake accomplishes nothing. The end result of planning for developmentally disabled individuals should be implementation of needed services that will occur only if the planning process is designed to that end. As Confucius said, "The way out is through the door,"—yet why is it that so few of us will use this exit?

Four underlying assumptions regarding developmentally disabled individuals form the conceptual basis for this chapter. They include:

1. Persons with developmental disabilities are sufficiently different from people with other types of handicaps that a separate definition of them is warranted, and are sufficiently similar to each other that grouping them together within a single concept is appropriate and helpful.
2. Substantial impairment in childhood that interferes with the acquisition of basic skills is qualitatively different from acquiring the same impairment in adulthood. It is assumed that by being impaired in childhood, developmentally disabled individuals differ from other substantially handicapped individuals, not only during childhood, but throughout their lives.
3. By the very nature of being developmentally disabled, people are likely to be underserved, inappropriately served, or unserved.
4. By their nature, many developmentally disabled individuals have limited ability to be self-advocates and frequently require others to represent their rights.

CLIENT NEEDS

Developmental Disability Defined

Who are developmentally disabled persons, and what are their needs? As defined in the Developmental Disabilities Assistance and Bill of Rights Act (Public Law 95–602):

> . . . the term developmental disability means a severe chronic disability of a person which: (a) is attributable to a mental or physical impairment or combination of mental or physical impairments; (b) is manifested before the person attains age 22; (c) is likely to continue indefinitely; (d) results in substantial functional limitations in three or more of the following areas of major life activity, including self-care, receptive/expressive language, learning, mobility, self direction, capacity for independent living, and economic self-sufficiency; and (e) reflects the person's need for a combination and sequence of special, interdisciplinary, or generic care, treatment, or other services which are individually planned and coordinated.

PL 95–602 (Section 503) changed the way developmental disabilities are defined. The categorical listing of specific conditions that were previously considered as developmental disabilities was discarded in favor of a functional definition. The primary impact of this change is that persons are now regarded as being developmentally disabled *only if* their conditions produce major functional limitations in designated "areas of major life activity." Developmental disability is no longer a label applied to persons who have particular conditions, such as cerebral palsy; it now applies to persons who have activity limitations that can result from a wide variety of medical, physical, or mental conditions. Moreover, the definition is a constitutive one in that it explains the meaning of the concept of developmental disability by relating it to other concepts, such as "impairment," "substantial functional limitation in capacity for independent living," etc. The modified definition lacks operational meaning, in that the indicators by which a developmentally disabled person are to be identified are not described in observable or measurable terms; the task of putting the definition into operational terms has been left to each state.

Estimated prevalence rates for developmental disabilities vary widely. For mental retardation alone, estimates range from 1% to 3% of the general population. Blatt (1976; Blatt et al., 1977), for example, estimates that 1% of the total population needs special services due to mental retardation, 1% due to behavioral disturbances, and another 1% due to sensory and/or physical disorders.

PL 95–602 incorporates the special services referred to above into four priority service areas—alternative community living arrangements, child development services, nonvocational social-development services, and case management services. It is interesting to compare the priority areas of the previous Act (PL. 94–103) with those of the current Act (PL 95–602), as outlined in Table 2.1.

Table 2.1. Comparison of priority service areas (PL 94–103 vs. PL 95–602)

PL 94–103 National Program Goal Areas:

1. **Deinstitutionalization:** The elimination of inappropriate placement in institutions of persons with developmental disabilities, and the improvement of the quality of care and the state of surroundings of persons who are appropriately placed in institutions.
2. **Community Alternatives to Institutionalization:** Community programs as alternatives to institutions designed to provide services for the care and habilitation of persons with developmental disabilities.
3. **Early Screening, Diagnosis, and Evaluation:** Early screening, diagnosis, and evaluation (including maternal care, developmental screening, home care, infant and preschool stimulation programs, and parent counseling and training) of developmentally disabled infants and preschool children, particularly those with multiple handicaps.
4. **Adult Programs:** Counseling, program coordination, follow-along services, protective services, and personal advocacy services on behalf of developmentally disabled adults.

PL 95–602 Priority Service Areas:

1. **Alternative Community Living Arrangements:** Services that will assist persons with developmental disabilities in maintaining suitable residential arrangements in the community.
2. **Child Development Services:** Services that will assist in the prevention, identification, and alleviation of developmental disabilities.
3. **Nonvocational Social-Developmental Services:** Services that will assist persons with developmental disabilities in performing daily living and work activities.
4. **Case Management Services:** Services that will assist persons with developmental disabilities to gain access to needed social, medical, educational, and other services.

NEEDED SERVICES

Three national studies provide valuable information as to the needs of developmentally disabled persons. One study (Scheerenbergeer, 1981) surveyed current trends in public residential facilities that offer comprehensive 24-hour services. The second (Bruininks et al., 1981) surveyed community residential programs regarding major problems and issues in community residential services. The third (Gollay, 1981) dealt with community adjustment of deinstitutionalized mentally retarded persons. The major results from these studies as related to client needs include the following:

1. *Public Residential Programs—Current Status and Trends (1978–79)*
   a. The average daily population was 139,410, with the largest single population group being composed of severely and profoundly retarded adults.
   b. Twenty-two percent of the new admissions to residential facilities were moderately and mildly retarded individuals of school age; 61% of new admissions were severely or profoundly retarded, and 35.8% of those were of school age.
   c. Approximately 40% of new admissions came from their own homes.
   d. Although 15.4% of the residents were estimated to be ready for placement, the anticipated placement rate was only 8%. Respondents (superintendents) suggested the low placement rate was due to critical problems

associated with availability of alternate community living facilities; adequacy of educational, special services (physical and occupational therapy, speech, counseling), and medical programs; adequacy of adult programming and behavior management (regardless of severity level); and adequacy of personnel training and competencies in meeting the needs of the more severely affected individuals.

2. *Community Residential Alternatives—Problems and Issues*
   a. As of June 30, 1977, a total of 76,250 residents lived in community residential facilities; 91% of these residents were mentally retarded persons. Most of the facilities were small, with 88% serving 20 or fewer residents; however, over one-half of the mentally retarded residents lived in residences that served 31 or more persons. Of the mentally retarded residents, approximately 62% were 22 years and older; 37% were of legal school age; and 65% were borderline, mildly, or moderately retarded persons. Over 50% of the facilities reported no movement into or out of their facilities during the 12 months covered by the survey.
   b. The major problems cited by facility administrators included: 1) recruitment of qualified staff, staff turnover, and staff training (85% of respondents); 2) funding problems, including client census, cash flow, and external control of salary/benefit issues (61%); 3) service issues, including lack of an available continuum of comprehensive services as well as development and implementation of individualized program plans (46%); 4) interagency problems, including licensing standards, regulations, administrative red tape, and lack of coordination among local, regional, and state services (22%); and 5) administrative problems involving maintenance of facility relationships with the board of directors, insurance problems, and admission policies (2%).
3. *Community Adjustment of the Mentally Retarded—Service and Training Needs*
   a. The following services are generally needed by mentally retarded persons: 1) medical and health care (medical, dental, physical therapy, speech therapy); 2) social and recreational (recreation, counseling, occupational therapy); 3) employment placement and support; and 4) housing and legal assistance.
   b. The following support services were indicated for families of retarded individuals: 1) support and/or training prior to the individual's entry into community living; 2) general counseling; 3) consultation for handling specific problems; 4) temporary relief from responsibilities; and 5) parent or professional associations.
   c. The major training needs relate to: 1) personal maintenance (eating, toileting, dressing, cleanliness, grooming); 2) sensorimotor development (hearing, vision, speech, and language); and 3) education and employment (preacademic, numbers and telling time, reading, writing, prevocational, vocational).

Note the the inclusion in the above listing of services for families of the community-based client. A recent study by Schalock, Harper, and Genung (1981) found that the two most significant predictors of successful community placement of mentally retarded persons were the family's acceptance of and involvement in a community-based program (in this case, the Mid-Nebraska Mental Retardation Services). Additional significant predictors of successful community placement included institutional size at placement, demonstrated skills in work behavior, sensorimotor skills, appropriate social-emotional behavior, gender (females were more successful than males), and community size (larger communities favored).

A common theme runs through the four studies summarized above: Deinstitutionalization involves more than simply placing a person into a community-based program (Note 1). Rather, deinstitutionalization encompasses the development of a continuum of living-training facilities and associated support services that extend from the institution to a community-based program, to semi-independent, and independent placement. This notion is developed more fully in Chapter 4.

MANDATED SERVICES

Comprehensive services for developmentally disabled persons are federally mandated through a number of mechanisms, including individualized habilitation plans (IHP) and interdisciplinary approaches to programmatic services. Each is discussed in detail below.

Individualized Habilitation Plan

The development and implementation of the client's individualized habilitation plan is essential in implementing the above-mentioned continuum of living-training-support services. Federal public laws mandate the development and implementation of such plans for the clients served by (re)habilitation programs. Six public laws that contain specifications for human service organizations in this regard include:

Education for All Handicapped Children Act of 1975 (PL 94–142)
Developmental Disabilities Assistance and Bill of Rights Act (PL 95–602)
Rehabilitation Act Amendments of 1974 (PL 93–156)
Title XIX (Medicaid) of Social Security Act (PL 92–223)
Title XVI of Social Security Act, Section 1615 (as amended by PL 94–566)
Title XX of Social Security Act (PL 93–647)

A number of elements must be included in the client's individualized habilitation plan (Note 2). These include:

1. *Assessment of Client Need* PL 94–142, for example, requires an assessment of the "child's present levels of educational performance including academic

achievement, social adaptation, prevocational and vocational skills, and self-help skills.''

2. *Development of Individualized Plan* PL 95–602 stipulates that

> . . . the Plan is developed by an interdisciplinary team for every individual served by the program, and requires at least the participation of the handicapped individual, the individual's parents, family or other representative, a joint development team of appropriate and relevant representatives, and/or staff of the agency, facility and/or program involved in serving the individual, and representatives and/or staff of other agencies involved in serving the individual.

3. *Content of Plans* Generalizing across the public laws, the plan's contents must include statements of need, goals, objectives relative to goal attainment, services to be provided, duration of services, strategies for achieving objectives, responsible person for the plan, and evaluation procedures.
4. *Plan Review Process* The plan needs to be reviewed and evaluated regularly (and at least annually) to determine the client's progress, to make modifications, and to evaluate appropriateness of placement in light of client progress. The individual receiving service and his or her parents or other representative have the opportunity to review the plan and participate in its revision.

Interdisciplinary Approach

Public laws and accrediting agencies such as the Accreditation Council for Services for Mentally Retarded and Other Developmentally Disabled Persons (ACMR/DD) and The Commission on the Accreditation of Rehabilitation Facilities (CARF) require an interdisciplinary approach to service delivery. This approach has a number of components including (cf. Golin and Ducanis, 1981; Johnson and Magrab, 1976; Valletutti and Christopolis, 1977):

1. *A unified and integrated approach to diagnosis, evaluation, individualized habilitation plan development and remediation* This approach should be based on the client's needs and should encompass such behavioral domains as cognitive, communication, perceptual-motor, self-help, social-emotional, and vocational.
2. *Team meetings* Habilitation plan implementation must involve a face-to-face team meeting in which participants share and discuss all information and recommendations regarding the client. Persons providing significant services to the person should be present; if not, a person competent to interpret and integrate the information must attend.
3. *Interdisciplinary team composition* There is no standard composition of an interdisciplinary team. In reference to the Title 19 standards (249.10; d-l-v) for example, ''active treatment'' is defined as:

> (a) Regular participation, in accordance with an individual plan of care in professionally developed and supervised activities, experiences, or therapies.
> (b) An individual ''plan of care'' which is a written plan setting forth measurable

goals or behaviorally stated objectives and prescribing an integrated program of individually designed activities, experiences or therapies necessary to achieve such goals or objectives. The overall objective of the plan is to attain or maintain the optimal physical, intellectual, social, or vocational functioning of which the individual is presently or potentially capable;

(c) An interdisciplinary professional evaluation consisting of complete medical, social and psychological diagnosis and evaluation, and an evaluation of the individual's need for institutional care, prior to but not to exceed 3 months before admission to the institution or, in the case of individuals who make application while in such institution, before requesting payment under the plan. The evaluation is conducted by a physician, a social worker and other professionals. At least one member of the team meets the requirements of 249.12 (c) (3).

The following represents the approach taken by the ACMR/DD (in standard numbers 1.1.1–1.1.3):

An interdisciplinary team is identified for each individual served.

Each individual's interdisciplinary team is constituted of persons drawn from, or representing, the professions, disciplines, or service areas that are relevant to identifying the individual's needs and designing programs to meet them.

Each individual's interdisciplinary team includes those persons who work most directly with the individual in each of the professions, disciplines, or service areas that provide services to the individual.

The interdisciplinary team process provides for and invites the active participation of the individual and, as appropriate, the individual's family and/or advocate.

The agency has written policies and procedures that specify the organization and operation of the interdisciplinary team process as it pertains to the individuals served.

As with client needs, a theme common to these mandated services is the focus on individualized, interdisciplinary program services based on the concepts of normalization and the developmental model. Since your organization may well be required to be accredited, it is wise for the administrator to keep informed on accreditation standards. This information can be obtained from:

Accreditation Council for Services for Mentally Retarded and Other Developmentally Disabled Persons, 5101 Wisconsin Avenue, NW, Suite 405, Washington, DC 20016 (202/363-2811)

Commission on Accreditation of Rehabilitation Facilities, 2500 North Pantano Rd., Tucson, AZ 95715 (602/886-8575)

COMMUNITY ATTITUDES

One of the most important issues today regarding services for developmentally disabled persons centers on the community's acceptance of group homes for handicapped people. Although community attitudes differ widely, a review of the literature indicates that public opinion on the following eight statements will significantly affect your community's acceptance of group homes:

1. Persons with mental retardation are childlike.
2. Group homes will lower the value of property.
3. Deinstitutionalization is too expensive.
4. Persons with mental retardation are better cared for in institutions than they are in the community.
5. Persons with mental retardation present a threat to the community.
6. Mental retardation is usually a hereditary condition and is not likely to occur in the typical family.
7. Persons with mental retardation are not capable of becoming productive members of society.
8. Persons with mental retardation are not capable of learning.

Chapter 6 analyzes these community attitudes and outlines a community education program designed to overcome attitudinal barriers and allow developmentally disabled persons to become "visible." Community attitudes will also be reflected in your constituents and the expectations they have of you and your organization. As shown previously in Figure 1.1, the basic constituents of most human service organizations include clients and their representatives (parents and/or advocates), staff and their representatives (unions and professional organizations), regulatory boards (including your board of directors), and funding/regulatory agencies. This author's experience with human service programs indicates that major expectations of each constituent group can be summarized as follows:

Clients and their representatives want quality services, regardless of cost.

Parents want protection and security for their family member along with assurance that the organization is permanent and stable.

Staff and their representatives want interdisciplinary services, job security, reasonable pay, and a minimum of paperwork and accountability requirements.

Regulatory and governing boards want face validity, safety, and an effective/efficient organization.

SUMMARY

Carl Haywood, in addressing the American Association on Mental Deficiency in 1981 (Haywood, 1981), referred to the vulnerability of mentally retarded individuals. According to Haywood, this vulnerability is manifested in factors such as accumulative mental age deficit, societies' reliance on institutionalization, restrictive ordinances, frequent exploitation, and active attempts to exclude developmentally disabled persons from a variety of social systems and institutions.

Haywood proposes that a reasonable goal for a service delivery system is a balance between maximum social participation and minimum social vulnerability. This requires a dual process of changing the environment to accommodate the needs of disabled persons and increasing disabled persons' behavioral skills in order to cope with the environmental demands. This chapter summarized critical input variables that will facilitate developing services to accomplish this dual process.

The first input variable relates to client needs and is reflected in the service priority areas of alternate community living arrangements, social-developmental training, and case management services. Specific needs were identified from recent studies dealing with deinstitutionalization. A second need, reflected in mandated services, relates to the development, implementation, and evaluation of an interdisciplinary team-developed individualized habilitation plan. The components of both the plan and team approach were outlined. Finally, the community's attitudes toward developmentally disabled persons were discussed, along with the expectations of an organization's heterogeneous constituency. Once an organization is sensitive to client needs, mandated services, and the community's attitudes, it can then begin to develop the appropriate services that will maximize disabled persons' social participation and minimize their social vulnerability. Chapter 3 begins that planning process.

DISCUSSION QUESTIONS

1. PL 95-602 lacks operational meaning in that the indicators by which a developmentally disabled person is defined are not described in observable or measurable terms. What are some measurable "substantial functional limitations" in the major life activities of a person that would result in a functional disability?
2. Analyze the alternative living arrangements and training services provided by your organization. Do they provide a meaningful continuum of services, and are they appropriate to the discussed needs of the developmentally disabled person?
3. The criteria of an individualized habilitation plan were discussed in this chapter. Which of these criteria are part of your plan, and which are not? What are the major problems involved in implementing a functional, easy-to-read and -evaluate individual habilitation plan?
4. What is the justification for an interdisciplinary team approach? What has been your experience with this approach, and do the advantages outweigh the disadvantages? How does this approach compare to a multidisciplinary one?
5. Survey your community's attitudes regarding developmentally disabled persons. How do the assessed attitudes compare with the eight attitude statements included in this chapter under "Community Attitudes?"

REFERENCE NOTES

1. Deinstitutionalization studies to date have evaluated a number of predictor variables related to successful community placement. These variables fall into one of four classes: Institutional factors, such as size, quality of training, and duration of institutionalization; client characteristics, including age, intelligence, and various personality descriptors; training variables related to vocational or independent living skills; and community characteristics, such as attitudes, support services, and residential service systems. Although few unequivocal relationships have been found between successful community placement and each of the above predictor classes, the following general statements can be made: Institutional factors, such as duration, prerelease training, and costs generally show a positive relationship (Heal, Sigelman, and Switzky, 1978; McCarver and Craig, 1974). Client characteristics, including personal appearance, vocational skills, social skills, age at release, and psychomotor ability also show a positive, albeit inconsistent, relationship (Bell, 1976; Crawford, Aiello, and Thompson, 1979; Heal et al., 1978; McCarver and Craig, 1974; O'Connor, 1976; Windle, 1962). In reference to training variables, prerelease training in vocational or independent living skills is associated with successful community adjustment (Bell, 1976; McCarver and Craig, 1974; Gollay et al., 1978). Finally, successful community placement of retarded persons has been related to community characteristics, including availability and access to community resources (Justice, Bradley, and O'Connor, 1971; Scheerenberger, 1976), a continuum of residential/programmatic services (Gollay et al., 1978), and the presence of an advocate or benefactor (Edgerton, 1975; Henshel, 1972; Kurtz, 1975).
2. The author is indebted to Ms. Cathy Smith and her excellent analysis of current public laws.

3

STRATEGIC PLANNING

Strategic planning directs an organization's resources, technology and manpower towards making people more independent, productive and socially integrated.

(Anonymous)

This chapter focuses on the strategic planning required to provide the services that will result in your clients becoming more independent, productive and socially accepted. Chapter 2 discussed client needs, mandated services, community attitudes, and the expectations of your heterogeneous constituency. This chapter attempts to integrate functionally these variables in light of your organization's philosophy, goals, objectives, and desired products. These four components to strategic planning are outlined in Figure 3.1. Before discussing each, let us look at the rationale for strategic planning.

As we enter the third decade of the deinstitutionalization movement for persons with developmental disabilities, we face the increasingly difficult task of integrating more severely handicapped individuals into the community. The necessity of adapting community programs to address the needs of multiply handicapped persons has been evident for some time. Whether this involves reintegration of individuals into the community, or enabling them to remain in the community, current data strongly indicate that a continuum of residential and training alternatives increases normalization and integration, and deflects people from institutionalization. Indeed, the literature increasingly points to the need for comprehensive systems of living-training components.

CONTINUUM OF LIVING-TRAINING ALTERNATIVES

Magrab and Elder (1979) define a delivery system as a general strategy for the mobilization and organization of all appropriate resources to provide for the prevention, intervention, and rehabilitation of human problems. Our current human service delivery system is composed of several separate systems, each the result of a categorical response to service needs. None of these single subsystems of education, health, welfare, rehabilitation, and housing satisfies the above definition of system, since none alone can solve the multiple problems of handicapped persons. Cooperation, coordination, and collaboration among these subsystems is necessary to achieve this.

PHILOSOPHY:
Normalization
Deinstitutionalization

GOALS:
Independent Living
Vocational Productivity
Community Integration

OBJECTIVES:
Living–Training Progressions
Behavioral Skills Training

PRODUCTS:
Increased Skills
Movement within Progressions
Living/Work Placement
Community-Based Services

Figure 3.1. Components of strategic planning.

The existence of a functioning system of community services would provide a range of living and training environments that facilitate client movement along a series of continua as reflected in Figure 3.2. Ideally, client movement would always be in the direction of less restrictive settings that promote increased independence and productivity. However, given the complexity of needs of severely and profoundly handicapped individuals, the system must be flexible enough to accommodate movement up and down the continuum as the individual's needs change. Intervention, (re)habilitation, and support services must be coupled with living alternatives in order for severely handicapped individuals to move within the continua.

As the name implies, a continuum involves a progression from one end of the spectrum to another. In terms of community living-training alternatives, this continuum generally ranges from highly structured, protective, restrictive environments to unstructured environments that facilitate freedom of movement and independence. Examples of the progression were shown in Figure 3.2. The two ends of the spectrum can usually be differentiated by the degree to which they conform to normalization principles. In delineating the service components for a continuum of community living-training alternatives, special consideration should be given to the following issues.

First, the essential role of a clearly articulated underlying philosophy must be stressed. The philosophy provides the rationale for the particular structure selected and dictates the direction that future service planning and provision should take. A continuum concept is based on the recognition that a full range of service environments and programs is required to address the diversity of needs characterized by the developmentally disabled population. In addition, the services provided through the continuum should reflect the current state-of-the-art in service de-

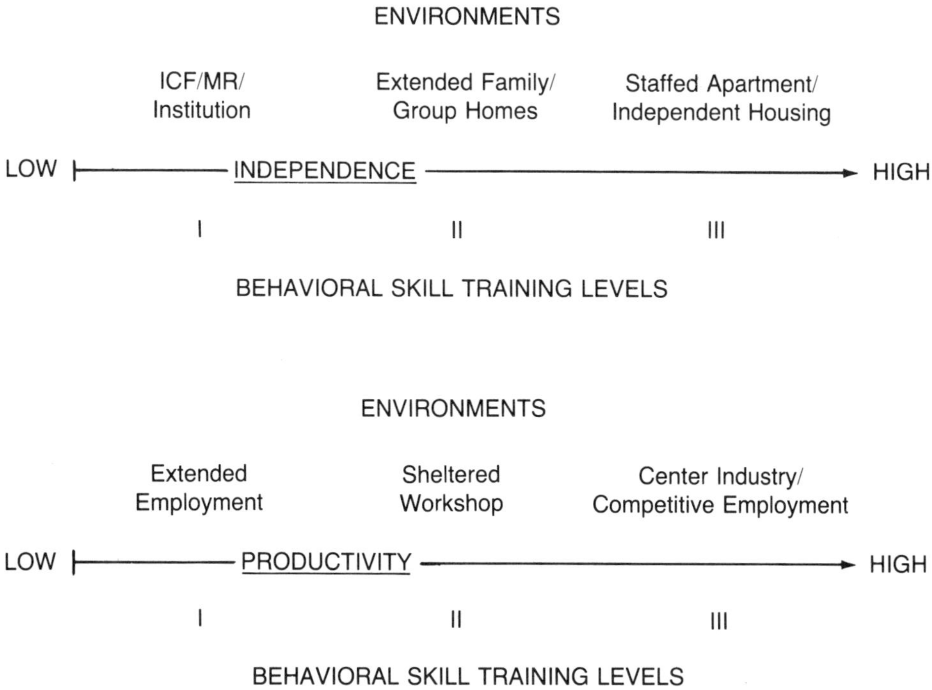

Figure 3.2. Living-training facilities and associated behavioral skill levels. (ICF/MR = Intermediate Care Facility for the Mentally Retarded.)

livery, including principles of normalization and an individualized approach to providing services.

Second, in keeping with the current orientation in the human services field, the following points are essential in structuring the continuum:

Natural environments (for example, home-like living arrangements, competitive employment options) should be the preferred service setting whenever possible.

Generic services (for example, medical, educational, legal, recreational facilities utilized by the general public) should be utilized to the greatest extent possible.

Assistance to the individual should be provided only at the level actually needed in order to promote independence and self-reliance.

Training provided an individual should focus on enhancing economic self-sufficiency to the extent possible, and on increasing the person's ability to live independently and to behave appropriately within the norms and values of the community.

Third, in designing the continuum, particular attention must be focused on the interface between generic and specialty service providers. A continuum should not result in a closed, self-contained system of special services to a population. Pluralism in services is normalizing. It is desirable for consumers to have multiple options via the generic system available to every other citizen. In addition, it is counterproductive to attempt to totally reorganize the human service network as it currently exists in order to meet the needs of any single consumer population.

Instead, mechanisms for building adequate linkages between specialized and generic services should be established (see Section II, "Implementing Services").

Given these caveats, the conceptualization of a continuum of services serves as a useful model in ensuring comprehensiveness in service delivery and eliminating traditional problems of fragmentation and duplication. To be complete, the continuum must encompass three major areas of services, including: 1) alternative living environments; 2) habilitation/training/educational alternatives; and 3) support services. Each of these should result from an interface of generic and specialty services. Services along the continuum are linked through one or more coordinating mechanisms that ensure that the appropriate array of programs and environments are available to meet all clients' needs at any given time.

The four strategic planning components—your organization's philosophy, goals, objectives, and desired products—discussed in the remainder of the chapter should serve as a model for conceptualizing the broad range of services needed to integrate individuals with all types of developmental disabilities into normalized community settings. However, models by their nature must be simple in order to communicate clearly their intent. They provide only a framework upon which a service delivery system is developed, and cannot encompass the multitude of critical dimensions that must be addressed in refocusing an existing network of services. Because each organization or service network will be designing a continuum of community living-training alternatives that corresponds to its unique needs, several factors must be considered in that process. These include:

The particular characteristics and needs of the developmentally disabled population in your service area

The generic and specialized services now in existence that address these current and future needs

Resources available to fill the gaps between what is needed and what is available

Factors that facilitate and/or inhibit the establishment of a continuum of community living-training alternatives

In applying the model's conceptual framework to a service delivery area, two major tasks face planners and providers. First, the extent of need in the community for those model components and the resources available to meet those needs must be determined. Second, plans for filling any gaps identified through this determination must be developed through interagency coordination and requests for funding of resources not currently available. These needed components can only be determined following a thorough assessment of the factors listed above (more on this in Chapter 4).

PHILOSOPHY

Current programs for developmentally disabled persons are based on normalization and integration principles that are generally translated into three major agency goals—that is, making persons less dependent, more productive, and more integrated socially. All too often, however, programs are hampered in accomplishing these goals because they lack a clear philosophy, focus, or program emphasis. As a result, clients and staff are stagnating, not because of lack of effort, but because of lack of direction. Hence, this chapter stresses the importance of an organization's internalizing a philosophical position regarding its clientele *before* developing its program.

Two of the cornerstones of any forward-looking program for developmentally disabled persons must be the concepts of normalization and deinstitutionalization. Yet, today some individuals have begun to question the wisdom and efficacy of these principles. Lest we lose sight of their importance, let us look again at these two concepts—why they developed, and why they are still relevant.

Normalization

Scheerenberger (1976) states, "the genuine goal of both deinstitutionalization and normalization is the increased independence and quality of life for the mentally retarded." Normalization originated in the Scandinavian countries and means that handicapped persons should be provided the same rights and benefits as are provided all citizens, and should be exposed, as well, to experiences that are likely to elicit or maintain normative behavior (Nirje, 1969; Wolfensberger et al., 1972). Normalization thus involves:

1. Providing handicapped persons with opportunities to have a normal daily rhythm (getting out of bed, getting dressed, and being involved in activities); and weekly rhythm (home, school, work, leisure)
2. Enabling handicapped persons to experience the normal rhythm of the year (having holidays and observing family days of personal significance)
3. Providing opportunities for handicapped persons to undergo the normal developmental experiences of the life cycle (early childhood, school age, adulthood, old age)
4. Respecting the choices, wishes, and desires of retarded persons and their right to self-determination
5. Enabling handicapped persons to live in a heterosexual world
6. Applying financial help available to others to enable mentally retarded persons to live as normally as possible
7. Modeling physical facilities serving retarded persons on those available in society for ordinary people
8. Integrating retarded persons into the mainstream of life in regard to their physical, social, spiritual, and interpersonal needs

Deinstitutionalization

Although it is impossible to review all court decisions regarding deinstitutionalization and mentally retarded individuals (Note 1), the major thrusts of federal court judgments have been toward: 1) preventing unnecessary institutionalization and 2) reforming current institutional services. In reference to each:

1. *Preventing Unnecessary Institutionalization* Court decisions have stressed three critical prevention measures.
   a. They have placed marked restrictions on who should be considered eligible for admission:

   > ''No borderline or mildly retarded person shall be a resident of the institution'' (*Wyatt* v. *Stickney,* 1972.)
   >
   > ''No person classified as borderline, mildly or moderately retarded according to the standards of classification at Cambridge shall be admitted unless that person suffers from psychiatric or emotional disorders in addition to his retardation. . .'' (*Welsch* v. *Likens,* 1974.)
   >
   > ''No person shall be admitted unless he is dangerous to himself or others'' (*Lessard* v. *Schmidt,* 1972.)

   b. Retarded persons, even those considered eligible under the court orders, should not be admitted to a residential facility until all other community resources have been explored:

   > ''No person shall be admitted to the institution unless a prior determination shall have been made that residence in the institution is the least restrictive habilitation setting'' (*Wyatt* v. *Stickney,* 1972.)
   >
   > ''No mentally retarded person shall be admitted to Cambridge State Hospital on civil commitment if services and programs are available in the community'' (*Welsch* v. *Likens,* 1974.)

   c. No retarded person should remain in a residential facility longer than necessary (Note 2).

   > ''Residents shall have a right to the least restrictive conditions necessary to achieve the purposes of habilitation. To this end, the institution shall make every attempt to move residents from: (1) more to less structured living; (2) larger to small facilities; (3) larger to smaller living units; (4) group to individual residence; (5) segregated from the community to integrated living'' (*Wyatt* v. *Stickney,* 1972.)

2. *Reforming Current Institutional Services* Federal court judgments have emphasized five broad aspects of institutional reform, including (Willer, Scheerenberger, and Intagliata, 1980):
   a. All retarded persons have basic rights that must be recognized. For example, in *Wyatt* v. *Stickney,* Judge C. Johnson's final document outlined minimum treatment standards concerning admission policies, residents' rights to treatment and habilitation, staffing patterns, records and review, physical plant and environment, medication, and resident labor.
   b. Large institutions should serve a very select population that probably will include two groups: 1) those who are severely and profoundly retarded with multiple handicapping conditions requiring constant medical super-

vision; and 2) those who are extremely difficult to manage who cannot function acceptably in the community.

c. Each resident is to have his or her needs met on an individual basis. For example, in *Welsch* v. *Likens,* the statement was made, "almost all of the residents, no matter the degree of severity of their retardation, are capable of some growth and development if given adequate care and suitable treatment."

d. Restraints and aversive treatment procedures are strictly circumscribed.

e. The residential facility must provide a humane physical and psychological environment. In June, 1982, for example, the U.S. Supreme Court established for the first time constitutional rights for persons committed to institutions for mentally retarded individuals, including unprecedented but limited guarantees of a minimum level of training and development. The court said in its decision that institutions have a legal obligation to provide a reasonable amount of physical freedom as well as safety for involuntarily committed patients. At the same time, Justice Lewis F. Powell, Jr., writing for the 8 to 1 majority, cautioned judges to respect the professional judgments and budgetary restraints of the institutions and not require them to "make each decision in the shadow" of possible lawsuits.

GOALS

Internalizing normalization and deinstitutionalization principles should lead to the planning of programs stressing independent living, vocational training and placement, and community integration. The details of such programs are presented in Chapter 4. Their importance in goal formulation and strategic planning is discussed below.

Increased Independent Living

The quantity and quality of training for independent or community living currently offered by community-based programs is frequently less than adequate (Crnic and Pym, 1979; McDevitt et al., 1978; Schalock and Harper, 1981b; Scheerenberger and Felsenthal, 1977). The training program is typically carried out in bits and pieces interspersed between contracts, recreation, survival academics, and the so-called "related instruction programming." This mixed message approach tends to require a multiplicity of skills on the part of staff and leads to confusion as to what is expected on the part of the clients. The burden of training for independent living is usually assumed by the residential staff after the day program is complete—a staff that is often the least paid, trained, or respected in the agency hierarchy. The picture is further complicated by the notion that continuing the training after 8 hours in the adult center is considered by some to be over-programming for those "lucky" clients who happen to be living in the group homes.

Positive changes are occurring, however, as reflected in the following legislative and programmatic trends:

Title 3 of PL 95–602 and Title 7 of the 1978 Amendments to the Vocational Rehabilitation Act of 1973 focus on independent living programs.

Title XX State Plans must address five basic needs including medical, shelter, social, clothing, and food.

PL 94–142 contains two focus areas dealing with social adaptation and self-help skills.

Systematic training and support programs for developing community living skills are available and have demonstrated that learned skills do generalize to a less restrictive living environment.

If independent living-training and placement is one of your organization's primary goals, it is important at the strategic planning stage to realize that both training and support services will be necessary. These include services such as housing, enabler/facilitator assistance, prosthetic procurement and repair, financial/legal advocacy, transportation training, deaf/blind services, and access to mental health services.

Increased Vocational Productivity

A recent report on "Training and Employment Services for Handicapped Individuals in Sheltered Workshops" (Whitehead, 1981) outlines problems that an organization might encounter in developing vocational programs and goals for its clients. The report, which summarizes a 1978 Office of Social Service Policy Analysis, was initiated in response to growing public concern regarding sheltered workshop services, as evidenced by congressional hearings before the U.S. House of Representatives Labor Standards Subcommittee during 1978–1980, and General Accounting Office investigations during the same period. The major problems and criticisms identified were:

1. Handicapped clients lacked movement from the workshop into the competitive labor market.
2. Handicapped persons had a dual relationship in workshops (that is, they were often both client and employee receiving a service and producing a commodity or service).
3. Federal wage and hour regulations were ineffective in assuring payment of appropriate, commensurate wages to handicapped workers.
4. Training and employment services in workshops typically were funded from several federal and state sources, resulting in poor coordination of service delivery and lack of accountability.
5. Linkages of sheltered workshops with private business and industry were generally limited or lacking in many facilities.

A recent analysis in 44 states of vocational opportunities for severely handicapped adults resulted in similar conclusions (Bellamy et al., 1980):

1. Adult day programs in 1980 provided the major daily habilitation for an estimated 105,000 severely handicapped persons.
2. The organization, funding, and service characteristics of these programs

generally reflect a welfare approach to services, characterized by ongoing dependence on social service and long-term care programs and a minor emphasis on job preparation.
3. Despite the appealing stepwise logic of the flow-through continuum of services, these programs have become indefinite placements for many severely handicapped persons.
4. The fiscal contingencies created by current policies result in disincentives to local service providers and state agencies that attempt to provide vocational opportunities.
5. Inertia and fragmentation have resulted from incoordinated funding sources and regulation by several different agencies and levels of government.
6. Although the number of severely handicapped people served in these programs has increased rapidly during the last decade, many individuals still do not have access to community-based services.

Given these problems and barriers to vocational training and placement, what might reasonably be done at the strategic planning phase to reach your goal of increased vocational productivity? One approach, as outlined in Chapter 4, is to implement a multiple-component vocational training and placement program that includes components related to extended employment, sheltered work, and competitive employment.

Increased Community Integration

The importance of social behavior in successful community adjustment is widely acknowledged. Results of several deinstitutionalization studies indicate that personality and social behaviors among retarded adults significantly affect community adjustment, acceptance, and integration (Note 3). Strategic planning can maximize a person's successful community adjustment by recognizing and planning the following "community integration programming areas":

1. *Social Skills Training* A number of techniques including operant conditioning, modeling, and role playing have been used to develop social and assertive skills in retarded persons. These techniques and the specific behaviors manipulated are discussed in Chapter 4.
2. *Extended Friendship Patterns* Recent literature regarding the social lives of retarded individuals suggest a definite need to increase our efforts at social acceptance and integration programming. One line of evidence (Reiter and Levi, 1980; Richardson, 1978) suggests that retarded persons, especially those living independently, have fewer friends than nonretarded persons. In a recent study of friendship patterns among former Mid-Nebraska Mental Retardation Services clients who are now living independently, for example, we found that

   > Females reported having an average of two friends who were most likely a roommate, advocate, or former instructor. Each friend was seen about 5 times per week socially, with activities most likely consisting of a movie, shopping, eating out, or going to church. Males reported an average of one friend who would most

> likely be a roommate or advocate. Visitations averaged 3 times per week, with common activities being a movie or athletic event. One-third of the clients interviewed reported having no friends (Schalock, Harper, and Carver, 1981, p. 175).

The above data do not mean necessarily that retarded persons are nonsociable. The data could suggest, rather, that retarded persons might prefer to interact with individuals of similar age, gender, and intellectual level. For example, Berkson and Romer (1981) recently summarized their work on affiliation and friendship patterns: "We have shown that mentally disabled people in community facilities are generally sociable. They interact mainly in dyads, and most of their social behavior with peers involves conversation."

3. *Benefactors and Assistance* Just as one line of evidence suggests that retarded persons have fewer friends within the community, other evidence indicates that having nonretarded friends is strongly related to social and community success. Reiter and Levi (1980), for example, found that among a group of moderately and mildly retarded adults studied in Israel, persons who had nonretarded friends showed better social-educational skills than those without nonretarded friends. Similarly, the work by Edgerton (1975) underscores the critical role that benefactors, family members, and program-based training assistants play in successful community adjustment, acceptance, and integration of developmentally disabled persons (Note 4).
4. *Mental Health Needs* Inherent in each of the three programming areas mentioned above is the reality that mere placement into a community setting does not insure that developmentally disabled persons will be personally satisfied, socially productive, or amenable to established behavioral norms. The very process of rapid deinstitutionalization has resulted in clients being placed into new, but sometimes highly stressful, environments without being adequately prepared. As a result, many remain passive, dependent, lonely, unmotivated, socially inept, highly anxious, compulsive, ritualistic, depressed and/or withdrawn. It is no wonder, then, that many seek out and affiliate with persons who have had similar experiences, and shy away from involvement in an environment designed to require more independence, assertiveness, decision making and self-expression. During an organization's strategic planning it is crucial that mental health services be procured and provided. The need for such services has to date been grossly underestimated (Gardner and Cole, 1981b; Menolascino, 1983).

OBJECTIVES

An organization's philosophy and goals provide the direction and thrust of a service delivery program; however, neither can occur without the next step in strategic planning—the establishment of specific, measurable objectives. Consistent with the previously defined goals of increased independence, productivity, and community integration, the following three objectives need to be met by a human service delivery program: 1) provide a continuum of living-training facilities that will permit both skill development and generalization training in environments commensurate with increased independence, productivity, and social integration; 2) provide systematic training in the behavioral skills associated with and required by each step on the continuum; and 3) prevent institutionalization or reinstitutionalization by providing or procuring those services needed to meet the client's environmental requirements. Each objective is discussed below.

Living-Training Progressions

Increasing a person's independence and productivity, in this author's opinion, requires the planning, development, and integration of sequential living-training environments culminating in less restrictive living and more productive working conditions. Thus, environments that require certain behaviors can be used in consort to develop and practice those required behavioral skills. The sequential living-training environments suggested to accomplish these aims were depicted in Figure 3.2. This author's observation has been that within many communities throughout the country, most of the alternatives in the two progressions toward productivity and independence are operating; what is usually lacking, however, is the integration of the living-training facilities into a comprehensive service delivery system. As discussed in Chapter 5, integrated services can be developed using mechanisms such as interagency agreements, regionalized services, or consortia.

Behavioral Skills Training

Table 3.1 reveals the relationship, based on this author's research to date, between living-training facilities and the behavioral skill levels associated with increased independence (community living skills), productivity (vocational skills) and community integration. Specific skills associated with successful placement from these two training components are outlined in Schalock and Harper (1978) and Schalock, Harper, and Carver (1981).

Preventing Institutionalization and Reinstitutionalization

Strategic planning that focuses on preventing institutionalization will stress procuring specialized services related to behavioral management, physical therapy, occupational therapy, speech, counseling, medical care, recreation, protective services, transportation, and advocacy. A service delivery program must also engage in strategic planning to prevent reinstitutionalization. For example, a recent study (Schalock, Harper, and Genung, 1981) analyzed the termination summaries and incident reports of 26 reinstitutionalized clients who either returned to a state mental retardation facility or were placed in a mental health facility. The reports for clients who returned to the state facility reflected high-frequency soiling, physical abuse of clients and staff, property destruction, and stealing. It is probably significant that a high percentage of this group's negative behavior occurred in a

Table 3.1. Behavioral skill training areas associated with living-training facility progressions

	Community Living-Facility Progression		
	ICF/MR[a]	*Group Home/Transitional Living*	*Staffed Apartment/Independent Housing*
CLS[a] training areas[b]	Grooming skills	Health care	Handles medication
	Dressing skills	Laundry skills	Clothing repair/replacement
	Independent eating	Meal preparation	Meal planning and shopping
	Self-referenced behaviors	Social integration	Interpersonal relations
	Expresses needs	Uses an expressive language system	Language generalizations
	Cleaning skills	Home safety	Coping skills
	Utility of money	Money concepts	Independent money usage
	Prompted daily routine	Unprompted daily routine	Independent scheduling
	Perceptual motor skills	Recreation and leisure activities	Uses community recreation facilities
	Community awareness	Community access	Independent communty use
	Vocational Training-Placement Progression		
	Extended Employment	*Sheltered Workshop*	*Center Industry/Competitive Employment*
VT[a] training areas[b]	Self-help skills	Job-related skills	On-the-job evaluation
	Personal/interpersonal behaviors	Work performance	On-the-job training
	Information processing	Work behavior	Industrial practicum
	Learning/coping strategies	Job-seeking skills	Job enabler-facilitator (assistance)
	Prevocational skills		

[a]ICF/MR = Intermediate Care Facilities for the Mentally Retarded; CLS = community living skills; VT = vocational training.
[b]Referenced to behavioral domains contained in Schalock (1980, 1981, Note 5).

group home, where less well-trained staff members were employed and where the staffing ratio was 8 to 10 clients to 1 staff (as compared to the training areas, where the ratio was 5 clients to 1 staff member). Incident reports for those clients placed in the mental health facility showed high-frequency temper tantrums, physical abuse of other clients, property destruction, and defiance. Built-in staff training and support services can prepare staff to deal more effectively with such behaviors and thereby reduce the chances of reinstitutionalization. The investment is well worth it, but does require foresight at the strategic planning stage.

PRODUCTS

Although we know something about the quantity and approximate cost of services being provided to the developmentally disabled, we still do not have a precise understanding of the outcome or product of the large investment made. This is, in part, because programs for developmentally disabled individuals historically have emphasized the needs of clients rather than the measurable results of services. In addition, the divergent opinions and perceptions of what is good for the client as viewed by funding sources, families, program staff, administrators, and regulatory agencies have mitigated against operationalizing and implementing client-centered outcome measures. Despite these problems, programs for developmentally disabled persons are increasingly required to account for their services and to evaluate the outcomes. This level of accountability is difficult when dealing with the severely and/or profoundly handicapped population, especially since the central problem today in program evaluation is the inadequacy of the output measures used (Noble, 1977; Sorensen and Grove, 1977). Good management and strategic planning incorporates measurement of an organization's products from the start. Some might say, "in human services you can't measure what we do—human behavior is too [choose one, depending on your audience] complex, subtle, precious, subjective, slow developing, vegatative." In 1983, however, the realistic response is, "we can (if we are sophisticated enough) and we must (if we are to survive)." What this means is that if we are true to our philosophy and goals, and have implemented our objectives as outlined above, then our organization's products will be reflected in one or more of the following client-referenced outcome measures or products:

Increased behavioral skills related to independence, productivity, and social behavior
Movement up the living-training progressions as outlined in Figure 3.2
Placement into independent living facilities and competitive employment positions
Services received in a community-based program rather than within an institution

SUMMARY

Strategic planning, which lays the groundwork for later program implementation, evaluation, and accountability, is both a science and an art that directs an organization's resources, technology, and staff capability toward making people more independent, productive, and socially integrated. This chapter stressed the critical need for systematic planning prior to program development and implementation, and summarized the normalization and deinstitutionalization philosophy that should guide current (re)habilitation services. From this philosophy stems appropriate programmatic goals of increased independence, vocational productivity, and community integration. The goals are meaningless, however, without the facilities and training areas necessary to develop and practice the skills. Interfacing sequential living-training facilities with appropriate behavioral skills training is an integral part of strategic planning, along with developing measurable products that reflect the organization's goals.

DISCUSSION QUESTIONS

1. Write a one-sentence definition of your organization's goal(s). What is the guiding philosophy, and is there concensus among staff regarding the goal(s)?
2. What are the measurable objectives of your organization? Are these objectives: a) related to the goal statement generated in Question 1, and b) presented in measurable terms?
3. Generate a list of specific organizational outputs (excluding staff efforts) that can be used to evaluate the effectiveness of your organization. In the process, evaluate the various reasons people say "this can't be done."
4. Generate a list of specific behaviors that can be used to evaluate the level of a person's independence, productivity, and community integration. Discuss how these behaviors can be developed and evaluated.
5. Watch for signs within your organization and elsewhere indicating a movement away from the principles of normalization and deinstitutionalization. What are the factors and forces pushing in that direction, and how can those forces be counteracted? (A parallel development regarding "euthanasia" of severely impaired persons is discussed by Wolfensberger, 1980).

REFERENCE NOTES

1. Comprehensive reviews regarding court decisions and mentally retarded persons can be found in Boggs (1972), Bradley (1978), Comptroller General (1977), Hanley-Maxwell and Heal (1980), Laski (1977), Laski & Spitalnik (1980), Willer, Scheerenberger, and Intagliata (1980).
2. Conversely, neither shall the retarded be returned to the community indiscriminately:

> No resident may be transferred to a community residential facility or foster home unless it has been duly licensed; and the defendants are to make a written determination of the eligibility of each resident at Cambridge for community placement and review such determination at least yearly. The defendants are to

provide the court with a written plan to develop alternative residential care for all residents (*Welsch* v. *Likens,* 1974).

3. Results of community adjustment studies can be found in Cohen (1961), Gollay et al. (1978), Kolstoe (1961), Nihira and Nihira (1975), Reiter and Levi (1980), Sali and Amir (1971), Schalock and Harper (1978), and Schalock, Harper, and Genung (1981).
4. The importance of community-placed persons having benefactors or enablers is discussed by Edgerton and Bercovici (1976), Gollay et al. (1978), Henshel (1972), Schalock, Harper, and Carver (1981), and Willer (1978).
5. Standardization information including test construction, reliability, validity, and normative data can be found in Schalock, R.L., 1981, *Vocational Training Standardization Manual;* and Schalock, R.L., 1980, *Community Living Skills Standardization Manual,* Mid-Nebraska Mental Retardation Services, Hastings, Neb. 68901.

4

PLANNING PROGRAMMATIC SERVICES

Independence in the sphere of working and independence in the sphere of living are inseparable parts of complete habilitation.
(Boyen, 1978)

Chapter 3 underscored the importance of a unifying philosophy to guide your organization's goals, objectives, programs, and products. The present chapter goes one step further and outlines how an organization can mobilize and integrate its resources, technology, and staff to implement its philosophy and accomplish its major goals, objectives, and products. Interfacing client training with your organization's goals is one of the most significant aspects of organizational planning, because it will greatly facilitate program implementation, monitoring, and evaluation. This chapter summarizes current thinking about relevant programmatic services for developmentally disabled persons and delineates systematic approaches to developing behavioral skills necessary for increased productivity, independence, and community integration (the three programmatic goals discussed in Chapter 3).

As the area of programmatic services could consume volumes, discussion in this chapter is restricted, first, to approaches for developing *adaptive behaviors* as related to the three above-mentioned goals. Early intervention or traditional education programs are not treated here. A description and evaluation of these are found in Gray, Klaus, and Ramsey (1981), Jenkins, Stephens, and Sternberg (1980), Lazar et al., (1981), Palmer and Anderson (1981), and Seitz, Apfel, and Rosenbaum (1981).

A second focus of this chapter is on adults rather than youth, an orientation that reflects the author's bias and is explained in a recent article entitled, "Kittens and Cats in Rural America" (Schalock and Harper, 1979a). It has been my experience that since almost everyone likes a kitten, but fewer people like cats, there are many more programs and programmatic materials available for youth than for adults. Yet America's population, including that of developmentally disabled persons, is aging. The focus on adults in this volume is not to imply that the adaptive behaviors and programmatic approaches discussed are inappropriate for youth, but, rather, to stress the need for programmatic services that are both age-appropriate and functional.

A third focus is to integrate support services such as transportation, counseling, legal/financial assistance, mental/physical health services, advocacy, and follow-along assistance into the job descriptions of instructional staff. These services are viewed as part of the environmental support network required to successfully place a client into an environment that is less restrictive and more productive, but frequently much more demanding.

The chapter is organized into four sections: first, a summary of trends affecting services to developmentally disabled persons; second, an outline of a vocational training model; third, a review of various approaches to developing community living skills, along with a model training program; and fourth, a discussion of efforts to date at social skills training and a proposed program to facilitate the social acceptance and community integration of developmentally disabled individuals.

RECENT TRENDS AFFECTING SERVICES TO DEVELOPMENTALLY DISABLED PERSONS

Focus on Adaptive Behavior

Adaptive behavior, according to the American Association on Mental Deficiency (AAMD), is the effectiveness or degree with which an individual meets the standards of personal independence and social responsibility expected of his or her age and cultural group (Grossman, 1977). The concept of adaptive behavior has become increasingly important in efforts to serve persons with developmental disabilities, for three primary reasons. First, it reflects the functional legal definition of developmental disabilities, which are defined in terms of ''inabilities or limitations in performing roles and tasks expected of an individual within a given environment'' (PL 95–602). Second, the concept is an integral part of the official definition of mental retardation that refers to ''significantly subaverage general intellectual functioning existing concurrently with deficits in adaptive behavior, and is manifested during the developmental period'' (Grossman, 1977). Third, adaptive behavior has been proposed as the basis for individual program planning and as an outcome measure for habilitative efforts (Bogen and Aanes, 1975; Smith and Polloway, 1979; Zigler and Trickett, 1978).

Operationally, adaptive behavior includes a number of skills encompassing those related to independent functioning, cognition, social behavior, sensorimotor development, and communication. Although adaptive behavior is a complex and ever-changing attribute, it can be assessed, quantified, and scaled into levels of impairment. Assessment is best done, in this author's opinion, on the basis of observing actual client behavior (Note 1). In this regard, the inventory approach, including criterion-referenced instruments, appears to be more popular than the developmental or psychometric approach because of the ease with which important target behaviors can be included and the greater ease in standardization (Mori and Masters, 1980; Switzky et al., 1979).

The most widely used contemporary observation instrument is the AAMD Adaptive Behavior Scale, with versions standardized on institutional residents (Nihira et al., 1975) and students in regular and special classes (Lambert and Nicoll, 1976; Nihira et al., 1975). There are an additional 100 or so instruments used in various settings for measuring adaptive behavior (Mayeda and Lindberg, 1980). To summarize, the major instruments include:

AAMD Adaptive Behavior Scales (Nihira et al., 1975)
Adaptation for Profoundly Retarded (Congdon, 1973)
Alpern-Boll Developmental Profile (Alpern and Boll, 1972)
Balthazar Scales of Adaptive Behavior (Balthazar, 1971)
Cain-Levine Social Competency Scale (Cain, Levine, and Elzey, 1963)
Fairview Behavior Evaluation Battery for the Mentally Retarded (Ross, Boroskin, and Giampiccolo, 1970–1974)
Newman-Doby Measure of Social Competence (Newman and Doby, 1973)
Vineland Social Maturity Scale (Doll, 1964)

These scales attempt to isolate the factors usually associated with adaptive behavior. In particular, 12 major areas of adaptive behavior are commonly assessed in the scales (Robinson and Robinson, 1976) including self-help skills, communication skills, socialization or interpersonal skills, locomotion, self-direction, occupational skills, economic activity, neuromotor development, personal responsibility, social responsibility, emotional adjustment, and health.

When comparing these major areas to the above AAMD definition of adaptive behavior, the deficits in adaptive behavior will be reflected in the following areas according to one's age and cultural group (Grossman, 1977):

1. During infancy and early childhood:
   a. Sensorimotor skills development
   b. Communication skills (including speech and language)
   c. Self-help skills
   d. Socialization (development of ability to interact with others)
2. During childhood and early adolescence:
   a. Application of basic academic skills in daily life activities
   b. Application of appropriate reasoning and judgment in mastery of the environment
   c. Social skills (participation in group activities and interpersonal relationships)
3. During late adolescence and adult life in vocational and social responsibilities and performances

Changing Conceptions of Developmental Disabilities

Developmental disabilities are now defined functionally, not categorically. This shift is seen in Table 4.1, which compares PL 94–103 with PL 95–602. Although

Table 4.1. Comparative definitions of developmental disabilities

PL 94–103 Sec. 102(7)	PL 95–602 Sec. 503b(7)
The term "developmental disability" means a disability of a person that:	The term "developmental disability" means a severe, chronic disability of a person that:
(A) (i) is attributable to mental retardation, cerebral palsy, epilepsy, or autism; (ii) is attributable to any other condition of a person found to be closely related to mental retardation because such condition results in similar impairment of general intellectual functioning or adaptive behavior to that of mentally retarded persons or requires treatment and services similar to those required for such persons; or (iii) is attributable to dyslexia resulting from a disability described in clause (i) and (ii) of this sub-paragraph;	(A) is attributable to a mental or physical impairment or combination of mental and physical impairments;
(B) originates before such person attains age 18;	(B) is manifested before the person attains age 22;
(C) has continued or can be expected to continue indefinitely; and	(C) is likely to continue indefinitely;
(D) constitutes a substantial handicap to such a person's ability to function normally in society.	(D) results in substantial functional limitations in three or more of the following areas of major life activity: (i) self-care, (ii) receptive and expressive language, (iii) learning, (iv) mobility, (v) self-direction, (vi) capacity for independent living, and (vii) economic self-sufficiency; and
	(E) reflects the person's need for a combination and sequence of special, interdisciplinary, or generic care, treatment, or other services which are of lifelong or extended duration and are individually planned and coordinated.

the pros and cons of functional versus categorical definitions can be debated, the new definition clearly emphasizes function and functional limitations.

Understanding of intelligence is also changing (Haywood and Wachs, 1981; Kamhi, 1981). People are increasingly becoming aware that intelligence is a multidimensional, multidetermined trait that can be viewed from a number of perspectives including psychometric, developmental, motivational, learning, and social. The reader is referred to Haywood and Wachs (1981) for an excellent review of these different perspectives.

Two significant implications for treatment of disabled persons result from the changing ideas on intelligence: First, contrary to popular attitudes and practice, intelligence is not a unidimensional, global entity. Rather, "intelligence consists of specific abilities, learning processes, or cognitive functions that may be organized hierarchically in a single-stage, multidimensional space, or in a structure integrating cognitive and motivational aspects'' (Haywood and Wachs, 1981). Thus, intellective, multidimensional components exist and may underlie different levels of adaptive behavior, therefore enhancing the possibility of altering behavior or of learning other behavior. A second implication is that there is evidence that the nature of intelligence changes as individuals develop. Therefore, habilitative efforts should be directed toward changing environments to provide appropriate experiences, toward structuring situations to maximize learning, and toward focusing staff and client attitudes on learning and functioning potential (Haywood and Wachs, 1981).

Emergence of an Ecological Perspective

Three major concepts have historically influenced services to developmentally disabled persons. The first emphasizes security and good health through adequate residential programming, nutrition, and physical care. The second emphasizes development of cognitive and social skills through education and training programs. The third, or social ecology approach, recognizes that the environment significantly affects persons' behavior (Berkson and Romer, 1981).

This ecological or ''person-environment perspective'' represents different ways of thinking about the developmentally disabled person, including:

1. Individuals cannot be separated from their living-training environments (Stucky and Newbrough, 1981).
2. Both persons and their environments can be assessed (Dokecki, 1977; Hobbs, 1975; Moos, 1974a, b; Newbrough, 1977).
3. Behavioral change and growth potential is possible (Feurenstein et al., 1980; Haywood, 1977; Schalock and Karan, 1979).
4. Intervention focuses on the caregivers and settings as much as on the disabled person (Karan and Schalock, 1982; Stucky and Newbrough, 1981).
5. The unique qualities of the person and the living-training environment can be matched, promoting a person-environment consequence that optimizes functional level (Richardson, 1981; Stucky and Newbrough, 1981; Sutton, Michael, and Wanner, 1981).

Application of Client-Referenced Technology

Technology refers to applied science. All too often human services agencies view themselves at the other end of the continuum—as practicing an art. Somewhere in the middle there is room for a ''humanistic scientist'' who is willing to use science and technology to improve our service delivery process and increase our client-referenced products. The wise administrator should be familiar with the technology at his or her disposal; human service organizations have the tools and techniques to revolutionize how we deal with client training—if we but use the available technology. The future is now. Application of both behavioral and engineering technology is discussed below.

1. *Behavioral Technology* The systematic application of applied behavioral analysis and teaching techniques has resulted in significant changes in the lives of developmentally disabled persons. Some of the more important analysis and training techniques are summarized in Table 4.2.
2. *Engineering Technology* Behavioral technology provides techniques that can be used to overcome a mismatch between persons and their environment. A second technology, engineering technology, involves providing an environment that eliminates the mismatch. For example, a visually impaired person who enters an elevator without braille-referenced floor indicators is at a disadvantage; the barrier is overcome, however, if the elevator has the indicators. What is the difference? Very simply, the environment was changed and thereby eliminated the mismatch (and the handicap to a large extent). Another type of engineering technology, which is stressed below, provides a prosthetic device that smoothes the interface between the person and the environment at the point of interaction (Marks and Wade, 1981; Weisgerber, Dahl, and Appleby, 1980). Prosthetic devices effectively remove functional handicaps; therefore process planning must involve determining the prosthetic needs of the client and then either altering the environment (to make it "barrier free") or procuring prosthetics to reduce the handicap. The technical aid categories outlined below were suggested by Weisgerber et al. (1980); in addition, commercial resources are found in the reference notes. Neither an endorsement nor evaluation is implied in these listings.
   a. *Aids for visually impaired persons* (Note 2), including: 1) Kurzweil Reading Machine—converts ink print into spoken output; 2) Digicassette—converts material into braille; 3) Votrax Electronic Voice System—provides a vocabulary for speaking computer-generated output; 4) magnification systems, including closed circuit television; 5) control knobs that can be adjusted by touch; 6) tactile markings on various types of equipment; 7) light probes that emit a tone that varies in pitch and can be used for gauging distance; 8) modified work tools; and 9) provision of sight by electrical stimulation of the brain
   b. *Aids for hearing impaired persons* (Note 3), including: 1) volume control dials attached to a standard telephone; 2) manual communication modules presenting output in visible form; and 3) auditory trainers—small wireless transmitters and receivers with the incoming information transmitted to the listener's ear by a plug
   c. *Aids for upper extremity difficulties* (Note 4), including: 1) devices that make knobs and buttons easier to use; 2) head wands and mouthsticks; 3) powered hooks; 4) robotic arms; and 5) eating, grooming, and dressing aids such as utensils, toothbrushes, and modified clothing

d. *Aids to facilitate communication* (Note 5), including: 1) artificial larynx—substitutes electronically generated vibrations for those normally produced by the larynx; 2) speech amplifier—attached to standard telephone handset and can be used to adjust the volume of the transmission; and 3) communication boards—involving either light-activated or touch-activated controls
e. *Aids to facilitate locomotion* (Note 6), including: 1) protheses and orthoses for upper and lower limbs; 2) artificial kinesthetic feedback; and 3) work station modification
f. *Aids to facilitate cognitive processing,* including; 1) instructional techniques that produce generalized improvement in cognition (Butterfield, 1981; Feurenstein et al., 1980; Haywood and Wachs, 1981); and 2) calculator- or computer-assisted instruction (Brebner, Hallworth, and Brown, 1977, 1981; Hallworth and Brebner, 1978; Smeets, 1981)

These four trends emphasizing adaptive behavior, the functionality of development and intelligence, the person-environment perspective, and the application of client-referenced technology have forced a reevaluation of how we have historically approached the handicapped person. The optimism regarding that person's potential, combined with the current legal and social emphasis on normalization and integration, provide the vehicles and conceptualization to develop appropriate, effective, and efficient programmatic services for the developmentally disabled population. The remainder of this chapter outlines three essential services reflecting an organization's goals of increasing the person's productivity, independence, and community integration. The services include systematic approaches to vocational, community living, and community integration skill development.

VOCATIONAL TRAINING

Planning vocational training and placement programs requires knowledge of recent trends and research findings regarding vocational (re)habilitation. These are summarized below.

Trends and Research Findings

The current approach to vocational training relies heavily on work activity and sheltered workshops. A number of factors suggest that we need to reform this approach (Note 7). One factor relates to serious concern about what is currently happening in sheltered workshops. O'Connor (1976), for example, reported that in her sample of 9,000 retarded individuals living in community-based facilities, only 14% were competitively employed and 52% were in sheltered work or work

Table 4.2. Suggested training techniques resulting from behavioral research

Research area/ learning theory	Suggested training/instructional techniques	Major references
General learning theory	1. In early learning, prevent incorrect responses and maximize correct responses. 2. Provide immediate feedback of results regarding correct or incorrect responses. 3. Teach the desired response in a variety of contexts and practice across persons, tasks, and situations. 4. Use distributed practice. 5. Increase motivation by using reinforcers. 6. Develop response chains from simple to complex behavior.	Denny, 1966; Popovich, 1981
Social learning theory	1. Provide opportunities for learning and success, and set realistic goals. 2. Consistently pair specific behaviors with consequences. 3. Avoid ambiguous feedback. 4. Reinforce statements that reflect an internal locus of control.	Bandura, 1976; Zigler, 1966
Modeling (Observation)	1. Reward the model and observers for the behavior to be imitated. 2. Punish the model for undesirable behavior. 3. Have the model verbalize the behavior being performed.	Mercer and Snell, 1977; Pomerantz et al., 1981
Applied behavioral analysis [a]	1. A behavior must be demonstrated before it can be modified by changes in environmental conditions. 2. A behavior may be strengthened through immediate and carefully scheduled reinforcement.	Mercer and Snell, 1977; Popovich, 1981

	3. Fading of support should follow acquisition of a behavior.	
	4. Contingent reinforcements rather than punishment should be regarded as the primary means of changing behavior.	
	5. Learning is facilitated when acquisition proceeds from simple to complex response demands.	
	6. Continuous measurement of the target behavior regulates the pace and direction of learning.	
Special education	1. Provide a detailed task and content analysis combined with systematic chaining of components.	Brown et al., 1976; Popovich and Laham, 1982; Wehman and McLaughlin, 1980
	2. Size discriminations are made more easily by matching a very large item with the standard size item.	
	3. Color coding helps orientation to the most critical parts of a task.	
	4. Pictorial instructions are effective with many nonverbal clients.	
	5. Massed practice may increase learning speed.	
	6. Positive reinforcement in the form of verbal praise, trainer proximity, graphs, tokens, money, edibles, or adjacent peer attention are positive influences on learning rates.	
	7. Training in the natural environment, or environment where the skill will be used, facilitates learning.	

[a] Applied behavioral analysis is composed of: 1) the direct observation of the individual's behavior; 2) continuous measurement of that behavior; and 3) systematic environmental changes consistent with the relevant principles of behavior (Mercer and Snell, 1977).

activity centers. Similarly, Bellamy et al., (1980 and Note 8) report that over 100,000 severely handicapped adults are served in day programs that typically lack vocational training and placement services. Among clients in workshops, Whitehead (1979) reports that in 1976, the average hourly wage of all workshop clients was 81 cents an hour, which at that time represented only 35% of the minimum wage. The annual earnings were even less favorable, showing an average of $666 for the total client population and only $417 for the largest disability group, mentally retarded persons.

These data are bothersome because they do not reflect what research practices in (re)habilitation have indicated during the last decade—specifically, that there is a technology for job training (Bellamy, Horner, and Inman, 1979; Gold, 1973; Karan, 1976; Rusch and Mithaug, 1980; Schutz and Rusch, 1981; Wehman and McLaughlin, 1980), rehabilitation engineering (Malick, 1979), and work station modification (Weisgerber et al., 1980). Research has also shown clearly that developmentally disabled persons can acquire complex skills and perform them at acceptable rates (cf. Bellamy et al., 1979; Gold, 1976; Karan, 1976).

A second factor suggesting the need for change relates to the orientation and management of sheltered workshop programs. In general, it has been this author's experience that most workshops for developmentally disabled persons are: 1) employers of last resort, in that referrals are usually hard to train, low-skill persons; 2) poorly administered with little if any sophisticated equipment, management techniques, or marketing activities; 3) reactive to available contracts regardless of their training or skill acquisition potential; and 4) deficient in developing a sequential training program that focuses on measurable objectives related to developing vocational skills, increasing wages and/or client movement.

A third and final factor indicating need for reform relates to the current political-social climate which is characterized by reduced public funds and increased dependence and focus on the private sector (Gatty, 1981). This climate is an essential component of the vocational training and placement model discussed below.

Vocational Training and Placement Model

Figure 4.1 diagrams the major evaluation, training, and placement components of the proposed model. As shown in the figure, the evaluation component consists of assessing both industry and the client—a process described more fully under "Steps to Implement . . . " below. The extended employment component deals with the more severely handicapped person whose disability is such that it prevents him or her from competing in the labor market or who is unable to compete equally because of labor market conditions. The major goals for Extended Employment are to increase the person's wages, vocational skills, and physical tolerance, and eventually to move the individual to the sheltered workshop component. Client training is the catalyst for the movement. Task-analyzed contracts provide both financial renumeration and training materials.

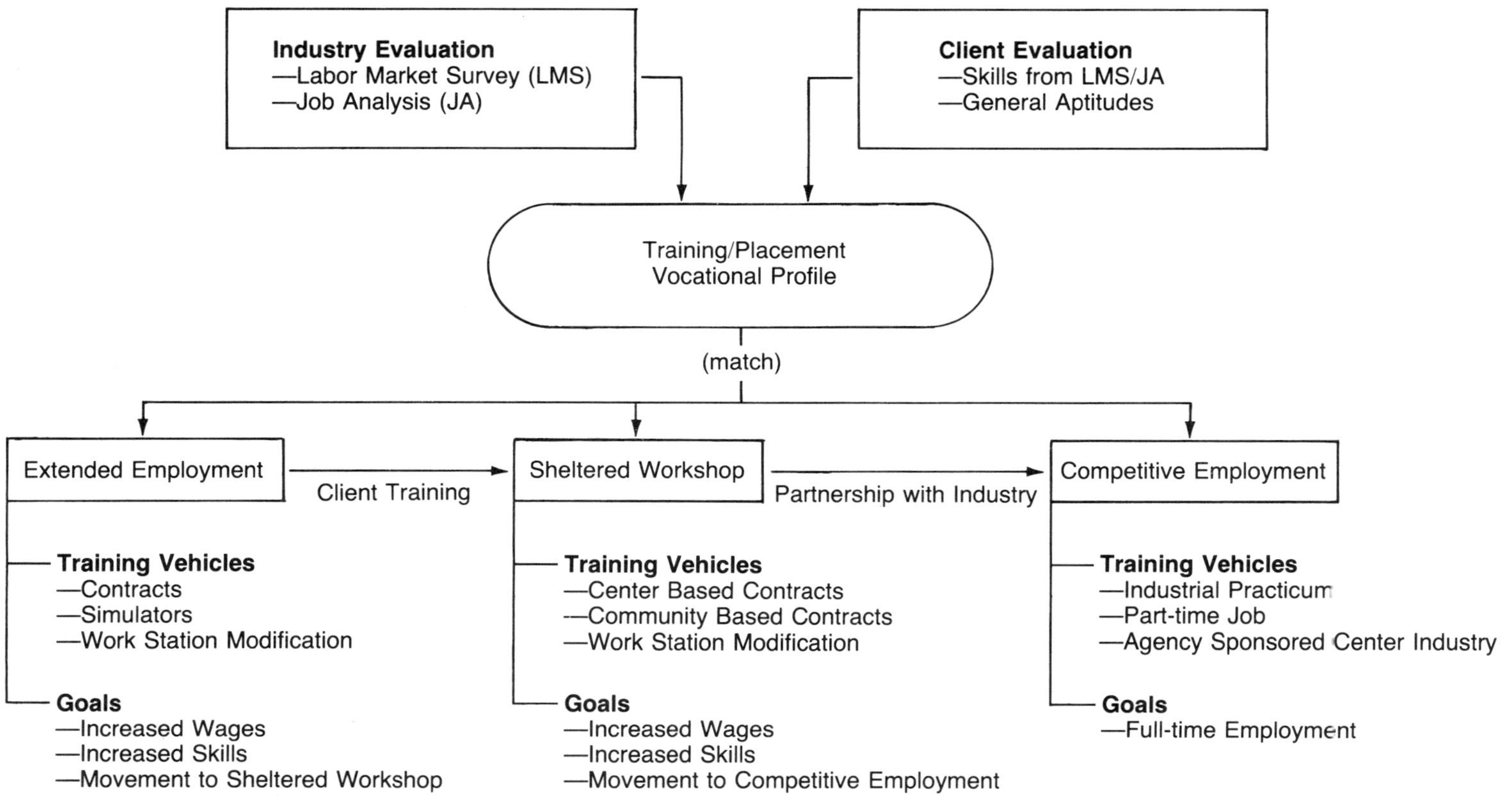

Figure 4.1. Three-component model of vocational training and placement.

The Sheltered Workshop component deals primarily with clients who are job-ready, or who can be with additional training. The major goal is competitive employment, with secondary objectives related to increased wages and vocational skills. Sheltered Workshop staff are in contact with local industry, updating their labor market surveys and job analyses. Contracts and potential private industry jobs are analyzed for required skills. Vocational training focuses on these required skills plus other competencies related to social and work behavior, interviewing, transportation, and physical stamina. The catalyst for movement from sheltered work to competitive employment might well be "partnership with industry," as embodied in one or more of the following private sector training-employment programs (Note 9).

Private Sector Training-Employment Programs

1. *Projects with Industry* Title III of the 1978 Rehabilitation Act (Section 621) authorizes cooperative arrangments with employers and organizations for the purpose of establishing projects designed to prepare handicapped persons for gainful and suitable employment in a competitive labor market. The intent of Section 621 is to bring the employer more directly into the rehabilitation process as a partner in the goal of restoring disabled persons to the world of work. The philosophical and pragmatic bases of the Project With Industry program include:

    Actual work settings provide the best situations for evaluating work potential for handicapped individuals.

    Rehabilitation personnel working more directly with the employer provide much needed assistance in the process of recruiting, hiring, and promoting the handicapped.

    Employers provide information about job requirements, needed aptitudes, and performance skills that are most adaptable to jobs for the handicapped.

    Under Section 621, an employer may enter into an agreement with the Rehabilitation Services Administration to establish jointly funded programs that provide disabled persons with opportunities for training and/or employment that would prepare them for full-time competitive employment. The federal share for such a program cannot be more than 80% of the total cost of the project. The wages paid to workers in such a program must meet federal minimum standards, the minimum rate required by the Fair Labor Standards Act, or the Walsh-Healy Public Contract, whichever is more appropriate. The program also requires necessary support programs for the workers, an adequate and safe work environment, and proper recordkeeping for the attendance, performance, and progress of the worker-trainees.

    Project with Industry programs also require local and business community involvement through advisory committees that are involved in technical training and job development. A common method is for an industry association to receive program funding to provide for anticipated industry needs. The association establishes a training program with federal money, but with local firms providing training assistance. Trainees are placed in jobs at the end of the training period. A second method is for the rehabilitation facility to establish relationships with local corporate sponsors to assist in specific job training. Since the specific industry specifies the type and nature of the training, this latter method is more germane to the company's needs and, therefore, is better suited to prepare the disabled person for employment.

2. *On-the-Job Training Program* This program is sponsored by the National Association for Retarded Citizens and funded from Title III of the Comprehensive Employment and Training Act of 1973, as amended in 1978 (PL 93–203 and PL 95–524). In this program, placement personnel match trainees with public- and private-sector jobs. A trainee's wages are subsidized for an 8-week period.
3. *Targeted Jobs Tax Credit Program* This program has been functioning for a number of years and offers wage subsidies in the form of elective tax credits for certain groups of disadvantaged workers in private-sector employment. Employers can receive tax credits for wages paid to certified employees equal to 50% of first-year wages and 25% of second-year wages (up to $6,000 each year). Filing forms are available through Department of Employment or Job Service offices.
4. *Title VII—Private Sector Initiative Programs for the Economically Disadvantaged* Title VII of the Comprehensive Employment and Training Act is designed to increase the involvement of the business community in employment and on-the-job training activities. The primary vehicle created to accomplish this goal is the Private Industry Council. Such councils are designed to work in cooperation with primary sponsors to achieve increased private sector employment, thus reducing sponsors' reliance on public and private nonprofit subsidized employment. To be eligible, participants must meet the requirements for Title II-B and C (CETA) that include:
   a. *Subpart B:* Eligible participants must be economically disadvantaged, unemployed, underemployed, or in school.
   b. *Subpart C:* Eligible participants must be operating at less than full skill potential and working at least 6 months in either entry level, unskilled, or semi-skilled positions, or positions with little or no opportunity for advancement.

Steps to Implement the Vocational Training and Placement Model

The following sequential implementation steps are suggested for those interested in developing the vocational training-placement model outlined above.

1. *Labor Market Survey* A labor market analysis (including both a labor market survey and job analysis) is essential in developing a valid vocational training program. Research has demonstrated repeatedly that vocational evaluation and training for developmentally disabled persons are best guided by clearly

identifying available jobs and the skills required of these jobs (Wehman and McLaughlin, 1980; Weisgerber et al., 1980).

The labor market survey focuses on the identification of industry, products, and jobs within an organization's geographical location. Such a survey should identify:

Industries that are willing to employ developmentally disabled individuals
Jobs that are available to the developmentally disabled clients served by the organization
Sources of contracts that may be procured from various industries within the area

2. *Job Analysis* A correct job analysis can reveal many aspects useful in vocational evaluation and training (McCormick, 1979; Weisgerber et al., 1980). Among these are a list of duties and tasks that are entailed; information about the tools, machines, and equipment involved; and a delineation of the required skills that can be taught if necessary.

   Although it may be impossible for vocational professionals in many jobs to thoroughly understand all jobs, they should understand the process by which jobs can be studied, analyzed, evaluated, and described. A working knowledge of the *Dictionary of Occupational Titles* (U.S. Department of Labor, 1977) will allow vocational professionals to understand the general requirements of almost all jobs in the U.S. economy. The *Dictionary* is based directly on actual job analyses of approximately 40,000 jobs. It identifies jobs within industries by expanding upon the constructs of data, people, and things, and further breaks down these constructs to indicate job complexity, with each occupation assigned a 3-digit code based on the classifications shown in Table 4.3.

   The *Dictionary* also analyzes desirable trait characteristics that a person should bring to the job that are likely to affect job success. These traits include general educational requirements, specific vocational preparation, aptitudes, interests, temperaments, working conditions, and physical demands. Techniques to assess these characteristics can be found in the *Dictionary*.

   Job analysis data should specify the entry level skills required of community-based jobs. Once the skills are identified, then task and content analysis can be used to design training programs that lead to skill acquisition and job placement.
3. *Vocational Evaluation* Figure 4.1 depicts vocational evaluation as interfacing client skills and job requirements. The result is a "Training/Placement Vocational Profile" that either matches the client's skill level to available jobs or indicates the skills to be acquired from additional training. Assessment tools that can be used to develop Vocational Profiles are summarized in Reference Note 10.

   Extended employment and sheltered work might be used in conjunction with vocational evaluation. Depending upon the intent, three types of certificates issued currently (1982) by the U.S. Department of Labor are appropriate:

Table 4.3. System of job classification used in *Dictionary of Occupational Titles*

Data	People	Things
0. synthesizing	0. mentoring	0. setting up
1. coordinating	1. negotiating	1. precision working
2. analyzing	2. instructing	2. operating-controlling
3. compiling	3. supervising	3. driving-operating
4. computing	4. diverting	4. manipulating
5. copying	5. persuading	5. tending
6. comparing	6. speaking-signaling	6. feeding-offbearing
	7. serving	7. handling
	8. taking instructions—helping	

Source: U.S. Department of Labor. 1977. *Dictionary of Occupational Titles*. 4th Ed. Washington, D.C.

Sheltered Employment—issued for the purpose of serving clients who demonstrate a higher level of production potential

Work Activities—issued to provide treatment and training programs in cooperation with work-for-pay programs

Evaluating and Training—allows the employer to pay less than minimum wages to a client who is working on a job for the primary purpose of receiving training

4. *Training/Placement* Clients should be placed in competitive employment if the vocational profile matches the person to an available job. If an immediate job is not available, sheltered work can be used until a job is available through a private sector training-employment program. If the client is not immediately job-ready, but will become so with additional training, a number of training-placement options are possible: For example, industrial practicums can be used with staff supervision for additional personal, social, or vocational skills training. Sheltered workshops can also be used for structured vocational training (Note 11) or prime manufacturing. In addition, new program models in provider organizations can be developed, such as:

Industrial employment programs (for example, see Jewish Vocational Service, 1978. *Program Models for Projects with Industry*. Research Utilization Laboratory, Jewish Vocational Service, Chicago; also JWK International Corporation, 1980. *Maximizing Employment Potential*. JWK International Corporation, Annandale, Va.)

Enclave work stations in industry (for example, see McGee, J., 1975. *Work Stations in Industry*. University of Kansas, Kansas University Affiliated Facility, Lawrence.)

Affirmative industry model (for example, see DuRand, L., and DuRand, J., 1978. *The Affirmative Industry*. Minnesota Diversified Industries, St. Paul.)

Specialized training programs (for example, see Bellamy, T., Inman, D., and Horner, R., 1979. Design of vocational habilitation services for the severely retarded: The specialized training program model. In: G. Hamerlynck (ed.), *Behavioral Systems for the Developmentally Disabled.* Brunner/Mazel, New York.)

COMMUNITY LIVING SKILLS TRAINING

Approaches to Independent Living

The term "independent living" has emerged as possibly the most dynamic development in the developmental disability field since the popularization by Wolfensberger of the normalization principle. To some, it is an emerging social or civil rights movement (DeJong, 1978; Roberts, 1977) that endeavors to counteract the devaluation experiences of disabled persons including being regarded as inferior, useless, burdensome, unesthetic, and generally "one down" (Vash, 1975). This view is well summarized by Stoddard (1978) who states:

> When those active in the disabled movement use the term 'independent living', they are referring to their ability to participate in society—to work, have a home, raise a family, and generally share in the joys and responsibilities of community life. 'Independent living' means freedom from isolation or from the institution; it means the ability to choose where to live and how; it means the person's ability to carry out activities of daily living that non-disabled people often take for granted (p. 2).

Two early developments in the independent living movement involved physical modification of aids for daily living (Stoddard, 1978) and independent living rehabilitation. One example of this development is the Center for Independent Living, Inc. (Berkeley, California), which describes itself in the following manner:

> The Center for Independent Living is a community-based nonprofit organization which provides a variety of support services to disabled and elderly individuals in order to enable them to live independently in the community.
>
> These support services include: peer counseling, housing referral, attendant referral, wheelchair repair, financial advocacy and counseling, transportation, deaf services, and blind services.
>
> The Center began as a very small corporation in 1972. Three severely disabled individuals developed the concept of an independent living program when the support services which they received were about to be terminated due to their graduation from the University.
>
> The Center was born as a result of these three persons coming to a crossroads in life. Rather than returning to dependency—living with their parents or in nursing homes, they chose to set up a system by which they could provide their own support services and thus could continue to lead independent lives in the communities of their choice.
>
> In its earliest years, the Center developed a strong philosophical base. This philosophy has two major points. The first is that independent living programs should serve all disabilities. The second point is that disabled persons should run and control any organization created to serve their needs.

Federal recognition of the significance of independent living is reflected both in the Comprehensive Vocational Rehabilitation Act of 1978 (Title 7), which specifies that the rehabilitation goal of severely handicapped persons will include training in independent living skills, and in Title III of PL 95–602, which establishes a new program—Comprehensive Services for Independent Living—focusing on persons who at present are too severely disabled to benefit from traditional vocational rehabilitation services. Unfortunately, neither of these Title programs has been well developed, and as a result, the quantity and quality of training for independent living currently offered by community programs for developmentally disabled persons is frequently less than optimal (Crnic and Pym, 1979; McDevitt et al., 1978; Scheerenberger and Felsenthal, 1977).

It is not surprising that as early as 1967 literature referred to the fact that jobs among developmentally disabled persons were being lost due to "problems of living rather than problems of working" (President's Committee on Employment of the Handicapped, 1977). To the author's knowledge, however, no one had determined empirically why this was so; or beyond that, endeavored to establish a program to address the issue. In addition, without an adequate data base or funding, people could only speculate as to the validity of establishing a systematic program for community living skills training.

The goal of training for community living was incorporated into the Mid-Nebraska Mental Retardation Services Program 8 years ago when it became obvious that the majority of clients failed their job placements because of living problems, not because of inadequate job skills. As a result, a separate, systematic training program directed toward the acquisition of specific community living skills was developed. The term "community living skills" (CLS) was purposefully chosen to distinguish it from the "independent living social movement" discussed above, as well as to stress that this was a systematic client training component (analogous to vocational training) whose primary goal is to develop those specific behavioral skills associated with living successfully within less restrictive environments.

A Model for Community Living Skills Training

During the last 8 years, the approach to training community living skills developed by this author has been based on a number of longitudinal studies associating community living placement success with variables related to placement environments, client characteristics, client skills, and necessary support services (Note 12). The current training model is outlined in Figure 4.2. The model's most important aspects include:

1. It specifies the goal of community living skills training, which is to allow persons to live in less restrictive and more independent environments.
2. It outlines a progression of living-training facilities currently within the service delivery system.

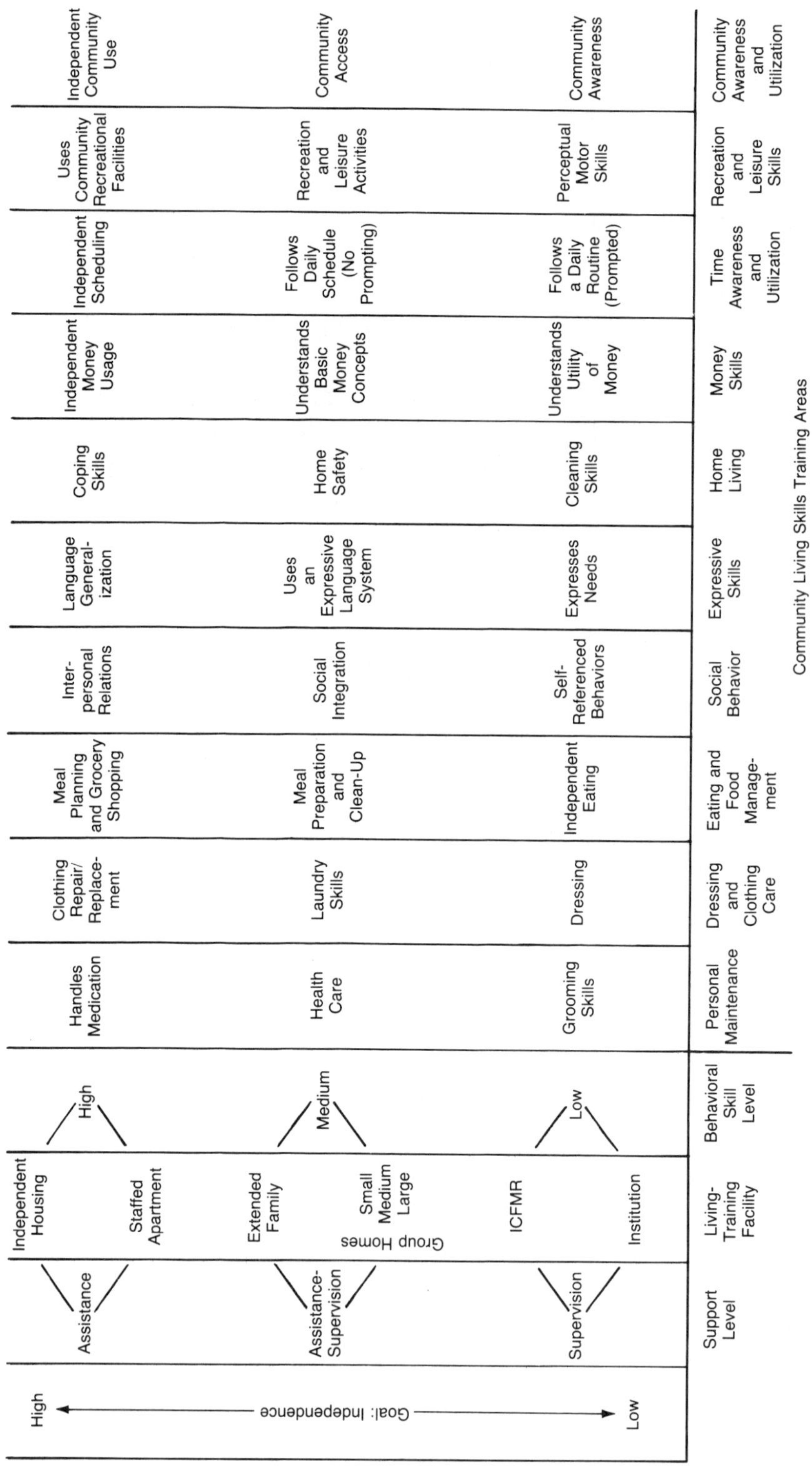

Figure 4.2. Community integration and skills training model.

3. It suggests the necessary support level required by the respective living-training facility.
4. It summarizes the behavioral skill level appropriate to the progression.
5. It interfaces proposed skill training areas with the above-referenced living-training facilities.

Implementation Steps

One of the priority service areas specified in PL 95–602 is the development of alternative community living arrangements defined as "services which will assist persons with developmental disabilities in maintaining suitable residential arrangements in the community." Implementing these arrangements will require at least the following steps:

1. *Develop progression* Deinstitutionalization does not end at the group home; rather it involves a progression from the institution to the community-based residence to living independently within the community. This movement requires a continuum of living-training facilities such as those outlined in Figure 4.2 and discussed more fully in Chapter 3.
2. *Establish training areas* Although the community living skills training model outlined in Figure 4.2 interfaces suggested skill training areas with a progression of living-training facilities, other suggested training areas and curricula are available (Note 13). In this regard, an analysis was recently completed on a number of independent/community living skill curricula. Each curriculum was evaluated in terms of focus (assessment or remediation), content (behavioral skill areas), number of skills covered, client functional level for which the curriculum was appropriate, and the environment toward which the curriculum was directed. The results of this analysis are presented in Table 4.4.
3. *Develop assessment and remediation approach* Once a service delivery system has determined its living-training progressions and the specific behavioral skills and domains with which it will deal, the assessment/training staff need to decide how those behavioral skills will be assessed and remediated if deficient. The author has found several parameters important in implementing the evaluation model presented in Figure 4.2. In reference to assessment, criterion-referenced assessment instruments have been developed (Schalock and Gadwood, 1980) that outline the evaluation procedure and the criterion behavior the client should demonstrate for each of the specific behavioral skills assessed. This criterion-referenced assessment, if done reliably and with validity, results in a profile of the client's skills relative to the objectives and goals previously discussed. The assessment process should also interface with the remediation approach outlined below and should reflect behavioral change through reassessment of the same behavioral skills at a later time.

Table 4.4. Independent living/community living curriculum analysis

Title[a]	Format[b]		Functional level[c]	Environment	Content-behavioral skill areas[d]								
	A	T			PH	SCS	FM	SB	C	HLS	FA	RL	CAU
An Activities of Daily Living Curriculum for Handicapped Adults (1978)		X	Moderate	Gr. Homes	X	X	X	X	X	X	X		X
Becoming Independent: A Living Skills System (1978)	X	X	Moderate	Gr. Homes/ Apt.	X	X	X	X	X	X	X	X	X
Community Living Skills: Assessment and Training (revised 1978)	X	X	Unavailable	Gr. Homes/ Apt.	X	X		X		X			X
Community Living Skills Screening Test and Remediation Manual (revised 1980)	X	X	Mild to Severe	All living facilities	X	X	X	X	X	X	X	X	X
Home and Family Living Laboratory (1978)	X		Mild/Moderate	Indep. Housing				X		X	X	X	X
Independent Living Behavior Checklist (1979)	X		Mild to Severe	Gr. Homes/ Apt.		X	X	X	X	X	X		X
Independent Living Skills Curriculum (1981)	X	X	Mild/Moderate	Gr. Homes	X		X			X	X		
Skills to Achieve Independent Living (1975)	X	X	Mild/Moderate	Gr. Homes/ Apt.	X	X	X	X	X	X	X	X	X
Social Perceptual Training Kit for Community Living for Trainable and Educable Retarded Citizens (1978)		X	Mild/Moderate	School			X	X	X	X	X	X	X
The Individual Assessment and Program Guide (1976)	X		Moderate	Gr. Homes	X	X	X	X	X	X	X	X	X
Toward Independent Living (1980)	X	X	Special needs children	Natural home	X	X			X		X		
Training for Independent Living (1975)		X	Mild/Moderate	Apt.	X		X	X	X	X	X		X

[a] See Reference Note 14 for bibliography.
[b] A = assessment; T = training.
[c] Functional level as stated in material.
[d] Behavioral skill abbreviations:
PH = personal hygiene; SCS = self-care skills; FM = food management; SB = social behavior; C = communication; HLS = home living skills; FA = functional academics (usually time and money); RL = recreation and leisure; CAU = community awareness and utilization.

In reference to remediation, the systematic, individualized approach recommended by the model is characterized by the following:

Establishes teaching or behavioral objectives for each of the deficit behaviors (from the assessment).
Relates specific materials and techniques to each behavior.
Implements an individualized intervention strategy to remediate each behavioral deficit. This strategy relates the behavioral objective to teaching materials, teaching strategies, acceleration-deceleration cycles, and the method used to quantify the results.
Quantifies the specific results of the remediation activity employed.

4. *Operationalize movement criteria* There is currently considerable emphasis on criterion-referenced assessment technology. There is also a need to develop a similar technology for criterion-indexed movement and placement, so that a client's progression along the continuum will be based on specific behavioral criteria. By defining the settings available and what is required to function in them, one can determine where clients should be placed; and training can then be initiated to allow persons to move forward toward less dependency and more productivity. Under the current system, clients are frequently placed on a space-available basis, rather than being placed according to their abilities. The situation is exacerbated by the fact that vendors tend to prepare the client to cope with the present environment with little regard for the next step on the progression toward community living. Preparing clients for the "next step" might well be facilitated if economic incentives were offered to programs that demonstrate a progression of clients toward increased independence and productivity. This would also facilitate client movement "through the system." Criterion-indexed norms will be necessary to indicate appropriate entry and exit behavioral skill levels. This author feels strongly that the norms should be flexible and based on functional skills that can be acquired through systematic remediation; otherwise, they will serve as barriers rather than norms.
5. *Expand instructional staff duties* Most human service programs use a traditional model of follow-along that provides maximum advice but minimum assistance to clients placed or terminated; however, increasingly studies show that the advice and minimum level of assistance provided by case management is not enough to maintain placement, especially for lower functioning clients. It is necessary, therefore, to implement a more intensive assistance program in which regular instructors provide skill training and assistance to the clients in their staffed or independent/shared apartment (Schalock, Harper, and Carver, 1981). This necessitates shifting from an "in-house" academic training model to one in which staff rotate throughout the day and evening as benefactors (Edgerton, 1975) or facilitators (Schalock, Karan, and Harper, 1980) to provide training and assistance as needed.

What CLS Evaluation Studies Tell Us

Although systematic training in community living skills has been implemented only recently, studies are beginning to evaluate this training on persons placed into semi- or independent living environments. Four generalizations from these studies are apparent:

1. *Skills do generalize*. Efforts to date indicate that behavioral skills associated with independent community living can be taught and do generalize to the person's new environment (Crnic and Pym, 1979; Justice and Close, 1980; Schalock and Harper, 1978; Schalock, Harper, and Carver, 1981; Sitkei, 1980). A recent study by the author (Schalock, Harper, and Carver, 1981), for example, found that 5 years after apartment placement, behavioral skills in personal maintenance, clothing care and use, and community utilization demonstrated during training are still related statistically to placement success. The data also indicate that with increasing placement duration, skills in food preparation, time management (personal schedule and leisure time), and communication become increasingly important. It is interesting to note that even though tested intelligence and functional academics (money, banking, time concepts) were not statistically related to placement success, the assistance provided by case management staff was primarily in activities requiring those skills (checkbooks, appointments, medication usage, and shopping).
2. *Assistance is necessary*. The evaluation data also suggest that community living skill training programs must do a better job of analyzing, teaching, and providing assistance in the skills necessary for adapting to less restrictive living environments. For example, if one considers that the institution provides a communal living environment, and large group homes represent an extension of this communal concept, it becomes clear that transition to a noncommunal environment will entail significant psychological adjustment on the part of clients (Carsrud et al., 1979; Gardner and Cole, 1981a). To facilitate this transition, it has become necessary to implement a more intensive assistance program such as that described above.
3. *Environmental variables are important*. Recent evidence suggests that different environments significantly effect the adaptive behavior of persons residing within those environments. For example, Hull and Thompson (1980) report that in reference to adaptive functioning within community settings for mentally retarded persons, client characteristics accounted for 21% of the variance, whereas environmental variables accounted for an additional 35%. Similarly, Romer and Berkson (1980a) found that across two settings (residence and workshops), setting variables accounted for 16% to 63% of the variance, independent of personal traits or mediating factors.

   Environments can also affect skill acquisition. For example, a recent study (Schalock, Gadwood, and Brown, 1983) compared skill acquisition indices (see Chapter 10) for two community living skill training programs that are within the same agency, but that use different approaches to client training. One approach was ''center-based'' and accomplished the majority of remediation programming within an adult developmental center; the second approach trained clients in their natural living environments. The two groups were compared after 1 year of training on the number of community living skills gained. Results indicated that clients trained in their apartments (natural living environments) gained three times the skills as those trained in the center and, furthermore, maintained their placements.

4. *Quality of life variables cannot be excluded.* The quality of life for clients placed into the community has recently received considerable attention (Edgerton, 1975; Landesman-Dwyer, Berkson, and Romer, 1979; McDevitt et al., 1978; Scheerenberger and Felsenthal, 1977; Throne et. al., 1977; Willer, Scheerenberger, and Intagliata, 1978). Most studies dealing with this issue present a mixed picture: On the one hand, the quality of life of clients placed into the community and terminated from active program involvement can generally be characterized as low-income and possibly lonely. On the other hand, community utilization occurs frequently and involves normal activities. Persons report that they are proud of their apartments and feel good about ''doing their own thing,'' but frequently indicate they would like more friends. The friendship patterns appear to be program-specific, in that clients continue after placement to associate with other clients or program staff (Romer and Berkson, 1980a, b; Schalock, Harper, and Carver, 1981). This mixed message regarding the clients' quality of life indicates a continued need to be sensitive not only to the development of skills necessary for more independent living, but also to the subjective feelings and wishes of clients placed into less restrictive, but often more complex, living arrangements.

COMMUNITY INTEGRATION

The previous section summarized studies reporting the effects of community living skills training. What these studies increasingly point out is that there is an important distinction between community *living* and community *integration*. In many cases, former clients are living in independent and semi-independent placements, but are still isolated from the mainstream of the community's activities and life. Therefore, we must do a better job not only of placing people into theoretically more independent living environments, but also of ensuring their true integration into the community. Three programmatic focuses and services should facilitate this integration: 1) attending to the client's mental health needs; 2) focusing on the training of social and interpersonal skills; and 3) developing community-oriented recreation and leisure skills. Each is discussed in detail below. First, however, a brief discussion of the importance of social behavior.

The Importance of Social Behavior

The importance of developing social and interpersonal behavioral skills in developmentally disabled persons cannot be overemphasized. The role of appropriate social behavior in both deinstitutionalized and community placement efforts has been well documented. For example, results of several community adjustment studies have reported that personality and social behaviors are among the major variables affecting successful community placement (Eyman and Call, 1979; Gollay et al., 1978; Heal, Sigelman, and Switzky, 1978; Nihira and Nihira, 1975; Reiter and Levi, 1980; Schalock, Harper, and Genung, 1981). Research has also demonstrated the importance of appropriate social-interpersonal skills in successful job and living placements (Baller, Charles, and Miller, 1967; Foss and Peterson, 1981; Kolstoe, 1961; Rosen, Clark, and Kivitz, 1977; Schalock and Harper, 1978; Wehman, 1981). Social-interpersonal competence and work success is furthermore reflected in the content of vocational assessment instruments. Walls and Werner (1977), for example, identify 24 relevant behavioral checklists, each containing from 1 to 56 items related to social-interpersonal behavioral skills.

Despite the documented importance of social-interpersonal behavioral skills, few programs for developmentally disabled persons have successfully developed a systematic approach to either meeting the mental health needs of their clients or developing appropriate social, interpersonal, and recreational skills in these persons. Programmatic approaches to these areas are outlined in the remainder of this chapter.

Meeting the Clients' Mental Health Needs

It is becoming increasingly evident (cf. Gardner and Cole, 1981b; Laski and Spitalnik, 1980; Menolascino, 1977, 1983; Szymanski and Tanquay, 1980) that community placement does not automatically insure the developmentally disabled person's participation in the new living arrangement in a personally satisfying and productive manner. Too frequently, community placement occurs before the person has been prepared adequately for the new, generally stressful environment. As a result, many persons remain (or become) passive, dependent, unmotivated, socially inadequate, anxious, depressed, withdrawn, and frequently aggressive toward self and others. In fact, a number of studies (Menolascino, 1977; Szymanski and Tanguay, 1980) report developmentally disabled persons living in community-based programs have a 20% to 35% higher frequency than others of obvious mental health problems, including: a) the severe disorders of personality disorganization seen in psychotic reactions; b) problems characterized mainly by excessive anxiety and related neurotic defensive reactions; and c) a range of disorders including those of conduct, passivity, dependency, withdrawal, helplessness, and depression (Gardner and Cole, 1981b).

The approaches used to date to meet the mental health needs of the developmentally disabled have generally been inadequate (Szymanski and Tanguay,

1980). Rosen et al. (1977) and Sternlicht (1977) report, for example, that personal counseling and psychotherapy have not been effective. This may reflect either the lack of training among mental health professionals in serving the disabled population or the categorical exclusion of developmentally disabled persons from mental health centers (Szymanski and Tanguay, 1980). Studies also indicate that 33% to 67% of developmentally disabled clients referred to community mental health facilities do not keep their appointments; and that 40% to 50% of those that do, fail to return after the first session (Anthony, 1980). Although chemotherapy is a valuable adjunct in mental health services, it is less than effective if it is the only specialized treatment used or is controlled by persons external to the ongoing training program (Rivinus, 1980; Sprague and Baxley, 1978). And finally, well-defined behavioral therapy approaches are either not available or involve the use of punishment procedures of questionable acceptance or feasibility within community-based programs (Gardner and Cole, 1980, 1981a).

Meeting the mental health needs of developmentally disabled persons will not be an easy task for your organization. The following guidelines and suggestions represent current thinking:

1. Interagency involvement is essential, including mental health agencies, regional centers, private practitioners, and other components of the service delivery system. Clients will need to move "in and out" of treatment-program facilities, analogous to admission and discharge from a community clinic or hospital.
2. Intervention should reflect an emphasis on habilitation and education rather than treating problems as an illness. In most instances, the mental health problems of the developmentally disabled person are best met by designing programs to teach the person new social competency skills within the person's natural environment.
3. Agency staff should be trained to identify and provide effective mental health intervention in the setting in which the mental health problems occur. Consultation with mental health agencies can thereby be reserved for the more difficult and chronic problems that require a more sophisticated intervention strategy.
4. Staff should be trained to monitor drug effects and communicate these to the prescribing physician.
5. A preventive attitude should be maintained. Specifically, many mental health problems can be prevented or reduced by sensitive attention to the person's emotional and interpersonal needs at the time.

Developing Social-Interpersonal Skills

Inadequate social and interpersonal skills are among the most important factors preventing the full integration of the developmentally disabled person into society's mainstream. The development of these skills, however, cannot be separated from the person's experiences. For example, Baroff (1974) suggests that all persons require certain kinds of psychological experiences that facilitate personality development. The primary ones include: 1) *structure*—that imparts the ability to predict events and to possess a sense of familiarity with one's life; 2) *self esteem*—a sense of usefulness and adequacy about oneself that is directly related to feelings of intimacy, success, and autonomy; and 3) *self expression*—in the form of activities and pursuits. With these experiences in mind, social-interpersonal skill training should focus on what the environment does to the person, what it tells the person about himself or herself, and which social-interpersonal skills are necessary to adapt successfully to the person's environment.

It is also important to realize that different environments require different social-interpersonal skills. For example, a recent study (Foss and Peterson, 1981) of the social-interpersonal skills relevant to job success among mentally retarded adults found that sheltered workshops personnel in 11 western states reported the following eight skills as most relevant to job tenure: following supervisor instructions; responding appropriately to supervisor criticism or correction; refraining from exhibiting bizarre or irritating behavior; working independently of direct supervision; maintaining an appropriate personal appearance; interacting appropriately with co-workers while on the job; controlling aggressive behavior; and requesting assistance as needed. Analogously, social-interpersonal skills related to community placement success include appropriate emotional expression, group participation, self-control, social etiquette (including self-help skills), motivation to initiate and complete reasonable activities, and appropriate use of leisure time (Schalock, Harper, and Genung, 1981; Schalock, Harper and Carver, 1981).

The above data suggest that social-interpersonal skills training programs are *environment specific*. This means that training staff should determine the skills required of the client's current and future living-training environments. Once these environments are analyzed (analogous to the job analysis procedure outlined in Figure 4.1), social-interpersonal skills training can begin. Some of the more popular social skills training areas, programs, and techniques are outlined in Table 4.5.

Developing Community-Oriented Recreation and Leisure Skills

Available data (Salzberg and Langford, 1981; Schalock, Harper, and Carver, 1981; Wehman, Schleien, and Kiernan, 1980) indicate that many clients placed into community-based facilities (including independent housing) spend most of their leisure time inside their residences rather than in the community interacting and participating in leisure time/recreational activities. In addition, one frequently finds few age-appropriate activities when walking through adult clientele housing and training programs. Hence, a two-part question: First, what should be the goals of an adult-oriented recreation and leisure program; and second, how can programs be implemented to reach the goals?

The answer to the first question is probably easier than the second. Recreation and leisure activities should promote community integration; be age-appropriate

(Wehman et al., 1980); be personally satisfying (Salzberg and Langford, 1981); develop active as well as passive activities (Katz and Yekutiel, 1974); and focus on everyday activities rather than large, special events (Corcoran and French, 1977).

Developing recreation and leisure activities to attain these goals will require one or more of the following adaptations:

1. *Material adaptations,* in which the usual equipment is adapted to the person's physical/functional level. Examples of this include bowling ball pushers, hand grip bowling ball, foam rubber ratchet handles, and so on (Wehman et al., 1980).
2. *Procedure adaptation,* in which the rules or procedures are adapted to the person's level. These changes or modifications can convert an impossible game into a highly enjoyable and feasible one (Weisman, 1982).
3. *Skill sequence adaptations,* by which the instructor alters the normal chain of behaviors to facilitate performance. For example:

> A hobby such as cooking provides a clear illustration. When boiling an egg, a nonhandicapped person may place the egg into a pot of boiling water. It is obvious that this could be a hazardous problem (i.e., scald hand) for an individual with physical and/or intellectual limitations. A remedy to this problem is to rearrange the sequence of the component steps of the skill by training the cook to initially place the egg into the saucepan and then filling the pot with cold water. The saucepan is then placed onto the burner and the water brought to a boil. This procedure does not alter the final results (i.e., boiled egg) when several minutes are added to the cooking time, but facilitates a safe and practical method of performing this worthwhile leisure pursuit.
>
> A modified skill sequence applicable to the manipulation of a camera can also be implemented. Typically, an individual will first raise the camera to eye level and then place his index finger over the shutter release button. However, individuals lacking sufficient fine motor coordination could initially be trained to position their finger over the shutter release button prior to lifting the camera. In this way, the individual would merely have to depress the button once the camera was appropriately positioned (Wehman et al., 1980; p. 400).

4. *Facility adaptations,* whereby community recreation/leisure facilities are made accessible to the nonambulatory person (ramps, enlarged doors, lowered drinking fountains, and so forth) or are designed from the beginning to be accessible. Designs for the latter can be found in *A Guide to Designing Accessible Outdoor Recreation Facilities* (Heritage Conservation and Recreation Service, U.S. Department of the Interior, Washington, D.C., 20043).
5. *Provide a facilitator,* who assists the person with initial entry, transportation, and encourages self-confidence. An example is provided by Salzberg and Langford (1981), who used volunteers—matched to the client on variables such as interests and previous leisure time experience—to provide at least weekly community-integrated leisure and recreational activities. Staff can also be used in this capacity.

While community-oriented recreation and leisure activities are an important vehicle for community integration, one should not overlook the age-

Table 4.5. Social skills training: techniques and behaviors manipulated

Technique	Specific behaviors manipulated	Pertinent references
Operant Reinforcement	Verbal social responding	McClure (1968)
	Environmental awareness, behavioral effectiveness, social interaction, and appropriate emotional expression	Schalock, Ross, and Ross (1976) Craighead, Kazdin, and Mahoney (1981) Levitt (1963);
	Self-help skills (grooming, hygiene)	O'Leary, and Kent (1973); O'Leary and Wilson (1975)
	Hyperactive, assaultive	
Role playing/ Personal adjustment Training	Conversation, cooperative work, assertion	Meredith et al. (1979); Friedman (1968); Goldsmith and McFall (1975)
	Avoidance behavior	
	Anxiety, phobias, obsessions	Lira et al., (1975)
	Social skills and assertion Social interactions	Curran (1981); McFall and Marston (1970); Eisler, Miller, and Hersen (1973); Fiedler and Beach (1978) MacDonald, et al., (1975)
	Social responses/behaviors Social roles and expectations	Gibson, Lawrence, and Nelson (1976) Zisfein and Rosen (1973, 1974)

Modeling[a]	Question-asking, smiling, appropriate conversation	Nelson, Gibson, and Cutting (1973); Matson and Adkins (1980)
	Verbalization, recreation, and cooperation	Gibson, Lawrence, and Nelson (1976); Bandura (1976)
	Eye contact, response latency, length of reply, appreciation, praise	Stacey, Doleys and Malcolm (1979); Gutride, Goldstein, and Hunter (1973)
	Listening	Ross, Ross and Evans (1971)
	Meal time responses	O'Brien and Azrin (1972)
	Problem-solving and planning skills	Kazdin (1975)
	Telephone skills	Matson and Zeiss (1978, 1979)
	Frustration tolerance	Bandura, Adams and Beyer (1977)
	Avoidance (phobia)	Coleman and Stedman (1974);
	Language	Risely and Wolf (1967)
	Movement	Baer, Peterson and Sherman (1967)
Locus of control	Group interaction	Rimm and Masters (1979) Heitman and Justin (1980)
	Self-instruction,-observation, -recording, -evaluation, -reinforcement punishment	Bialer (1961); Hargrett (1981);
	Weight control (self monitoring)	Chambliss and Murray (1979)
	Goal setting	Matson and Stephens (1978)
	Attempting new responses	Rotatori, Switzky and Fox, (1981)
	Accepting responsibility	Matson (1979)
	Coping styles	

[a] Frequently combines modeling instruction, behavioral rehearsal, and feedback.

appropriateness and normalizing qualities of the activities. It is a delicate balance between recreation/leisure and "children's play." Additional references to help develop appropriate recreation and leisure activities are found in Reference Note 15.

SUMMARY

The final step in an organization's planning is to design its programmatic services. Three proposed training programs were outlined that focused on the development of vocational, community living, and personal-interpersonal social skills. These programs reflect recent changes in the way we approach developmentally disabled persons, including the focus on adaptive behavior, the emergence of an ecological perspective, and the availability of client-referenced technology. The proposed vocational training and placement model stresses the concepts of productive extended employment and a partnership with industry—both of which are consistent with current demands for workshop reform and involvement with the private sector. The community living skills model focuses on the need to develop a progression of living-training facilities and then to interface training with the requirements of those environments. Implementing the model will probably require interagency agreements and a significant expansion of instructional staff's responsibilities. The chapter also outlined techniques and programs used to increase a person's social and interpersonal skills. The reader was cautioned, however, that social skills training is only part of an organization's responsibility to the social and emotional needs of the client; in addition, programs for developmentally disabled individuals must do a better job of meeting the mental health needs of the population.

DISCUSSION QUESTIONS

1. What are the differences between an adaptive behavior approach, a development approach, and a trait approach to defining behavior? What are the implications of each to an organization's philosophy, training programs, and needed services?
2. A concept stressed in the chapter is that different environments expect and require different behavioral skills. In reference to Figures 4.1 and 4.2, generate a list of behaviors that you consider important to a client's successful functioning. How does your list compare with the behavioral domains outlined in Table 3.1?
3. Evaluate your current approach to vocational training in reference to some of the criticisms of workshop programs. (Major criticisms center around low wages, insignificant skill development, and lack of client movement.) In addition, have your local industry council discuss its answers to the following checklist developed by the U.S. Council for the International Year (1981) of Disabled Persons:

Do job requirements screen out disabled persons? Can such candidates qualify in spite of their disabilities?
Do training programs offer full opportunities for handicapped workers?
Do your disabled workers need car pools or special parking?
Is your firm's employment office accessible to handicapped job seekers?
Have receptionists been given training in the basics of dealing with disabled visitors? They should know the rudiments of sign language, be able to guide blind persons, and feel comfortable with persons in wheelchairs.
Have you developed contacts with local schools, colleges, and rehabilitation agencies? They can supply qualified disabled men and women for your job openings.
Have you contributed equipment and machinery to local rehabilitation and training establishments so disabled persons can get updated, hands-on training?
Have you met with local educational and rehabilitation leaders to coordinate training programs with the company?
Are all employee meetings fully accessible to handicapped workers (this includes ramps into meeting halls, sign interpreters for deaf employees, and cassettes instead of printed material for blind men and women)?

Use this forum to discuss and implement a Partnership With Industry Program.

4. The community living skills training model presented involves the development of living-training facilities, behavioral skills training, and criterion-indexed movement. What would be required among the service delivery agencies in your community to develop these three aspects of the model?
5. What are the social-interpersonal skill deficits of your clients? Of the deficits identified, how many are skill deficits per se, and how many relate to unmet mental health needs?

REFERENCE NOTES

1. Characterization and conceptualization of adaptive behavior are summarized by Coulter and Morrow (1978) and Meyers, Nihira, and Zetlin (1979). Discussions of the recommended procedures and qualities of scale development, including item selection, reliability, validity, and reference norms can be found in Carver (1974), Meyers et al. (1979), and Ysseldyke and Salvia (1974).
2. Aids for visually impaired persons are available from:
   Kurzweil Computer Products, Inc.
   68 Rogers St.
   Cambridge, MA 02142

Elfina, Inc.
1725 K Street, NW, Suite 1114
Washington, DC 20006
(Braille Converter)

Votrax Electronic Voice System
500 Stephenson Highway
Troy, MI 48084

American Foundation for the Blind
15 West 16th St.
New York, NY 10011
(magnifiers, sensory aids, stopwatches)

Electronic Hardware Corporation
320 Broad Hollow Rd.
Farmingdale, NY 11735
(adjustable knobs)

American Printing House for the Blind
1839 Frankfort Ave.
Louisville, KY 40206
(light probes)

Current research status of providing sight to the blind by electrical stimulation of the brain can be found in: Dobelle, W. H., 1977. Current status of research on providing sight to the blind by electrical stimulation of the brain. Journal of Visual Impairment and Blindness 71, (7): 290–297.

3. Aids for persons with hearing impairment are available from:

Micon Industries
252 Oak St.
Oakland, CA 94607
(manual communications module)

Telex Communications, Inc.
9600 Aldrich Ave. S.
Minneapolis, MN 55420
(auditory trainers)

4. Upper extremity aids are available from:

Independence Factory
P. O. Box 597
Middletown, OH 45042
(general prosthetics)

Bulletin of Prosthetic Research
(published quarterly by the Veterans Administration)
Superintendent of Documents, Government Printing Office,
Washington, DC 20402

Rancho Los Amigos Hospital
Rehabilitation Engineering Center
7601 East Imperial Highway
Downey, CA 90402

Sister Kenny Institute
Department of Research and Education
Office of Continuing Education
811 East 27th St.
Minneapolis, MN 55407

Fred Sammons, Inc.
Box 32
Brookfield, IL 60513

Skill Development Equipment Co.
1340 North Jefferson
Anaheim, CA 92807

Preston, J. A. Corporation
71 Fifth Ave.
New York, NY 10003

Cleo Living Aids
3957 Mayfield Rd.
Cleveland, OH 44121

5. Communication aids are available from:

Vanderheiden, G. C., and Grilley, K. (eds.), 1976. Nonvocal Communication Techniques and Aids for the Severely Physically Handicapped. University Park Press, Baltimore.

Snell, M. E. (ed.). 1978. Systematic Instruction of the Moderately and Severely Handicapped. Charles E. Merrill Publishing Co., Columbus, Ohio.

Hamre-Neitupski, S., Stoll, A., Holtz, K., Fullerton, P., Ryan-Flottum, M., and Brown, L. 1977. Curricular strategies for teaching selected nonverbal communication skills to severely handicapped students. In: L. Brown, J. Nietupski, S. Lyon, S. Hamre-Neitupski, T. Crowner, and L. Gruenewald (eds.), Curricular Strategies for Teaching Nonverbal Communication, Functional Object Use, Problem Solving and Mealtime Skills to Severely Handicapped Students, Vol. 7, Part I. University of Wisconsin-Madison and Madison Metropolitan School District, Madison.

Harris, S. I. 1975. Teaching language to nonverbal children with emphasis on problems of generalization. Psychol. Bull. 82:565–580.

Harris-Vanderheiden, D. 1975. Blissymbols and mentally retarded. In: G. Vanderheiden and K. Grilley (eds.), Nonvocal Communication Techniques and Aids for the Severely Physically Handicapped, pp. 120–131. University Park Press, Baltimore.

Bio-Dynamics, Inc.
33 Cambridge Parkway
Cambridge, MA 02142
(Instructasette and Instructacard)

6. Locomotion aids are available from:

Sheridan, T. B., and Mann, R. W. 1978. Design of control devices for people with severe motor impairment. Hum. Factors 20:321–338.

Abbey Medical Equipment Co.
Medical Catalog Sales Department
13500 South Figueroa St.
Los Angeles, CA 90061

Ortho-Kinetics, Inc.
1225 Pearl St.
Waukesha, WI 53186

Contourpedic Corporation
1106 Edgewater Ave.
Ridgefield, NJ 07657

Schmid, H. P., and Bekey, G. A. 1978. Tactile information processing by human operators in control systems. Transactions on Systems, Man and Cybernetics, 8(12):860–866.

Nowak, E. 1978. Determination of spatial reach area of the arms for workplace design purposes. Ergonomics 21(7):493–507.

7. The need for reforming the sheltered workshop program has come from divergent groups such as the federal government (U.S. Department of Labor, 1979; General Accounting Office, 1980; Training and Employment Services Policy Analysis, 1979), advocacy groups (Laski, 1977; *The Wall Street Journal,* 1979), rehabilitation professionals (Bellamy et al., 1980b; Pomerantz and Marholin, 1977; Whitehead, 1979), and research institutes (JWK International Corporation, 1980; Urban Institute, 1979).
8. Bellamy, G. T., Rhodes, L. E., Bourheau, P. E., and Mank, D. M. 1982. Mental retardation services in sheltered workshops and day activity programs: Consumer benefits and policy alternatives. Paper presented at the National Working Conference on Vocational and Employment Opportunities for Mentally Retarded Citizens, March 8–10, Madison, Wis.
9. The reader is cautioned that, although the Job Training Partnership Act (PL 97-300) was passed October 13, 1982, it is not yet implemented. The Act encourages private sector initiatives and involvement with the (re)habilitative process. The author is indebted to Michael W. Stumbaugh and Frederick C. Collingnon, whose discussion papers (presented at the President's Committee on Mental Retardation National Working Conference on Vocational and Employment Opportunities for Mentally Retarded Citizens, Madison, Wis., March 8–10, 1982) were used as a basis for this section on "Private Sector Training-Employment Programs."
10. Vocational assessment and evaluation techniques are described in the following publications (see References): Bellamy, Horner, and Inman (1979), Bolton and Cook (1980), Botterbusch (1980), Brolin (1976), Karan (1976), McCray (1980), Mithaug and Hagmeier (1978), Schalock (1981), Wehman (1981), Wehman and McLaughlin (1980).
11. Vocational training programs are described in Bellamy et al. (1979), Bellamy et al. (1980a), Bellamy and Wilcox (1981), Brolin (1976), Close et al., (1978), Gold (1973), Horner, Wuerch, and Boomer (1981), Mori and Masters (1980), Rusch and Mithaug (1980), Schalock (1981), Stern-Otago

(1980), Wehman (1981), Wehman and McLaughlin (1980), and Weisgerber et al. (1980).

12. The major results of these studies have been reported in Schalock and Harper (1977, 1978, 1979b, 1981a); Schalock, Harper, and Genung (1981); and Schalock, Harper, and Carver (1981).

13. Descriptions and information regarding community living skills programs can be found in:

Counts, R. (ed.). 1978. Independent Living Rehabilitation for Severely Handicapped People: A Preliminary Appraisal. Urban Institute, Washington, D.C.

President's Committee on Mental Retardation. 1978. Mental Retardation: The Leading Edge. Service Programs That Work. Superintendent of Documents, Washington, D.C.

13. President's Committee on Employment of the Handicapped. 1980. Rehabilitation for Independent Living: A Selected Bibliography. Washington, D.C.

14. Bibliography for independent living/community living curriculum analysis (Table 4.4):

An Activities of Daily Living Curriculum for Handicapped Adults (1978), by Chuck Tiller.
Magic Valley Rehabilitation Services, Inc.
Rt. 2, Eastland Dr. S.
Twin Falls, ID 83301

Becoming Independent: A Living Skills System (1978), by Ann Westaway and Tony Apolloni.
Edmark Associates
P. O. Box 3903
Bellevue, WA 98009

Community Living Skills: Assessment and Training (revised 1978), by Robert L. Conroy.
Hope Enterprises, Inc.
1536 Catherine St.
P. O. Box 1837
Williamsport, PA 17701

Community Living Skills Screening Test and Remediation Manual (revised 1980), by Robert L. Schalock and Linda S. Gadwood.
P. O. Box 1146
522 East Side Blvd.
Hastings, NE 68901

Home and Family Living Laboratory (1978), by Patricia Tramp.
Saint Paul Public Schools
Bridge View School
360 Colborne St.
St. Paul, MN 55102

Independent Living Behavior Checklist (1979), by Richard T. Walls, Thomas Zane, and John E. Thuedt.
West Virginia Rehabilitation Research and Training Center
509 Allen Hall, West Virginia University
Morgantown, WV 26506

Independent Living Skills Curriculum (1981), by V. Taylor, D. Close, C. Carlson, and D. Larrabee.
Materials Distribution
Rehabilitation Research and Training Center in Mental

Retardation
Second Floor Clinical
Services Building
University of Oregon
Eugene, OR 97403

Skills to Achieve Independent Living (1975).
Melton Peninsula, Inc.
1949 Stemmons Freeway, Suite 690
Dallas, TX 75207

Social Perceptual Training Kit for Community Living for Trainable and Educable Retarded Citizens (1978).
Educational Activities, Inc.
P. O. Box 392
Freeport, NY 11520

The Individual Assessment and Program Guide (1976), by Gary Fisher.
Developmental Services, Inc.
Residential Services Division
Box 1023
Columbus, IN 47201

Toward Independent Living (1980), by B. Baker, A. Brightman, and S. Hinchaw.
Research Press
2612 North Mattis Ave.
Champaign, IL 61820

Training for Independent Living (1975), by Jim White.
Ventura County Association for the Retarded, Inc.
P. O. Box 646
1732 Lewis Rd.
Camarillo, CA 93010

15. Adams, R., Daniel, A., and Rullman, L. 1975. Games, Sports, and Exercises for the Physically Handicapped. Lea & Febiger, Philadelphia.

Adkins, J., and Matson, J.L. 1980. Teaching institutionalized mentally retarded adults socially appropriate leisure skills. Ment. Retard. 18(5): 249–252.

Brown, L., Branston, M. B., Hamre-Nietupski, S., Pumpian, I., Certo, N., and Gruenewald, L. 1979. A strategy for developing chronological-age-appropriate and functional curricular content for severely handicapped adolescents and young adults. The Journal of Special Education, 13(1): 81–90.

Corcoran, E., and French, R. 1977. Leisure activity for the retarded adult in the community. Ment. Retard. 15:21–23.

Gunn, S., and Peterson, C. 1978. Therapeutic Recreation Program Design: Principles and Practices. Prentice-Hall, Englewood Cliffs, N.J.

Johnson, S. M., and Bailey, J. S. 1977. The modification of leisure behavior in a half-way house for retarded women. J. Appl. Behav. Anal. 10:273–282.

Koegel, R. L., Firestone, P. B., Kramme, K. W., and Dunlap, G. 1974. Increasing spontaneous play by suppressing self-stimulation in autistic children. J. Appl. Behav. Anal. 7:521–528.

Kraus, R. 1973. Therapeutic Recreation Service: Principles and Practices. W. B. Saunders Co., Philadelphia.

Section II

IMPLEMENTING SERVICES

By now, you should have a good understanding of a human service organization—of what goes into an organization's planning process regarding client needs, mandated services and environmental demands; how to develop the philosophy, goals, and objectives of an organization; and how to plan programs that channel your available resources, technology, and staff into an effective service delivery system that increases clients' independence, productivity, and social acceptance. Once the planning is done, it is time to put these plans into action. This is the major purpose of the next three chapters. Chapter 5 outlines the most important steps involved in becoming operational from a legal, financial, interagency, and information system viewpoint. Chapter 6 discusses the major barriers you are likely to encounter in implementing services, and suggests strategies that will help to break down the barriers. Chapter 7 presents a number of human resource development programs designed to maximize staff efficiency.

5
BECOMING OPERATIONAL

Becoming operational involves taking an idea and making it a reality.

(Schalock and Harper, 1979a)

Becoming operational is easier said than done. It requires considerable leadership skills on your part and major assistance from members of your supplemental resource management team. It also necessitates working with funding sources, legislative groups, accountants, lawyers, zoning boards, boards of directors, advisory groups, interagency councils, and staff. Interacting with these groups demands that an administrator dislay intangible leadership qualities such as getting heterogeneous groups and organizations to trust one another, developing a spirit of working together toward something better (a ''vision'' if you will), and demonstrating how your organization can solve a number of problems whose solutions are impossible or improbable without the organization's aid. Clearly, becoming operational will be hard work and will require your best efforts.

Why is becoming operational so important? For two critical reasons: to become more effective and efficient. Frequently, organizations become mired in leadership, legal, financial, or interagency problems and lose sight of their primary task, which is to provide quality services to their clientele. The following guideposts of service performance indicators proposed by Sorensen and Grove (1977) can be used to keep the organization on track: availability and awareness of services; comprehensiveness and appropriateness of services; efficiency and effectiveness of services; acceptability of services; and social and economic benefit of the services. The more operational the organizaion, the clearer and more relevant these guideposts will become. Through the process, your organization will become financially viable, legally constituted, functional, and it is hoped, effective in providing services to developmentally disabled persons.

A number of assumptions underlie the material presented in this chapter. First, most of you will not be starting a human services program from its inception; rather, you will probably be expanding programs, entering into interagency agreements, or attempting to secure funding, licensing, or accreditation. Second, most human services programs will continue to be government-sponsored; increasingly, however, other types of sponsorship (private, not-for-profit, and private for-profit) will characterize human services programs. Therefore, legal and financial requirements for various types of sponsorship are presented in the chapter. Third, human services programs need to demonstrate programmatic measurability, reportability, and accountability. The components of a management information system are therefore included to assist you in meeting this critical organizational need.

AN OVERVIEW

The specific procedures involved in becoming legal, financially solvent, and comprehensive are discussed later in the chapter. Following is an overview of the organizational and programmatic aspects of "becoming operational."

Assessing Client Needs

The needs assessment process should provide information to assist you in setting priorities for the service network. An effective process should incorporate data on client needs to ensure that the service delivery system is responsive to its consumers. This information, combined with data on the current status of services, is then compared to the conceptual framework to identify major inadequacies. Goals for the expenditure of available resources and strategies for obtaining needed resources can then be established. The assessment should provide data that can be aggregated for all developmentally disabled clients served by the program, such as:

Number of clients by age
Number of clients by functional and disability status
Number of clients by current living arrangement
Number of clients by needed living arrangement
Number of clients by current day program
Number of clients by currently unmet primary and secondary health and therapy needs
Number of clients by behavioral impediments
Number of clients by unmet community support needs

Inventorying Current Program Resources

This involves developing a resource inventory of available services, which can best be accomplished by requesting components of your program or other agencies to describe programs according to services provided, level of funding available by source, staff resources, number of clients served, number of clients on waiting list, number of slots unfilled, location of facility(ies), and preconditions to participation in program.

Comparing Available Program Resources to Service Needs

These data can be summarized in a number of ways useful to you and your organization. Comparisons of available program resources to needed services will result in a profile of gaps in the service delivery area related to the vocational, community living skills, and community integration programmatic components outlined in Chapter 4. When examining the data, keep the following points in mind: First, adopt a problem-solving strategy that focuses on determining the validity of the data compiled. Apparent gaps or surpluses may well indicate need for collaboration in establishing client-use patterns for the services in question. Second, examine duplicated services among program components or agencies to determine whether total resources can be used effectively to accommodate clients in need. Pooling resources may contribute a synergistic effect to the service delivery system. Third, place needed services in order of priority according to the philosophy, goals, objectives, and desired outcomes discussed in Chapter 3.

Assessing Heterogeneous Constituency

Assessing client needs and current programs generates important needs assessment data. In addition to these data, it is wise operational strategy to obtain a variety of perspectives on the same issues from funders, providers, consumers, clients, and the general public. The information can be gleaned in a number of ways, such as telephone surveys or personal interviews. A procedure referred to as "convergent analysis" will assist in this compilation and is described in Baum et al. (1982).

Developing an Operational Plan

The operational plan should be viewed as an "ideal plan" that will allow you to fill the gaps between needed (and desired) services and what is actually in place. Implementing this plan will probably involve one or more of the following specific steps—namely, becoming legal, financially solvent, interagency oriented, and accountable.

BECOMING LEGAL

Forming a Corporation

The chances are good that your organization will incorporate, since today this is by far the most popular form of organization for the majority of group enterprises. A corporation is a legal entity with its own name and membership, yet is regarded by law as an aggregate body distinct from its members. Hence, the corporation has a continuing existence even if its membership changes; it also insulates its members from personal liability. Incorporation requires establishing your legal organizational structure through articles of incorporation filed with your secretary of state, after which a charter is granted. The charter is a written document setting forth the facts prescribed by law and asserting that the corporation has complied with legal requirements. This charter is the base on which the corporation's authority rests. It is a contract between the corporation and the state. As long as the corporation complies with the terms of the contract, the state cannot alter the charter in any material way without obtaining the consent of the members. However, states frequently reserve the right when granting a charter to amend or modify it if necessary. During the period for which the charter is granted, the existence of the corporation is continuous, a characteristic sometimes referred to as "perpetual or continuous succession." A corporation has the right to buy, sell, and hold property that is necessary in its functioning as a corporation and that does not contradict the purpose for which it was created. In addition, a corporation must have a corporate name, bylaws and rules, and a corporate seal.

1. *Kinds of corporations* Corporations can be classified in many ways depending upon their emphasis. A common classification system is presented below (Lane, 1980; Wyatt and Wyatt, 1971):
   a. *Government corporations*, which are created for public purposes. These include municipalities that are used in the administration of government; and businesses, such as the Tennessee Valley Authority, that are used to operate and conduct a public business.
   b. *For-profit corporations*, which are ordinary business corporations created and operated for the purpose of making a profit that is distributed to the shareholders in dividends. There are a number of variants of this type of corporation, including "closed" and "public-issue." Although different, both types are generally incorporated in pursuance of and governed by the general corporation statutes of the state in which they were formed. You will need to pursue this further if you are incorporating as a for-profit corporation.
   c. *Not-for-profit corporations*, which include charitable, educational, (re)habilitation, recreational, social, and similar organizations. Such corporations do not distribute dividends to their members on invested capital; thus, they are frequently referred to as nonstock or membership corporations. Most human service organizations today that are not state agencies are not-for-profit corporations.
2. *Incorporation process* The rules for forming a corporation are prescribed in the authorizing state statutes (Lane, 1980). Generally the statutes outline two process steps: a) obtaining a certificate of incorporation and b) organizing the corporation.
   a. *Obtaining a certificate of incorporation* typically involves the following steps:
      (1) "Articles of Incorporation" are drafted that include corporate name, principal place of business, name and address of the resident agent of the corporation, purpose and nature of the business, number of shares and other information regarding the capital structure, the names and addresses of each of the incorporators, and whether the corporation is to have perpetual existence or only for a specified number of years.
      (2) The signed articles are usually sent to the secretary of state, together with the necessary filing fees and the organization tax. If approved, a charter is granted, but in some states, the articles may still have to be filed in the county of principal corporate business. When the articles are thus approved, the corporation becomes a body corporate. However, the organization remains to be perfected.
   b. *Organizing the corporation* can usually be accomplished by holding two meetings:

(1) The first formal meeting is held by the incorporators or shareholders for the purpose of electing directors and adopting bylaws. Bylaws provide for the internal management of the corporation and are subordinate to both the statutes of incorporation and the articles of incorporation.

(2) The board of directors then holds its first formal meeting to elect officers, adopt the form of share certificate and corporate seal, accept subscriptions to shares of stock, and perform whatever else needs to be done to begin operation.

3. *Tax status* Once the corporation is properly established, application is made to the Internal Revenue Service (IRS) for tax status. To qualify for exemption under the Internal Revenue Code, one must be organized for one or more purposes specifically designated in the Code. Human service agencies fall under one of the categories (typically 501-C-3) found in Publication 557 (U.S. Department of the Treasury, 1978).

State Licensing and Zoning Ordinances

Becoming operational also involves obtaining facilities, licensing, and dealing with zoning commissions. Hanley-Maxwell and Heal have recently (1980) published a summary of state statutes, licensing regulations, and zoning ordinances affecting community residential facilities. Much of the following material is based on that summary.

1. *State Licensing Regulations* Licensing regulations current in 1978 were obtained by surveying the coordinator for community residential services in all 50 states. The coordinator was requested to send information regarding state licensing regulations covering structures, personnel, and programming for community living facilities (group and foster homes, intermediate care facilities, half-way houses, supervised apartments, and nursing homes) for developmentally disabled adults. Surveys were returned by 42 states. The pattern of regulations was found to be similar across facilities:

    a. Zoning and building codes were generally taken for granted.
    b. Few facilities had general health regulations, but many had dietary and medical requirements.
    c. Fiscal standards were generally not specified.
    d. Program standards and staff competencies were not specified, although there generally were requirements for the administrator.
    e. Facility size was ordinarily specified.
    f. About 58% of all facilities had specific admission policies.
    g. The overriding concern appeared to be the physical plant.

    State and federal licensing, certification, and accreditation standards also stress staff qualifications and staffing ratios that have developed out of the need to protect the rights, health, and welfare of persons receiving services. Initially, the standards focused on the physical attributes of the person's environment, such as room size, fire escape, and physical safety. More recently, standards have been set for professional training and for staff-to-client ratios (Carlin et al., 1981). Standards for professional qualifications can be found in:

State Regulations for Health Power (U.S. Department of Health, Education and Welfare; Public Health Service, 1977).

Standards for Services for Developmentally Disabled Individuals—ACMR/DD (Accreditation Council for Services for Mentally Retarded and Other Developmentally Disabled Persons, 1980).

Standards for Intermediate Care Facilities for The Mentally Retarded—ICF/MR (Code of Federal Regulations; Title 42, Part 442, Subpart G, 1979).

Standards Manual for Rehabilitation Facilities—CARF (Commission on Accreditation of Rehabilitation Facilities, 1980).

Standards covering staff-to-client ratios vary according to each state, type of clientele, program, and licensing/accreditation agency. Three sets of standards are used consistently across states and are relevant to administrators' needs. These include those ratios that must be met for Title 19 funding (ICF/MR) and for accreditation (ACMR/DD and CARF). The proposed ratios are presented in Table 5.1. These ratios will probably change as we develop a better understanding of client training needs, environmental requirements, and optimal staffing ratios.

2. *Local Zoning Ordinances* Zoning regulations have been in existence in every state since 1928; their intent is to improve the general welfare of the community by placing restrictions on things potentially harmful to health, morals, safety, or welfare. The zoning regulatory power given to counties or cities gives them wide discretion as to the exact requirements of their ordinances (Chandler and Ross, 1976). Zones are labeled according to the type of structures permitted as follows (Chandler and Ross, 1976; Hanley-Maxwell and Heal, 1980):

R-1: a zone restricted to single-family dwellings and for residential use only
R-2: allows for residential use only, single and two-family dwellings
R-3: permits multiple dwellings and apartment houses that are for residential use only

The zoning application procedure is fairly standard and includes application review by a local or county planning board (or administrator); recommendation from the planning board to the planning commission; formal recommendations by the planning commission in an open hearing; and if approved, an amendment of the standing ordinance. Appeal of the planning commission's decision can be made, usually to the city council.

Family and group care facilities in most communities are considered as special or conditional uses within the zoning district. In that sense, these facilities may be located in the district once it has been demonstrated to the planning commission that the spirit of the ordinance is met by the facility in question (Lauber and Bangs, 1974). Conversely, the typical legal basis for excluding community residential facilities is the restriction of a residential zone to a family unit (Hopperton, 1975). In these instances the family unit is typically defined either in broad terms (housekeeping unit), traditional terms (related by blood, marriage, or adoption), or in reference to the number of unrelated persons residing. This definition tends to prevent the placing of group or foster homes in ''R-1'' zones. For example, of 400 planning department directors surveyed by the American Society of Planning officials, only about 40% reported that even small (serving seven or fewer residents) group homes were allowed in R-1 districts (Lauber and Bangs, 1974).

The time and effort required to fulfill licensing and zoning requirements can be considerable. Indeed, such matters are two of the largest hurdles your organization will need to surmount. A third hurdle, finances, comes next.

BECOMING FINANCIALLY SOLVENT

Human service programs typically have multiple funding sources. While each funding source usually has its own application or request procedure, the accounting

Table 5.1. Staffing ratios (ICF/MR, ACMR/DD, and CARF)

Settings	ICF/MR[a]	ACMR/DD[a] 1st Shift	ACMR/DD[a] 2nd Shift	ACMR/DD[a] 3rd Shift	CARF[a]
Units serving residents who are severely or profoundly retarded, moderately or severely handicapped, aggressive, assaultive, severely hyperactive, or exhibit psychotic behavior.	1:2	1:4	1:4	1:8	
Units serving residents requiring training in basic independent living skills.	1:2.5	1:8	1:4	1:16	
Units serving residents in educational training, vocational training, and sheltered employment programs.	1:5	1:16	1:8	1:16	
Facilities where vocational evaluation and/or work adjustment services are provided.					3:10[b]
Facilities with work activity programs.					3:15[b]
Facilities with extended employee programs.					3:15[c]

[a]ICF/MR=Intermediate Care Facilities for the Mentally Retarded; ACMR/DD=Accreditation Council for Services for Mentally Retarded and Other Developmentally Disabled Persons; CARF=Commission on Accreditation of Rehabilitation Facilities.

[b]Add one additional direct service employee for each additional 10 clients.

[c]Add one additional direct service employee for each additional 15 clients.

and reporting procedures required by funding sources are similar. This section focuses on the latter two points—how to secure funds and how to account for funds.

Securing Funds

Obtaining funding is frequently a matter of being in the right place at the right time. Seldom will money come to an administrator unsolicited; rather, most of the time you must go "chasing the buck." You will be more successful if you remember two things: First, know where the money is; and second, know how to get it.

The 1977 *Guide to Federal Resources for the Developmentally Disabled* (edited by M. Litvin and W. Russem, Federal Programs Information and Assistance Project, Washington, D.C.) summarizes the variety of funding sources available to either clients or programs for developmentally disabled persons. In general, these programs fall under the following headings:

1. *Income support*, such as that provided through the Supplemental Security Income Program, the Social Security Disability Insurance Program, and the Social Security Childhood Disability Beneficiary Program.
2. *Health care*, which is most commonly provided through Medicare and Medicaid.
3. *Social services*, such as may be provided through the Social Service Block Grant (attendent care, recreation activities, counseling, mental health services, and protective services).
4. *Residential care*, such as that provided through the Intermediate Care Facilities for the Mentally Retarded component of Medicaid.
5. *Rehabilitation and (re)employment services* to train persons to be able to perform a wider variety of jobs and to assist in matching persons with jobs.

Figure 5.1 shows the relationships among current (1982) funding sources and various living (residential) and training (day) programs. The reader is cautioned that funding mechanisms and priorities change rapidly at the federal level, and that each state uses differently the various funding sources listed in Figure 5.1.

Despite belief to the contrary, funds are available for programmatic services, provided you know where to look and whom to ask. Table 5.2 outlines the most important resource guides indexing potential funding sources. Applying for those funds is your next task.

The format of written proposals varies somewhat depending upon the source and purpose of the requested monies. However, there are common elements to any grant proposal, including (Note 1):

Introduction—includes a description of your organization's goals, objectives, history, importance, and community acceptance. This is where to stress your organization's credibility and potential to accomplish the proposed project or program.

Problem identification—includes documentation of the problem or needed services; definition of the specific problem area or needed services; and

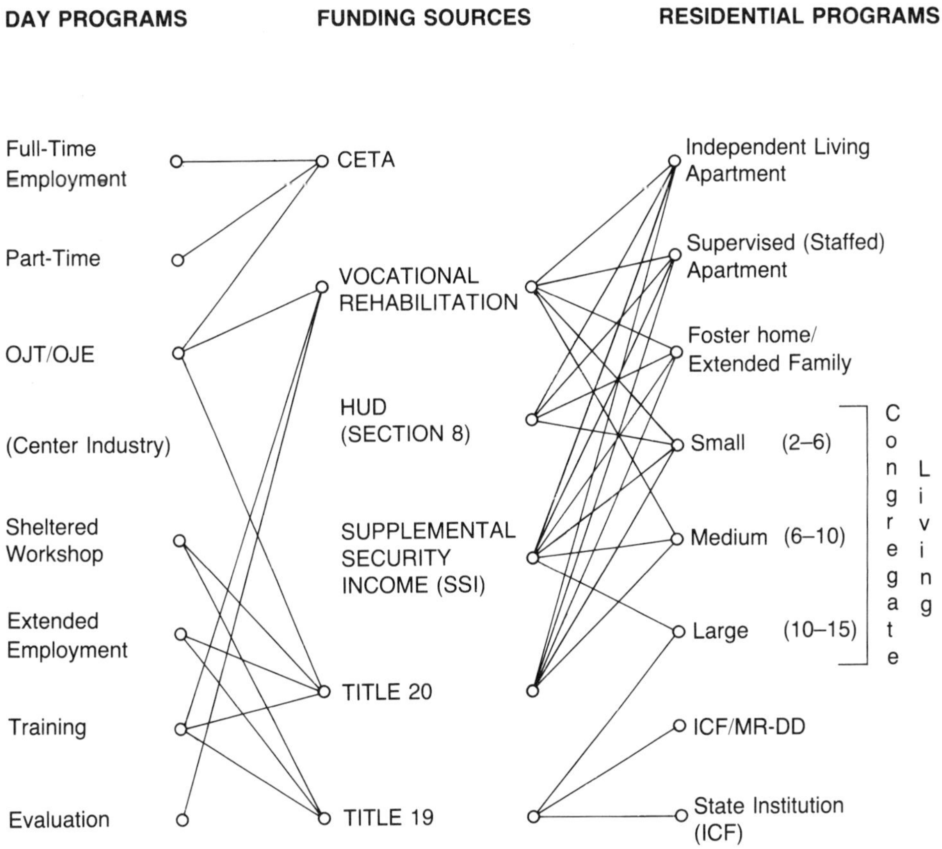

Figure 5.1. Relationship between funding sources and day-residential programs. (From Harper, 1979. Reprinted with permission.)

demonstration of a logical connection between your organization, its background, and its ability to lessen the problem or provide the needed services.

Program objectives—stated in specific, measurable outcome terms.

Methods—includes answers to questions on the "who, what, where, when, and how" of accomplishing the objectives; and a literatue review reflecting awareness of the problem area and reasons for proposing the activities outlined.

Evaluation—is based upon the specified, measurable objectives.

Budget—includes direct and indirect costs and future funding sources.

Following the above format obviously does not guarantee funding. However, most submitted proposals that are rejected are disapproved for one or more of the following reasons (Note 1): 1) problem statements that are unclear, or unrelated to measurable objectives or testable hypotheses; 2) methods and procedures that are vague, inconsistent with objectives, or experimentally inadequate; 3) budgets that are too high for anticipated outcome; and 4) investigators or organizations that are inexperienced, unknown, or inadequate to accomplish the proposed project.

Proposal writing is another one of those "but I wasn't trained to do that" phenomena. And probably you were not; yet proposal and report writing is an

Table 5.2. Indexes of potential funding sources[a]

Resource	Information provided	How to obtain
1. *Catalog of Federal Domestic Assistance*	1. Grants, loans, loan guarantee scholarships, mortgage loans, and insurance or other types of financial assistance 2. Assistance in the form of provision of federal property, facilities, and equipment goods or services, including the donation of surplus real and personal property 3. Technical assistance, counseling, and training 4. Statistical and other expert information 5. Service activities of regulatory agencies	Superintendent of Documents, Government Printing Office, Washington, DC 20402
2. *Fund Finders*	1. *The Guide to Federal Benefits and Programs for Handicapped Citizens and Their Families* 2. *Guide to Federal Resources of the Developmentally Disabled*	The Governmental Affairs Office, National Association of Retarded Citizens, 1522 K St. NW, Suite 576, Washington, DC 20005 Federal Programs, Information and Assistance Project, 1522 K St. NW, Washington, DC 20005
3. *The Federal Register*	*The Federal Register* is the Federal government's daily newspaper of the legal activities of federal agencies, containing the following: 1) proposed rules and regulations that an agency is considering issuing along with procedures for citizen input; and 2) updated rules and regulations.	Office of the *Federal Register*, National Archives and Records Service, Washington, DC 20408
4. *Code of Federal Regulations*	The *Code* is where regulations published in the *Federal Register* are codified. In using the *Code*, the number preceding "CRF" is the volume number. The Code is divided into volumes that correspond to subject areas. For example, Title 19 is 42 and Title 20 is 45.	Available in most major libraries or from the Superintendent of Documents, Government Printing Office, Washington, DC 20402
5. *Commerce Business Daily*	The *Daily* lists all potential contracts federal agencies plan to initiate; contract awards that exceed $25,000; and upcoming sales of government surplus property.	Regular subscription

6. The Foundation Center[b]	The Foundation Center makes available factual information on philanthropic foundations through programs of library service, publication, and research. Foundation Center libraries contain all of the Center's standard reference works, recent books, and reports on foundations, foundation annual reports on microfiche, and information returns filed by foundations with the Internal Revenue Service. Each collection contains the IRS returns for most foundations located within its state, while several also cover foundations in adjacent states. A complete set covering all U.S. foundations can be found at the national libraries.	1. Foundation Center National Libraries: The Foundation Center, 888 Seventh Ave. New York 10019 The Foundation Center, 1001 Connecticut Ave. NW, Washington, DC 20036 2. Foundation Center Field Offices: The Foundation Center— San Francisco, 312 Sutter St., San Francisco, CA 94108 The Foundation Center—Cleveland, Kent H. Smith Library, 739 National City Bank Building 629 Euclid Ave., Cleveland, OH 44114 3. National Cooperating Collection: Donors Forum of Chicago, 208 South LaSalle St., Chicago, IL 60604
7. *The Foundation Directory*	The *Directory* is the basic resource for information about the country's major foundations. Its 6th edition lists 2,828 foundations with assets of at least $1 million or annual grants of $100,000 or more. The data are arranged by states, fields of interest, and alphabetically. Information includes address, donor, date, and place of incorporation, financial data, range of grants, and names of officers and trustees.	Columbia University Press, 136 S. Broadway, Irvington, NY 10533
8. *The Foundation Grants Index*	The *Index* is organized into the following four sections: 1. Alphabetical list by state of foundations and recipients 2. Alphabetical list of recipients 3. Description by subject category of grants provided by the foundations 4. Subject areas	The Foundation Center, 888 Seventh Ave., New York, NY 10019

Table 5.2. *(continued)*

Resource	Information provided	How to obtain
9. *Internal Revenue Service: Circular* 990-AR	In section 6056 of the IRS Code, private foundations are required to provide information in 10 general categories: 1. Address of the foundation's principal office and of the location of its books and records 2. Total contributions and gifts received during the year 3. Gross income for the year 4. Annual disbursements (including administrative expenses) 5. Expenses attributable to gross income incurred within the year (broker's fees, bank or trust charges, property management, etc.) 6. Names and addresses of its managers 7. A list of managers who are also substantial contributors or who own 10% interest 8. A balance sheet showing assets, liabilities, and net worth 9. An itemized account of all securities and other assets, including both book-and market value 10. All grants made or approved during the year, the name and address of each recipient, the amount and purpose of the grant, and the relationship, if any, between any recipient and the foundation's managers or substantial contributors	Internal Revenue Service

[a]State resources are not listed. However, most states have directories of fundable programs and available monies; in addition, each state is required to have state plans for the various entitlement programs.

[b]Organizations need to be sensitive to the following aspects of foundation grants: 1) many foundations make grants in certain geographic areas only; 2) foundations have their own priorities that determine the types of programs, organizations and population they support; and 3) foundations often make their money available for certain specific purposes.

important skill that may make the difference between whether your organization receives funding to initiate and maintain vital programs. Often continuing education programs at local colleges or universities offer courses in proposal writing. However, if you still find such writing difficult or impossible, frequently another member of your supplemental management resource team can provide assistance.

Identification of possible program funds, however, is only the first step in planning or expanding programs. Overcoming start-up costs and the inevitable 60- to 90-day receivable problem when one deals with the government present a significant "Catch 22" for the establishment of new or expanded programs. Add to this the prohibition of the use of federal title and state general funds for capital construction, and an agency is forced to seek methods of financing that are charity-based or that are obtained through conventional leveraging mechanisms. This situation is further complicated by the notion by some funding authorities that substantial cash reserves in any agency are reason for lowering the per diem reimbursement. This naturally prevents an agency from acquiring the down payment needed for getting a loan approved.

It is doubtful that the above-described situation will be addressed or remediated by the present Congress or administration. The cost of federally financing appropriate facilities on a nationwide scale is politically impossible. With this in mind, the following alternative facility funding options are suggested:

Donations for constructing a new facility or rehabilitating an old one
A "Hand-me-down" of an old facility that has been used and can be acquired for free
Federal, state, or local government grants for which no pay-backs are required
Rent or lease
Lease-purchase or "buy-back" from an investor(s)
Contract sale
Purchase utilizing a bank or a savings and loan company
Government loans—Small Business Administration: handicapped assistance loan or 502; Farmers Home Administration: rural rental housing or community facilities loan; U.S. Department of Housing and Urban Development: Section 202 or community development block grant programs
Bonds—industrial development, hospital authority, local housing authority (11b program), state housing finance agency
Client use fees

Recently, there has been significant activity on the part of HUD in the area of facilities for nonelderly handicapped persons. The most recent allotment for HUD's Elderly/Handicapped Direct Loan Program, authorized under Section 202 of the Housing Act of 1959 (as amended), amounted to 67.4 million dollars for handicapped housing projects. In addition, there has been some activity in the area of day facilities under The Community Development Block Grant Program, by the Farmers Home Administration in the areas of community facilities loans and rural rental housing, and via the Small Business Administration's Handicapped Assistance Loan Program. In addition, two of the least utilized and best resources available at the local level are the local and state housing authorities. Their enabling legislation is sufficiently general to allow creativity on the part of their boards in the area of facilities.

Revenue bonds are an excellent way to finance facilities. Such bonds have been used almost exclusively in medical rehabilitation, where they have proven to be a successful approach to facility construction. The use of bonds in constructing residential facilities for the elderly has likewise been the dominant financial strategy for facilities for this group. Some conditions required to get the bonds issued include the ability to repay, certified audit and certified public accountant firm involvement, bond authority and authorization, bond underwriter-investment banker, and bond counsel. The majority of the expenses incurred in developing the bond package can be paid out of the bond itself. This feature is usually sufficient to attract accountants, attorneys, and investment bankers. The field of rehabilitation has been remiss in not conveying the needs of the disabled population to this critically important group of financial experts, and in not capitalizing on the resources they offer. As Christopher Callahan (1979) states:

> The attitude of the accounting profession toward non-profit organizations in this country has historically been one of benign neglect. While accounting firms concentrated their energies on business, where the big bucks were, non-profits struggled along with no direction or guidelines, borrowing methods where they found them. With no uniformity in accounting and reporting practices, neither contributors nor creditors could tell how much of an organization's revenue was actually expended on its programs. Confusion reigned. Credibility suffered. . . . (p. 27)

Accounting for Funds

Getting the funds to operate the organization is one thing; accounting for those funds is quite another. As an administrator, you will spend considerable time with accountants, auditors, and management letters. Most if not all administrators deal with some public or tax money; therefore, it is important to be familiar with governmental accounting principles (Note 2).

In 1968 the National Committee on Government Accounting set forth basic principles to be applied in accounting for governmental operations. These principles were updated and published by The Municipal Finance Officers Association in 1979 under the title *Governmental Accounting and Financial Reporting Principles, Statement 1* (Beams, 1979). The 12 basic accounting principles in "Statement 1" that underlie accounting and reporting for governmental operations are outlined in Table 5.3.

WORKING WITH OTHER ORGANIZATIONS

A number of economic and administrative pressures currently faced by human services organizations are spurring interagency cooperation and formal interagency agreements. Among the most salient pressures include the inability of single

Table 5.3. Accounting principles that underlie accounting and reporting for governmental operations

Principle	General requirements[a]
1. Accounting and reporting capabilities	A governmental accounting system must make it possible both: a) to present fairly and with full disclosure the financial position and results of financial operations of the funds and account groups of the governmental unit in conformity with generally accepted accounting principles; and b) to determine and demonstrate compliance with finance-related and contractual provisions.
2. Fund accounting systems	Governmental accounting systems should be organized and operated on a fund basis. A fund is defined as a fiscal and accounting entity with a self-balancing set of accounts recording cash and other financial resources, together with all related liabilities and residual equities or balances, and changes therein, which are segregated for the purpose of carrying on specific activities or attaining certain objectives in accordance with special regulations, restrictions, or limitations.
3. Types of funds	*Governmental funds include*: 1. The General Fund—to account for all financial resources except those required to be accounted for in another fund 2. Special Revenue Funds—to account for the proceeds of specific revenue sources (other than special assessments, expendable trusts, or for major capital projects) that are legally restricted to expenditure for specified purposes. 3. Capital Projects Funds—to account for financial resources to be used for the acquisition or construction of major capital facilities (other than those financed by proprietary funds, Special Assessments Funds, and Trust Funds). 4. Debt Service Funds—to account for the accumulation of resources for and the payment of general long-term debt, principal, and interest. 5. Special Assessment Funds—to account for the financing of public improvements or services deemed to benefit the properties against which special assessments are levied. *Proprietary funds include*: 6. Enterprise Funds—to account for operations a) that are financed and operated in a manner similar to private business enterprises, where the intent of the governing body is that the costs (expenses, including depreciation) of providing goods or services to the general public on a continuing basis be financed or recovered primarily through

Table 5.3. *(continued)*

Principle	General requirements[a]
	user charges; or b) where the governing body has decided that periodic determination of revenues earned, expenses incurred, and/or net income is appropriate for capital maintenance, public policy, management control, accountability, or other purposes. 7. Internal Service Funds—to account for the financing of goods or services provided by one department or agency to other departments or agencies of the governmental unit, or to other governmental units, on a cost-reimbursement basis. *Fiduciary funds include*: 8. Trust and Agency Funds—to account for assets held by a governmental unit in a trustee capacity or as an agent for individuals, private organizations, other governmental units, and/or other funds. These include a) Expendable Trust Funds, b)Nonexpendable Trust Funds, c) Pension Trust Funds, and d) Agency Funds.
4. Number of funds	Governmental units should establish and maintain those funds required by law and sound financial administration. Only the minimum number of funds consistent with legal and operating requirements should be established, however, since unnecessary funds result in inflexibility, undue complexity, and inefficient financial administration.
5. Accounting for fixed assets and long-term liabilities	*Fixed assets* related to specific proprietary funds or Trust Funds should be accounted for through those funds. All other fixed assets of a governmental unit should be accounted for through the General Fixed Assets Account Group. *Long-term* liabilities of proprietary funds, Special Assessment Funds, and Trust Funds should be accounted for through those funds. All other unmatured general long-term liabilities of the governmental unit should be accounted for through the General Long-Term Debt Account Group.
6. Valuation of fixed assets.	Fixed assets should be accounted for at cost or, if the cost is not practicably determinable, at estimated cost. Donated fixed assets should be recorded at their estimated fair value at the time received.
7. Depreciation of fixed resets	Depreciation of general fixed assets should not be recorded in the accounts of governmental funds. Depreciation of general fixed assets may be recorded in cost accounting systems or calculated for cost finding analyses; and accumulated depreciation may be recorded in the General Fixed Assets Account Group. Depreciation of fixed assets ac-

	counted for in a proprietary fund should be recorded in the accounts of that fund. Depreciation is also recognized in those Trust Funds where expenses, net income, and/or capital maintenance are measured.
8. Accrual basis in governmental accounting	The modified accrual or accrual basis of accounting, as appropriate, should be utilized in measuring financial position and operating results. *Governmental fund* revenues and expenditures should be recognized on the modified accrual basis. Revenues should be recognized in the accounting period in which they become available and measurable. Expenditures should be recognized in the accounting period in which the fund liability is incurred, if measurable, except for unmatured interest on general long-term debt and on special assessment indebtedness secured by interest-bearing special assessment levies, which should be recognized when due. *Proprietary fund* revenues and expenses should be recognized on the accrual basis. Revenues should be recognized in the accounting period in which they are earned and become measurable; expenses should be recognized in the period incurred, if measurable. *Fiduciary fund* revenues and expenses or expenditures (as appropriate) should be recognized on the basis consistent with the fund's accounting measurement objective. Nonexpendable Trust and Pension Trust Funds should be accounted for on the modified accrual basis. Agency Fund assets and liability should be accounted for on the modified accrual basis. *Transfers* should be recognized in the accounting period in which the interfund receivable and payable arise.
9. Budgeting, budgetary control, and budgetary reporting	An annual budget(s) should be adopted by every governmental unit. The accounting system should provide the basis for appropriate budgetary control. Budgetary comparisons should be included in the appropriate financial statements and schedules for governmental funds for which an annual budget has been adopted.
10. Transfer, revenue, expenditure, and expense account classification	Interfund transfers and proceeds of general long-term debt issues should be classified separately from fund revenues and expenditures or expenses. Governmental fund revenues should be classified by fund and source. Expenditures should be classified by fund, function (or program), organization unit, activity, character, and principal classes of objects. Proprietary fund revenues and expenses should be classified in essentially the same manner as those of similar business organizations, functions, or activities.
11. Common terminology and classification	A common terminology and classification should be used consistently throughout the budget, the accounts, and the financial reports of each fund.

Table 5.3. *(continued)*

Principle	General requirements[a]
12. Interim and annual financial reports	1. Appropriate interim financial statements and reports of financial position, operating results, and other pertinent information should be prepared to facilitate management control of financial operations, legislative oversight, and, where necessary or desired, for external reporting purposes.
	2. A comprehensive annual financial report covering all funds and account groups of the governmental unit—including appropriate combined and individual fund statements; notes to the financial statements; schedules; narrative explanations; and statistical tables—should be prepared and published.
	3. General purpose financial statements may be issued separately from the comprehensive annual financial report. Such statements should include the basic financial statements and notes to the financial statements that are essential to fair presentation of financial position and operating results (and changes in financial position of proprietary funds and similar Trust Funds).

[a]General requirements reprinted from: National Council on Governmental Accounting. 1979. *Governmental Accounting and Financial Reporting Principles, Statement 1*. Municipal Finance Officers Association of the United States and Canada. Copyrighted 1979 by the Municipal Finance Officers Association of the United States and Canada.

agencies to satisfy the demand for comprehensive services, a retrenched economy that increases demand for services but reduces available funds, changes in federal and state entitlement programs, and agency dysfunction as reflected in waiting lists and insignificant client movement. In response to these conditions, agencies are beginning to pursue one or more of the following types of multi-institutional arrangements (Magrab and Elder, 1979; Mason, 1979; Zuckerman, 1979):

1. *Formal Affiliation*—a close association under formal agreement, most commonly used for conducting joint educational activities.
2. *Shared or Cooperative Services*—formal or informal agreement to share or provide one or more administrative or clinical services. These can be provided by one agency or a group of agencies in a geographic area, or through a separate newly formed special purpose agency outside the geographic area.
3. *Consortia*—a voluntary alliance of agencies within the same geographic area organized for a specific purpose.

Regardless of the arrangement, human service organizations are increasingly recognizing the need and potential of working together. This concept is relatively new in human services; however, both hospitals (Brown and Lewis, 1976) and education (Grupe, 1974; Nelsen, 1972; Schwenkmeyer and Goodman, 1972) have been involved for years in such cooperative efforts. The major benefits anticipated from cooperative arrangements are outlined in "Benefits of Interagency Cooperation" below (Zuckerman, 1979):

Benefits of Interagency Cooperation

Economic Benefits

—Operating advantages (increased productivity, improved utilization of resource capacity, lower staffing requirements, and reduced unit costs from joint activities)
—Financial advantages (access to capital markets, improved credit standings, reduced borrowing costs)

Manpower Benefits

—Improved recruitment and retention of clinical and management staff
—Strong clinical and management capability

Organizational Benefits

—Organizational growth (extend referral networks, penetrate new geographical areas, expand existing services)
—Organizational survival (financial improvements, accreditation standards, greater political power)

Service Delivery Benefits

—Improved resource allocation
—Improved distribution of health staff
—Increased availability of services
—Broader, more comprehensive scope of services

The author has recently been involved in developing procedures for consortium formation, operation, and evaluation (Baum et al., 1982). Rather than review those procedures, a more general approach to working with other organizations is summarized below, focusing on interagency linkage mechanisms and interagency agreements.

Interagency Linkage Mechanisms

Interagency cooperation can range from agreements between state agencies for coordinating state planning to agreements between local service providers to coordinate facilities, training programs, information processing, and case management. To facilitate this process, a series of interagency linkage mechanisms are outlined in Table 5.4. These mechanisms are grouped according to an organization's planning, service provision, monitoring, and evaluation activities. Regardless of the mechanisms chosen, there needs to be a written interagency agreement that specifies the conditions and outlines respective responsibilities.

Interagency Agreements

Interagency agreements can vary from a broad statement of commitment to work together to a detailed description of the roles and responsibilities of each party to the agreement. A compilation of the information elements contained in a number of interagency agreements reviewed is presented in Table 5.5 (Note 3). Not all of the elements listed in the table need to be included in every type of interagency agreement. The following elements seem to be most important (Aram and Stratton, 1974; Barnard, 1971; Baumheier, 1979; Gross and Skopin 1977):

1. Statement of clear purpose of agreement between parties with delineation of goals and measurable objectives for the terms of the agreement
2. Definitions of any terms that could be ambiguous between the parties
3. Clear delineation of specific program, service, or focus for the agreement to facilitate clear communication of the need for and intent of the agreement
4. Specific actions, roles, and responsibilities of each party to the agreement
5. Designation of specific staff within each agency to implement and monitor the agreement

Table 5.4. Interagency linkage mechanisms

Organizational activity		Performance indicators
1. Planning	1.	Administrators from two or more agencies work together to develop plans for implementing shared policies.
	2.	Administrators from two or more agencies share responsibility for making certain policy decisions.
	3.	Staff from two or more agencies work together to develop and implement specific programs designed to meet shared planning objectives.
	4.	Personnel from two or more agencies work on policy level solution of problems.
	5.	Personnel from two or more agencies or divisions within the same governmental unit work on policy level solution of problems.
	6.	Interagency development of a program budget.
	7.	Joint conduct of needs determination by two or more agencies focusing on problems rather than services.
	8.	Budgeting/allocating resources according to jointly determined needs to a number of agencies dealing with the same problem.
	9.	Two or more agencies utilize the same grants management facilities as a conduit for shared funds.
	10.	Use of planning strategies including: a) performance evaluation review technique (PERT); b) critical path method (CPM); c) management by objectives (MBO); d) planning program budget system (PPBS).
2. Service provision	1.	Support services operated by a single unit for two or more agencies.
	2.	Written agreements on the handling of certain types of clients.
	3.	An agency that cannot provide needed services to a client refers the client to another agency where the needed services can be obtained.
	4.	Operation of a single program by two or more agencies.
	5.	Provision of needed services to clients through giving the client vouchers that can be exchanged for services from other agencies.
	6.	Staff members from one agency are stationed in the facilities of another agency.
	7.	Two or more agencies deliver services through the same staff members.
	8.	Two or more agencies plan and conduct a cooperative training program for their staffs.
	9.	Two or more agencies cooperate in efforts to identify and contact new clients.
	10.	Two or more agencies pool their intake procedures so that a client's access to and/or eligibility for services from each agency may be determined on the basis of common data.
	11.	Staff members from two or more agencies meet on an ad hoc or regular basis to discuss the progress of particular clients.
	12.	Staff members from two or more agencies work together on a systematic basis to provide services to particular clients.
	13.	Staff members from two or more agencies assume responsibility for guiding particular clients through the service system.
	14.	Staff members from one agency provide advice to another agency concerning the progress of particular clients.
3. Monitoring	1.	Two or more agencies utilize the same support services such as auditing, purchasing, and management information systems (MIS).
	2.	Common data developed and operated by two or more agencies.
	3.	Two or more agencies maintain common records on a set of clients.
	4.	Budgeting for general agencies or programs by a single unit with the budget making by the several units (centralized budgeting).

Table 5.4. *(continued)*

Organizational activity	Performance indicators
	5. Two or more agencies utilize the results of a shared client follow-up procedure.
	6. Two or more agencies share access to agency records or to a common data system.
4. Evaluation	1. Two or more agencies develop and operate a program evaluation system.
	2. Evaluation of jointly agreed upon outcomes for programs dealing with the problems covered by two or more agencies.
	3. Two or more agencies utilize the results of one client evaluation procedure.

Adapted in part from:

1. Aiken, M. 1975. Coordinating Human Services. Jossey-Bass, San Francisco.
2. American Society for Public Administration. 1978. Human Services Integration. Washington, D.C.
3. Baumheier, E. C. 1979. Interagency linkages in the field of developmental disabilities. In: R. J. Adams, C. B. Smith, and C. Travis (eds.), Readings on Interagency Evaluation. Nisonger Center — Ohio State University, Columbus, Ohio.
4. Department of Health, Education and Welfare. 1976. Integration of Services in HEW, Vol. I. Washington, D. C.
5. Maloof, B. A. 1979. The government sponsor as a key determinant of advancement in the state-of-the-art in program evaluation. In: R. J. Adams, C. B. Smith, and C. Travis (eds.), Readings on Interagency Evaluation. Nisonger Center — Ohio State University, Columbus, Ohio.
6. Mermis, W., and Chenault, J. (eds.). 1979. Handbook for Professional Development in Human Services. U.S. Department of Health and Human Services. Washington, D. C.

6. General administrative procedures including time lines, revision/termination procedures, meetings, confidentiality safeguards, referral mechanisms, and information sharing
7. Evaluation procedures and guidelines for the utilization of evaluation data
8. Assurances that each agency will maintain its autonomy

DEVELOPING A MANAGEMENT INFORMATION SYSTEM

Determining an organization's data needs is not easy. However, the recent emphasis on critical performance factors makes the job easier (Rockart, 1979). The focus of this process is to identify the critical data needs of the organization and to interface them with specific performance factors that can be operationalized, quantified, and computerized. The benefits to management from such an approach include:

1. It determines those factors management should concentrate on and monitor.
2. It allows a clear definition of the amount of information that an organization collects, and thereby precludes collecting costly, meaningless data.
3. It forces an organization to focus on and collect data that might not be "easy to collect," but are essential for the organization's success and survival.
4. It acknowledges that some factors are temporal and that an organization's information system should be expanded as needs or demands change.

Table 5.5. Common elements of interagency agreements

Basis for developing the written agreement, such as previous/on-going relationship between parties, identification of common need, institution of new service as foundation for current agreement and/or legal authority based on federal or state legislation
Definitions for agency or program-specific terms used in the agreement
Description of purpose to be achieved through agreement
Mutually agreed-upon goals and/or objectives of the agreement
Eligibility criteria/description for population to be serviced or affected by agreement
Delineation of specific roles and responsibilities of each party to the agreement
Mutual/shared responsibilities of all parties to the agreement
Specific actions (''action plan'') to be taken relative to the program/service identified in agreement
Specific services to be provided by each party
Designation of Responsible Party or Liaison Person for implementation of agreement and functions of that role
Specification of meetings (times, dates, frequency) relative to terms of the agreement
Specification of reporting mechanisms between parties of the agreement
Confidentiality and assurances relative to sharing of information
Agreement among parties for notification in cases of changes in agency operations
Specification of time period for agreement to remain effective
Schedule for periodic review of agreement
Procedure for modifying or terminating written agreement
Additional assurances
Specification of additional incentives to be provided as a result of the written agreement (i.e., funding additional staff, work space, etc.)
Signatures of all parties involved in agreement

5. It assists in program planning, monitoring, and evaluation.
6. It requires management during the operational stage to ''think through'' the system and to interface input with process and output.

Data needs and performance factors vary across organizations. This author has found, however, that service delivery programs typically require data related to client characteristics, services performed, reimbursement, client tracking, record keeping, fiscal monitoring, and programmatic outcomes. These data needs become the parameters, or subcomponents, of your management information system. Performance indicators associated with 11 system parameters are outlined in Table 5.6. The table also indicates each parameter's importance to management.

In addition to these parameters, a number of contextual criteria should guide development of your organization's management information system. As discussed by Sutherland (1977), these criteria include:

1. The system should be a staged one, such that the organization may implement any of its options, as demanded, without having to pay an overhead penalty for those options not required during a particular period.
2. The design should permit a hybridized system, one that may be entirely computerized or entirely manual or any combination; as the number of transactions and/or available budget increase, the extent to which computerization can be economically defended increases.

Table 5.6. Management information system parameters

Parameter	Performance indicators	Parameter's importance to management
1. Access	1. Current printout of potential, active, follow-along, and terminated clients 2. Interagency transfer agreement(s) 3. Available enrollment forms (''computer access forms'') 4. List of openings among available programs 5. Policies/procedures for emergency/respite access (''contingency enrollment'') or self-enrollment	The proportion of clients who access the service delivery system relative to available services, openings, and type of enrollment (regular or contingent)
2. Qualification and enrollment	1. List of current eligibility criteria 2. Documentation of client's eligibility and potential funding sources (third-party or copayer) 3. List of persons requesting services but who do not meet current eligibility criteria (this is equivalent to a ''demand function'' in for-profit organizations) 4. Verification that eligible client is enrolled 5. List of persons who qualify for services but for whom there are no openings (''waiting list'')	A maintenance of a favorable balance between client population and the resource base. A by-product is the generation of a waiting list of potential clients
3. Screening	1. Assessment of level of functioning at enrollment 2. Interdisciplinary assessments (if required) obtained 3. Prognosis of duration of needed services (acute, short-term, indeterminant, or chronic) 4. Generation of ''Client's Need Profile''	The client's current functioning level; interdisciplinary assessments; estimate of the duration of required services; and development of a ''Client's Need Profile'' based on the collective information
4. Assign to coverage modality	1. Listing of funding sources for residential services 2. Listing of funding sources for day-training programs 3. Listing of health care reimbursement sources including Title Programs and third-party payers	Reimbursement for services provided
5. Referral	1. Listing of available service components (''agency information index'') 2. Documentation of list of referrals requested and successfully made	Permits client referral to service components (agencies) who meet the following criteria: a. Qualified to meet the particular ''needs configuration''

	3. List of client problem/need categories or diagnostic codes	b. Proximate as possible to the client c. Most cost-effective (or adequately cost-effective) for client's condition and geographic location d. Has had the fewest referrals in the past, so as to distribute referrals evenly among a large number of providers
6. Optimal client/provider match	1. Interface between client needs and available modules or service components 2. Documentation of referral if currently constituted consortium does not have needed services	Provides an optimum match between the person's needs and the provider's programmatic services developed to meet those needs
7. Client tracking	1. Demographic printout indicating client-referenced variables such as: a. Name or reference number b. Birthdate/gender c. Functional level/diagnostic information d. Program entry/exit dates e. Skill acquisition and client movement history 2. Service/module components client is currently receiving service from, and units of service being received 3. Documentation of: a. Reassessment (screening) b. Continued eligibility c. Appropriate coverage modality d. Referral to another module when appropriate e. Recertification of optimal client/provider match	The organization's ability to monitor the client's entry into, processing through, and exiting from the service delivery system
8. Record keeping	1. Client-referenced data, including demographics, services being received, and units (amount) of those services ("client profile") 2. Staff activity reports, including services rendered 3. Referral sources and referrals/placements made 4. Client disposition	Provides the products of training program, staff activities, client movement, and current provider/referral sources
9. Reimbursement system	1. Funding source listing and current reimbursement rates	Identifies revenue sources and implements billing procedures

Table 5.6. *(continued)*

Parameter	Performance indicators	Parameter's importance to management
	2. Financial transactions (referenced to agency) including: a. Invoices b. Disbursement c. Accounts receivable (depending on funding source) 3. Client/agency/staff-referenced treatment or services provided invoices	
10. Fiscal control system	1. A chart of accounts including: a. Current assets b. Fixed assets c. Liabilities d. Fund balance e. Income f. Salary expense g. Employee benefit expense h. Operating supplies i. Operating expenses 2. Financial analysis capability including: a. Budget b. Purchase orders c. Invoices and invoice register d. Cash disbursement journal e. Receipts journal f. Bank reconciliation 3. Financial statements including: a. Cost reports b. Fund summary c. Revenue expenditure statements d. Statement of operations e. Balance sheet f. Statement of changes in financial position	The equitable distribution and utilization of resources across time and programmatic services

	4. Ratio analysis including: a. Working capital ratio (current assets/current liabilities) b. Quick ratio (cash and accounts receivable/current liabilities) c. Debt-asset ratio (total liabilities/total assets) d. Equity-asset ratio (fund balance/total assets) e. Accounts receivable turnover (revenue/average acccounts receivable) 5. Units of service provided to each client during the month and cost per unit. Computation determined by: a. Recording unit (hours) of service per client, per day from each program component (module) b. Prorate and assign to that respective component all direct costs (staff wages and benefits, operating expenses and supplies, travel, and capital outlay) *and* indirect (administration and other overhead) costs	
11. Evaluation system (see Chapter 10 for complete listing)	1. Assessment of client needs and available resources 2. Process (or formative) evaluation activities such as: a. Client change indicators b. Services provided c. Service costs d. Environmental evaluation 3. Outcome (or summative) evaluation activities such as: a. Financial/performance audits b. Licensing/certification c. Peer review (quality assurance, quality control, utilization review) d. Accreditation	Provides the information necessary for an organization to be measured, reported, accountable, and improved through the use of program evaluation data leading to management hypotheses (see Chapter 10)

Adapted in part from the following sources:

1. Alexander, M. J. 1974. Information Systems Analysis: Theory and Applications. Scientific Research Associates, New York.

2. Ryan, K. R. 1979. Establishing an effective human service agency cost accounting system. In: R. L. Schalock (ed.), MR/DD Services in Rural America. . .It is Time. Institute for Comprehensive Planning, Washington, D.C.

3. Sutherland, J. W. 1977. Managing Social Service Systems. Petrocelli Books, New York.

3. The system should have the capability to produce reports of a widely differing nature on demand. The information stored in data bases should permit complete histories to be developed on any or all of the critical performance factors.
4. The system should be modular in that it can accommodate without structural alteration any performance factor added.
5. The system should be horizontally expandable in that its logic can extend to the management of additional program/agency/module components.
6. The system should be portable in that it can be implemented without modification in other communities and for additional agencies who join the anticipated consortium.
7. The system should be internally buffered, such that errors occurring in one place do not resonate throughout the whole program; or when one system aspect must be shut down, the remaining aspects of the system are unaffected and will continue to operate.
8. The system should have some level of information protection; client data should be secure from outside access through a method of functional encoding, and subusers may use the systems facilities in a way that will protect their data from other subusers and also from the system manager if desirable for some reason.

It is at this point in operational planning that you should call upon a critical member of the supplemental management resource team, namely, an information processing (or computer) specialist who can take your information needs, along with the critical performance factors you have chosen, and develop an affordable, functional, and effective management information system. Start up costs will be high; however, long-term benefits to the organization and its management justify it. But a word of caution as reflected in "The Ten Commandments of Computer Buying" (Makower, 1981):

1. Know thy business. The biggest mistakes often are made not in choosing a computer that's bad, but in choosing one that's bad for your organization.
2. Do not hold false hopes. A computer won't solve all your problems. If you've got problems now, a computer will make them worse. A computer will find better ways to do what your organization already does right.
3. Thy patience shall be rewarded. Don't buy a computer with the idea that everything will work out immediately. It's going to take a year or more.
4. A bargain beckons only fools. If you're basing your buying decision solely on price, you'd best forget the whole thing and save your money.
5. Weigh thy options. If you end up with the wrong piece of equipment, you've no one to blame but yourself. Satisfaction comes to those who explore all possibilities.
6. Sustain thy computer. A vital step to successful computing is planning sufficient personnel to manage and operate the system.
7. Embrace the future. The future is now when it comes to computers. One does more harm than good by becoming locked into an inflexible arrangement with a computer system. A good system is one that adapts to change.

8. Fear not tradition. On the other hand, don't be side-tracked by the fact that your system may be "obsolete." If it still provides the services required, its obsolescence is only a state of mind.
9. Thou shalt take charge. Computers may be manipulated. Make sure you or your management is managing your system.
10. Thou shalt make thine own blunders. Repeat this three times: "Computers do not make mistakes. People do" (pp. 94–95).

SUMMARY

Becoming operational allows one to exert power and influence; it also allows increased efficiency and effectiveness. No one wants to be part of an ineffective organization. Becoming operational involves fulfilling legal and financial requirements along with demonstrating ability to plan services, work with other organizations, and implement a data-based management information system. Each of these were discussed in detail including incorporation, Internal Revenue Service status, boards of directors, licensure, obtaining and accounting for funds, establishing interagency arrangements, and the parameters of an information system. Since human service money is getting tighter, the chapter stressed the importance of interagency cooperation agreements, and linkage mechanisms. The chapter also emphasized the relationship between becoming operational and the resultant increased effectiveness and efficiency.

DISCUSSION QUESTIONS

1. Outline the relationship between your current funding sources and residential and day programs. Compare this interface with that provided in Figure 5.1. What are the apparent gaps; could these potential resources be used to provide additional or expanded services?
2. Analyze the available services and agencies in your community. How much duplication is there, and is there collectively a progression of needed services? If not, how could one be developed? Would a consortium facilitate that process?
3. Evaluate your local zoning ordinances, especially their definition of a "family." Has this definition prevented the development of community-based residences? If not, have other parts of the zoning ordinances prevented their development?
4. Which of the proposed interagency linkage mechanisms (Table 5.4) are operational within your service delivery network? What has facilitated and hindered their development? If there are barriers, how can they be overcome?
5. Generate a list of your organization's major data needs and the critical performance factors most useful in your planning, monitoring, reporting, and

evaluation functions. What is required to integrate these needs and factors into a usable management information system?

REFERENCE NOTES

1. Summarized from ''Program Planning and Proposal Writing'' by N. J. Kiritz. The Grantsmanship Center, 1015 W. Olympic Blvd., Los Angeles, CA 90015.
2. A comprehensive statement of current, generally accepted accounting principles can be found in: Miller, M.A. 1980. *Comprehensive GAAP Guide*. Harcourt Brace Jovanovich, New York.
3. The author is indebted to Cathy Smith for her willingness to share her unpublished work on ''Interagency Coordination: The Development and Application of a Model.'' The material was part of the Planning and Evaluation Project, DHEW Region V DD Consortium, 208 McCampbell Mall, The Ohio State University, 1580 Cannon Drive, Columbus, OH 43210.

6

IDENTIFYING AND OVERCOMING BARRIERS

In the 1980's, we will see a dramatic shift in the way services are funded and delivered . . . we will be facing challenging times; times which will demand creativity, particularly when addressing the needs of dependent populations.

(Morrissey, 1981).

It is a safe wager that the 1980s will be a frustrating decade for program administrators, who will face and, it is hoped, overcome barriers to effective and efficient client services. Barriers will involve competing messages from the heterogeneous constituency, lack of funds and facilities, and the administrators' own perceived inability to make a significant difference in the system. This chapter attempts to identify such barriers and suggests techniques to surmount them. The suggestions are not automatic panaceas; however, they can be effective, and generally confirm that "the best defense is a strong offense." The chapter begins with a discussion of general operating guidelines that may help to prevent the formation of barriers, followed by a discussion of a number of major service delivery barriers that may block or hinder an organization from implementing its philosophy, goals, objectives, and achieving its desired products. The chapter concludes by outlining specific strategies that will help you as an administrator overcome barriers, whether they be obvious, hidden, or personal to you or others.

SOME GUIDELINES THAT MAY PREVENT BARRIERS

Delegate and Support

A number of responsibilities will need to be delegated to persons, groups, or agencies to maximize your organization's effectiveness. To insure development and implementation of the components or tasks delegated, it is important to strive to maintain the following "rules of conduct" in gaining commitment from program personnel:

1. Be certain to delegate authority and resources to the responsible entity or personnel who will meet the demands of the assigned responsibility.
2. If expectations about anticipated products or outcomes are clear and understood, there is little need to meddle in how those outcomes are accomplished.

There is a distinct difference between exercising keen interest in the progress of tasks, and "suggesting" in detailed and potentially annoying fashion how the responsible entity should proceed at the work accomplishment level.

3. Decisions about how to proceed in component development should be made in conjunction with a direct observation and assessment of current program operations.
4. If the operational plan presented in Chapter 5 is followed, the need for additional procedural rules is lessened. Productive workers love a skinny rule book!
5. Be sure to express recognition of accomplishment and effective performance, not only to the responsible entity, but to the supervisory or governing bodies to which the entity is organizationally related.
6. Before final assignment of responsibility to an individual or group, discuss with that party(ies) what the responsibility entails. Such discussion helps to clarify the intent and scope of the work, and may provide the policy level with information about needed organizational changes from the delivery level that will enhance the organization's effectiveness.

Facilitate the Organization

An effective organization encounters fewer barriers than an ineffective or dysfunctional one. The organization can enhance or detract from its credibility throughout the service area by the extent to which it adheres to the principles listed below. Note that most of these apply to leadership and to the performance of executive functions. These principles are complementary to the management skills discussed in Chapter 8.

1. Debunk (or upgrade to fact if they appear valid upon investigation) all rumors, whether they reflect positively or negatively on the current or future status of the organization.
2. Make decisions when they are needed without undue delay, vacillation, or appearance of indecisiveness. Do not change decisions or back off from them when you feel the immediate heat of negative reaction. The lack of administrative courage is highly visible. Also, be certain to seek out and consider views about decisions before making them. Pay special attention to opposing points of view in decision areas that are known to be controversial.
3. Readily and forthrightly admit errors; assume full blame for the wrong ones and do not bask in credits for the right ones. Guard especially against passing the buck to the unspecified "they," or to the "system," or to "factors beyond our control."
4. Follow through on major details in implementing a decision. This conveys interest on your part, but more importantly, impresses the significance of the details upon those responsible for getting the work done.
5. Discourage bypassing of directors, boards, or legitimate, legally responsible authorities on the part of program personnel. Any gain for the organization is not usually worth the cost.

6. Guard against the development and appearance of cliques and/or "in group, out group" configurations. Especially in its early stages, the organization will appear fragile enough from the program personnel and consumer perspectives. Perceived splintering promotes avoidance of commitment.
7. While enabling adaptation to unusual or unforeseen circumstances, do not implement every decision as if practicing management by exception.

MAJOR SERVICE DELIVERY BARRIERS

A recent computer search by Stark (1978) produced an abundance of books, articles, monographs, and congressional reports discussing the numerous barriers that limit the quantity and quality of services to developmentally disabled persons. The *Resource Guide to Literature on Barrier-Free Environments,* published by The Architectural & Transportation Barriers Compliance Board (for address, see Note 2, Chapter 7) lists close to 100 periodicals alone that publish information in this area. In addition, there are 144 national or international organizations concerned about barriers that preclude services to handicapped individuals. Barriers related to each of the strategic planning components outlined in Chapter 3 are discussed below.

Philosophical and Policy Barriers

1. *Philosophical Differences* There is currently a revitalization of the historical debate concerning the quality, quantity, and location for services to developmentally disabled persons. One end of the continuum argues that maximum development occurs when the physical and programmatic environment is community-based, since the community is less restrictive and more normalizing. Institutions, from this perspective, are unnecessary because they are dehumanizing, more restrictive, and abnormal. The other end argues that 24-hour institutional care is required for some individuals and is a necessary element in the continuum of services to developmentally disabled individuals (Note 1). This philosophical barrier is interesting to examine in relation to the political theories of thesis, antithesis, and synthesis (Harper, 1979):

Thesis →	Antithesis →	Synthesis =	Community programs serve mildly and moderately handicapped persons
Institution (total segregation)	Community program (total integration)		Institutions serve severely and profoundly handicapped individuals

Although the synthesis does not fully satisfy the needs of the proponents on the left or right, it is usually considered satisfactory to those who take a middle ground. Since the "middle ground" is generally occupied by a majority of the population, this could be the reason that some political policymakers are taking the position that "there is a place for both the institution and the community program."

2. *Lack of Coherent Policy and Services* One of the primary reasons why the federal government lacks a coherent, unified policy regarding developmentally disabled citizens is the large number of federal (and corresponding state) agencies involved in funding and regulating training, employment, and support services. This cornucopia includes (see Table 6.1 for specific programs and references):

Social Security Administration—funding of rehabilitation services for disabled recipients and beneficiaries of Titles II and XVI of the Social Security Act.
Office of Human Development Services—support for training and employment services utilizing Title XX of the Social Security Act, and planning and services provision through the Developmental Disabilities Act.
Health Care Financing Administration—funding of habilitation services through Title XIX (Intermediate Care Facilities for the Mentally Retarded—ICF/MR) of the Social Security Act.
Public Health Service—support for training and employment services through the Mental Health Systems Act.
Employment and Training Administration (U.S. Department of Labor)—support through the Comprehensive Employment and Training Act.
Rehabilitation Services Administration (U.S. Department of Education)—funding allocated under the Rehabilitation Act of 1973.
Office of Special Education (U.S. Department of Education)—funding for education and training under the Education for All Handicapped Children Act of 1975.
Office of Vocational and Adult Education (Department of Education)—funding for training handicapped children and adults through the Vocational Education Act and the Adult Education Act.

Each of these agencies has developed its own operational policies, frequently disregarding the impact of such policies on other federal, state and local efforts (Gettings, 1977; Ross, 1980). The result is reflected in a recent General Accounting Office (GAO) report (1980) that concluded:

> A basic problem at the Federal, State and local levels is that those agencies primarily responsible for the mentally disabled do not have the funds needed to develop adequate . . . care systems . . . (nor) the responsibility for . . . the standards of care in communities. Therefore, they have approached deinstitutionalization by relying on the many social, welfare, and other programs that affect such target groups as the poor, the aged, children, or the disabled,

to accomplish deinstitutionalization individually without any central guidance or management.

We found that, in the absence of a national strategy or management system to implement deinstitutionalization, Federal officials responsible for other programs that affect deinstitutionalization generally: (1) were not aware of the national goal or had not received instructions on implementation; (2) had not implemented their programs to help achieve the goal; (3) had not undertaken joint efforts directed at deinstitutionalization; or (4) had not monitored or evaluated their programs' impact on deinstitutionalization (p. 30).

3. *Litigation and Implementation Barriers* Litigation has led to the articulation of the Constitutional rights of developmentally disabled individuals to a free public education, adequate habilitative services, access to the least restrictive living and programming environment, and freedom from involuntary servitude. Although this litigation has been significant, barriers will continue to remain if we do not take the proper follow-up measures. These steps include (Gettings, 1977):
   a. Legislative and executive action. As U.S. Circuit Court Judge D. Bazelon reminds us that court orders will not usher in the millennium. Courts are ill-equipped to assume de facto operational authority for complex state and local service delivery programs (Bazelon, 1973).
   b. Develop client services. Producing social change through litigation is both complex and, to date, has not proven to be a particularly successful method for creating fundamental changes in the quantity, quality, or range of services to developmentally disabled persons. Specifically, the time and effort expended in the litigation has forced administrators, legislators, and agency personnel to spend an inordinate portion of their time responding to the litigation process, rather than developing and implementing appropriate client services.
   c. Implement change systematically. One cannot deinstitutionalize, for example, unless community programs are available. Otherwise, the clients affected might end up in settings where the services are as bad or worse than those in an institution.

Barriers Related to Goals and Objectives

Stark (1978) clustered the major barriers obtained from over 1,500 citations into the following eight categories including:

1. *Transportation* Barriers include either complete absence or inaccessibility to transportation systems.
2. *Architectural* These barriers involve buildings, stairs, escalators, toilets, doors, water fountains, counter tops, elevator buttons, light switches, aisles, and sidewalks that are either inaccessible or lacking in most buildings.
3. *Employment* Employment barriers generally relate to lack of jobs, society's stereotyping of "appropriate jobs," inadequate or inappropriate job training, and common employer fears regarding higher insurance rates, absenteeism,

accidents, seizures, extra supervision, and negative reactions from co-workers and the public.

4. *Housing* Lack of appropriate and sufficient community-based facilities due to: neighbors who desire to put developmentally disabled persons ''elsewhere, where they are safer or won't devalue my property''; parents who may fear their family member will be less protected, more vulnerable and more apt to fail in a community living facility; and/or public administrators who issue rigid regulations, threaten loss of funds, insist upon multiple agency inspections, and do not plan for either sufficient funding or coordinated services.
5. *Funding* Inadequate or unavailable monies due to:
    a. Federal funds for community residential programs that are frequently inadequate, inconsistently funded, or funded so that construction funds and start-up support are more difficult to obtain than are operational funds.
    b. Social Security payments that meet board and room costs only, so that the person must therefore be supported financially by the state or some other source. This support is frequently marginal at best. Moreover, there are disincentives to higher wage earnings resulting from the Supplemental Security Income and Disability Insurance programs that provide income support to a large proportion of clients within community based programs.
    c. Housing and Human Development Section 8 (Housing Assistance Payments) Regulations that require that Section 8 housing be consistent with the local community's Housing Assistance Plan. This means that sponsors must convince their communities to include small-group housing for developmentally disabled individuals in their housing plans. HUD also requires that Section 202 sponsors obtain Section 8 operating subsidies, which sometimes presents conflicting regulations for housing handicapped persons.
    d. With Title XX funds capped, Title XIX becomes a funding option. However, the ICF/MR standards and regulations are based on a medical model and are generally inappropriate to the service delivery style of the typical group home. Also, many states are using Title XIX funds for their larger residential facilities, and therefore will not use those funds for community-based services.
6. *Education and Training* Inappropriate education and training provided to clients is frequently a major barrier to (re)habilitation programs, since many of these programs are inflexible and overly academic (Flynn, 1981). Similarly, the content of many special education programs is frequently a watered down version of regular classroom curricula (Schalock, 1981; Switzky et al., 1979). A number of social, economic, and political factors have also contributed to the paucity of appropriate training programs, especially for the severely impaired disabled person. These factors include historical reliance on state agencies and institutions; logistical and resource needs to deal effectively with hard-to-train individuals; the community's attitude toward developmentally disabled individuals; and other, frequently more pressing or vocal demands for the community's attention and resources (Morrissey, 1981).

7. *Attitudes* A number of subtle and not-so-subtle attitudes represent additional barriers. These include notions such as:

   Achievement is usually equated with jobs or work. This makes it "virtually impossible for the handicapped person to achieve any measure of satisfaction or success in activities that do not produce financial reward" (Park, 1975).

   Beneath the public's acceptance of the harmless child is still the concern of some that the child will become a threatening adult whose differences are viewed with exaggerated alarm and whose presence in the community makes many uncomfortable—especially if one sees the handicapped adult as a threat to the wage structure or to property value.

   Disabled individuals are different, threatening, contagious, or less worthy because they are retarded (Haywood, 1981).

8. *Interagency Cooperation* Constraints to the development of interagency coordination include factors such as lack of interest by administrators; fear of losing autonomy (O'Toole, 1972); failure to develop written policies and procedures (Magrab and Elder, 1979); lack of sufficient authority or clout in the lead agency (Gross and Skopin, 1977); and lack of effective communication and trust (Smith and Cooney, 1979).

Barriers to Measuring Outcomes

Many (re)habilitation programs are reluctant to measure the client-referenced outcomes for a number of reasons. One reason relates to the perceived inadequacy of many outcome measures used in program evaluation (Noble, 1977; Sorensen and Grove, 1977). A second is that (re)habilitation programs historically have emphasized the needs of their clients rather than the cost or effectiveness of those services. A third reason relates to the esoteric yet real goal conflict that exists in human service agencies. The perception of what is good for the client is viewed divergently within and among funding sources, clients' families, staff, management, regulatory agencies, and agency boards. In addition, standardized outcome measures are hampered by the variety of vendors, training strategies, reporting requirements, and diverse client characteristics. Attempting to overcome these outcome barriers is the central focus of Chapter 10 ("Evaluation Strategies").

BARRIER REMOVAL STRATEGIES

Overcoming one's own ignorance is one way to overcome barriers; encouraging other people to overcome their ignorance is a more difficult but equally important aspect in removing barriers to human service organizations. Barrier removal frequently involves the altering of our own and others' perceptions and of semantics as part of the education process. As administrators, we must also ensure that we are properly informed. This section therefore begins with a "short course" in the basics of legislation related to handicapped persons. Thereafter, specific legal, legislative, and community education strategies are discussed.

Legislative Intent

The intent of most legislation for handicapped individuals is to remove one or more of the barriers discussed in the previous section. Ignorance may be bliss, but an ignorant administrator can cause untold damage. Specifically, administrators need to keep constantly up-to-date on existing legislation related to handicapped persons. A recent report issued by the U.S. Department of Education (Note 2) summarizes the essential components of existing legislation related to developmentally disabled persons. These components are outlined in Table 6.1.

Legal Strategies

Frank Laski has been an instrumental force in the legal advocacy movement. The section following incorporates much of his work regarding constitutional and statutory claims to services (Laski, 1977, 1980). Laski suggests that four legal strategies—including education, vocational rehabilitation, community services, and best technology—singly, or in combination, hold promise for securing entitlement for services to handicapped persons.

1. *Education Strategy* The requirement to provide free, appropriate public education in the most normalizing setting is based on statutes (Section 504 of the Rehabilitation Act of 1973 and the Education for All Handicapped Children Act of 1975), the equal protection clause of the United States Constitution, and recent litigation (*PARC* v. *Commonwealth of Pennsylvania,* 1972; *Mills* v. *D.C. Board of Education,* 1972; and *Lebanks* v. *Spears,* 1973). As suggested by Laski (1977), p. 14), an education litigation strategy to provide integrated and effective education will probably focus on the following conditions and issues:

    Teachers, aides, psychologists, and therapists who are untrained in design and use of multidisciplinary assessments for handicapped persons.

    Teachers and aides who are untrained in use of the diagnostic/prescriptive method of teaching.

    Absence of developmentally sensitive curricula for severely handicapped persons.

    Total lack of vocational education programs for severely/profoundly retarded persons.

    Unnecessarily separate and segregated schools for mentally retarded persons.

    Lack of quality standards for education of severely/profoundly retarded persons.

    Absence of a system to monitor delivery of education to severely/profoundly retarded persons and to enforce quality standards.

    Lack of effective control over federal and state resources available to provide the proper environment, personnel, and equipment for appropriate education of severely/profoundly retarded persons.

Table 6.1. Summary of existing federal legislation related to handicapped persons

Legislative act	Major programs affecting handicapped persons	References
Education		
1. Education for All Handicapped Children of Act 1975 (PL 94–142)	a. Basic state grants for handicapped education	Part B, 94–142 as amended:
	b. Preschool incentive grants	PL 89–750, 90–247, 91–230, 93–380, and 94–142; U.S. Code: 20 U.S.C. 1411; C.F.D.A.: 13.499
	c. Regional resource centers	Part C, PL 94–142, as amended; PL 90–247, 91–230, and 95–49; U.S. Code: 20 U.S.C. 1421; C.F.D.A. 13.450
	d. Centers and services for deaf-blind children	Part C, PL 94–142, as amended; PL 90–247, 91–230, and 95–49; U.S. Code: 20 U.S.C. 1422; C.F.D.A. 13.445
	e. Early childhood education	Part C, PL 94–142, as amended; PL 90–538, 91–230, and 95–49; U.S. Code: 20 U.S.C. 1423; C.F.D.A.: 13.444
	f. Innovative programs for severely handicapped children	Part C, PL 94–142, as amended; PL 90–247, 91–230, 95–49; U.S. Code: 20 U.S.C. 1424; C.F.D.A.: 13.568
2. Higher Education Act (PL 89–329)	a. Community services and continuing education	Title I, Higher Education Act of 1965, as amended; PL 89–329, 90–575, 92–318, 94–482, and 95–43; U.S. Code: 20 U.S.C. 1001; C.F.D.A.: 13.491 and 13.557
3. Vocational Education Act (PL 88–210)	a. Basic grants to states for vocational education	Part A, Vocational Education Act of 1963, as amended; PL 88–210, 90–576, 94–482, and 95–40; U.S. Code: 20 U.S.C. 2301; C.F.D.A.: 13.493
	b. Consumer and homemaking education	Same as above, except: U.S.C. 2380

Table 6.1 *(continued)*

Legislative act	Major programs affecting handicapped persons	References
4. National Library Service for the Blind and Physically Handicapped	a. Free braille and recorded materials to blind and physically handicapped persons	Act to Provide Books for the Blind, as amended; PL 89–511 and 89–522; U.S. Code: 2 U.S.C. 135; C.F.D.A.: 42.001
Employment		
5. Comprehensive Employment and Training Act (PL 93–203)	a. Comprehensive employment and training services	Title II, CETA of 1973, as amended; PL 93–203 and 95–524; U.S. Code: 29 U.S.C. 801; C.F.D.A.: 17.232
	b. Special target population	Title III; U.S. Code: 29 U.S.C. 871; C.F.D.A.: 17.243
	c. Employment demonstration programs	Title IV: U.S. Code: 29 U.S.C. 891; C.F.D.A.: 17.239 and 17.241
	d. Job Corps	Title IV; U.S. Code: 29 U.S.C. 923; C.F.D.A.: 17.211
6. Fair Labor Standards Act (of 1938)	a. Certificates for special minimum wages b. Employees of an enterprise engaged in commerce c. Minimum wage commission and study	Fair Labor Standards Act, as amended; PL 89–601 and 95–151; U.S. Code: 29 U.S.C. 203
7. Small Business Act (of 1953)	a. Workshop loans	Small Business Act of 1953, as amended; PL 92–595 and 95–89; U.S. Code: 15 U.S.C. 636; C.F.D.A.: 59.021
	b. Handicapped-owned business	Same as above
	c. Procurement set asides	Same as above, except: 15 U.S.C. 637; C.F.D.A.: 59.009
Health		
8. Maternal and Child Health and Crippled Children's Services	a. Crippled children's services	Title V, Social Security Act, as amended; PL 88–156, 89–97, and 90–248; U.S. Code: 42 U.S.C. 704; C.F.D.A.: 13.211

	Program	Services	Authorization
		b. Maternal and child health services	Same as above, except: 42 U.S.C. 703; C.F.D.A.: 13.232
9.	Health Insurance for the Elderly and Handicapped (Medicare)	a. Hospital insurance	Part A, Title 18, Social Security Act Amendments of 1965, as amended. PL 89–97, 90–248, 92–603, 93–233, 94–182, 94–437, 95–210 and 95–292. U.S. Code: 42 U.S.C. 1395. C.F.D.A.: 13.773
		b. Supplementary medical insurance	Same as above, except: Part B and C.F.D.A.: 13.774
10.	Grants to States for Medical Assistance (Medicaid)	a. (*Note:* States have broad flexibility in developing their medical assistance programs.) States are mandated under Title 19 to provide some amount of the following services to categorically-needy Medicaid recipients: (1) Inpatient hospital services (excluding mental hospitals) (2) Outpatient hospital services (3) Laboratory and X-ray service (4) Skilled nursing facility and home health services for persons 21 and over (5) Physician services (6) Early periodic screening, diagnosis, and treatment services for persons under 21 (7) Family planning services (8) Certain rural health clinic services	Title 19, Social Security Act Amendments of 1965, as amended; PL 89–97, 90–248, 91–56, 92–223, 92–603, 93–66, 93–233, 93–368, 94–182, 95–142, and 95–210; U.S. Code: 42 U.S.C. 1396; C.F.D.A.: 13.714
11.	Community Mental Health Centers Act	a. Inpatient, outpatient, and emergency mental health services b. Screening regarding alternatives to institutionalization c. Follow-up care to deinstitutionalization	Community Mental Health Centers Act of 1963, as amended; PL 88–164, 89–105, 90–31, 91–211, 93–45, 94–63, and 95–622; U.S. Code: 42 U.S.C. 2681; C.F.D.A.: 13.925
12.	Public Health Service Act	a. Prevention (1) Communicable diseases that lead to disability	Title III, Public Health Services Act, as amended; PL 92–449, 94–317, and 95–626. U.S. Code: 42 U.S.C. 247 b-c; C.F.D.A.: 13.268

Table 6.1 *(continued)*

Legislative act	Major programs affecting handicapped persons	References
	(2) Prevention of lead-based poisoning	Same as above, except: 42 U.S.C. 4801; C.F.D.A.: 13.266
	(3) Genetic screening	Part A, Title XI, as amended; PL 92–414, 92–294, 94–278, and 95–626; U.S. Code: 42 U.S.C. 300b; C.F.D.A.: 13.862 and 13.890
13. Military Medical Benefits Act (CHAMPUS)	a. Diagnosis b. Inpatient, outpatient, and home treatment c. Training, rehabilitation, and special education d. Institutional care and transportation to and from such facilities when necessary	Military Medical Benefits Act, as amended; PL 89–614 and 92–58; U.S. Code: 10 U.S.C. 55
Housing		
14. United States Housing Act of 1937	a. Rent subsidies	Housing Act of 1937, as amended; PL 93–383, 94–375, and 95–557; U.S. Code: 42 U.S.C. 1437F; C.F.D.A.: 14.156
	b. Congregate housing (Section 7)	Same as above, except: 42 U.S.C. 1437e
15. Housing Act of 1949	a. Rural housing for elderly and handicapped persons	Title V, Housing Act of 1949, as amended; PL 89–754, 93–383, and 95–128; U.S. Code: 42 U.S.C. 1485; C.F.D.A.: 10.415
	b. Rural rental assistance payments.	Same as above, except: U.S. Code: 1490a; C.F.D.A.: 10–427
16. Housing Act of 1959	a. Section 202—authorizes long-term direct federal loans to private nonprofit corporations and consumer co-operatives to provide housing and related services for elderly and handicapped persons	Title II, Housing Act of 1959, as amended; PL 88–560, 93–383, 94–375, 95–128, and 95–557; U.S. Code: 12 U.S.C. 1701f; C.F.D.A. 14.157

17. Housing and Community Development Act of 1974	a. Title I authorizes formula grants to cities and urban countries to remove architectural barriers and construct special public facilities	Title I, Housing and Community Development Act of 1974, as amended; PL 93–383, 95–128, and 95–557; U.S. Code: 42 U.S.C. 5301; C.F.D.A.: 14.218
18. Consolidated Farms and Rural Development Act (PL 92–419)	a. Section 306 authorizes a program of loans for rural community facilities	Consolidated Farms and Rural Development Act of 1972; U.S. Code: 7 U.S.C. 1926; C.F.D.A.: 10.423
Income Maintenance		
19. Social Security Disability Insurance	a. Disability insurance benefits	Title II, Social Security Act of 1935, as amended; PL 89–97, 90–248, 92–603, 93–66, 93–233, and 95–216. U.S. Code: 42 U.S.C. 401; C.F.D.A.: 13.802
	b. Adult disabled child program (Section 202-d)	Same as above
	c. Rehabilitation services (Section 222)	Same as above, except: 42 U.S.C. 422
20. Supplemental Security Income	a. Basic supplemental security income program (disabled, blind, aged)	Title 16, Social Security Act of 1935, as amended; PL 92–603, 93–66, 93–233, 94–566, and 94–569; U.S. Code: 42 U.S.C. 1381; C.F.D.A.: 13.807
	b. Rehabilitation, treatment, referral and counseling services	Same as above, except: 42 U.S.C. 1382d
Nutrition		
21. National School Lunch Act	a. School lunch program	National School Lunch Act of 1946, as amended; PL 90–302, 91–248, 92–153, 92–433, 93–150, 93–326, 94–105, 95–166, and 95–627; U.S. Code: 42 U.S.C. 1753; C.F.D.A.: 10.555

Table 6.1. *(continued)*

Legislative act	Major programs affecting handicapped persons	References
	b. Commodity distribution program	Same as above, except: 7 U.S.C. 612; C.F.D.A.: 10.550
	c. Summer food service program	Same as above, except: 42 U.S.C. 1761; C.F.D.A.: 10.559
	d. Child care food program	Same as above, except: 42 U.S.C. 1766; C.F.D.A.: 10.558
22. Child Nutrition Act	a. School milk program	Child Nutrition Act of 1966, as amended; PL 91–295, 93–150, 93–347, 94–105, and 95–166; U.S. Code: 42 U.S.C. 1772; C.F.D.A. 10.556
	b. School breakfast program	Same as above, except: 42 U.S.C. 1773; C.F.D.A. 10.553
23. Food Stamp Act	a. Food coupons may be used to purchase food for Social Security Disability Insurance or Supplemental Security Income recipients residing in small (under 16) group homes	Food Stamp Act of 1977, as amended; PL 95–113 and 96–58; U.S. Code: 7 U.S.C. 2012; C.F.D.A. 10.551
Social Services		
24. Child Welfare Services	a. State grants for child welfare services	Title IV-B, Social Security Act, as amended; PL 90–248 and 92–603; U.S. Code: 42 U.S.C. 620; C.F.D.A.: 13.645
25. Social Services Program (Title XX)	a. Basic social services program. Title XX authorizes formula grants to assist designated state social service agencies to support activities directed at: (1) Achieving or maintaining economic self-support (2) Achieving or maintaining self-sufficiency (3) Preventing or remedying neglect, abuse, or exploitation	Title XX, Social Security Act, as amended; PL 93–647, 94–401, and 95–600; 42 U.S.C. 1397; C.F.D.A.: 13.642

		(4) Preventing inappropriate institutionalization by providing community-based care (5) Referral and institutional care when necessary	
	b.	Social services training (staff)	Title XX, Social Security Act, as amended; PL 93–647; U.S. Code: 42 U.S.C. 1397; C.F.D.A.: 13.644
26. Developmental Disabilities Assistance and Bill of Rights Act	a.	Basic grants to states for planning services	Developmental Disabilities Act, as amended. PL 88–164, 91–517, 94–103, and 95–602; U.S. Code: 42 U.S.C. 6061; C.F.D.A.: 13.630
	b.	Grants to protection and advisory systems	Same as above, except: 42 U.S.C. 6012
	c.	Special project grants	Same as above, except: 42 U.S.C. 6081; C.F.D.A.: 13.631
27. Domestic Volunteer Service Act of 1973	a.	A number of programs (Foster Grandparents, Action, Helping Hand) aimed at harnessing the resources of volunteers to help handicapped persons	Domestic Volunteer Service Act of 1973, as amended; PL 91–69, 93–113, 94–135, 94–293, 95–478, and 96–143; U.S. Code: 42 U.S.C. 5011; C.F.D.A.: 72.001 and 72.008
Transportation			
28. Urban Mass Transportation Act	a.	Section 16 (b) requires transportation facilities and services to be available to and usable by elderly and handicapped persons	Urban Mass Transportation Act of 1964, as amended; PL 91–453, 93–87, 93–503, and 95–599; U.S. Code: 49 U.S.C. 1601; C.F.D.A.: 20.504, 20.505, and 20.506
29. Federal-Aid Highway Act	a.	Provides adequate and reasonable access across curbs	Federal-Aid Highway Act of 1973, as amended; PL 93–87, 93–643, 94–280, and 95–559; U.S. Code: 23 U.S.C. 402; C.F.D.A.: 20.205

Table 6.1 *(continued)*

Legislative act	Major programs affecting handicapped persons	References
Vocational Rehabilitation		
30. The Rehabilitation Act of 1973 (PL 93-112)	a. Basic federal-state vocational rehabilitation grants	Title I, Rehabilitation Act of 1973, as amended; PL 93–112, 93–516, 94–230, and 95–602; U.S. Code: 29 U.S.C. 701; C.F.D.A.: 13.624
	b. Innovation and expansion grants (special services to the most severely handicapped persons)	Part C, Title I, same as above, except: 29 U.S.C. 740; C.F.D.A.: 13.649
	c. Construction grants and loans for rehabilitation facilities	Title III; 29 U.S.C. 771
	d. Special programs and supplementary services	Title III; 29 U.S.C. 770; C.F.D.A.: 13.626
	e. Employment opportunities	Title VI; 29. U.S.C. 795
	f. Comprehensive services for independent living	Part A, Title VII, Rehabilitation Act of 1973; PL 95–602; U.S. Code: 29 U.S.C. 796
	g. Centers for independent living	Part B, Title VII; 29 U.S.C. 796; C.F.D.A. 13.653
	h. Protection and advocacy	Part D, Title VII, 29 U.S.C. 796
31. Wagner O'Day Act	a. Procurement of selected commodities and services from qualified workshops serving blind and other severely handicapped persons	Wagner O'Day Act of 1938, as amended; PL 92–28, 93–76, and 93–358; U.S. Code: 41 U.S.C. 46

Material summarized from: U.S. Department of Education. 1980. *Summary of Existing Legislation Relating to the Handicapped*. Publication No. E-80-22014. U.S. Government Printing Office Washington, D.C. 20402.

[a] Abbreviations: PL = Public Law; U.S.C. = United States Codes; C.F.D.A. = *Catalog of Federal Domestic Assistance*.

2. *Rehabilitation Strategy* The Rehabilitation Act of 1973 (29 U.S.C. 701) requires that priority be given in vocational rehabilitation services to "those with the most severe handicaps." Section 503 of the Act requires government contractors to take affirmative action to employ disabled persons, including the severely disabled. Section 504 provides further that: No otherwise qualified handicapped individual in the United States . . . shall solely by reason of his handicap be excluded from the participation in, be denied benefits of, or be subject to discrimination in any program or activity receiving Federal financial assistance (29 U.S.C. 794).

   As discussed by Laski (1977), by imposing statutory equal protection duties on recipients of federal funds, Congress did much more than enact a nondiscrimination law. The consequences of Section 504 for disabled persons go beyond limited notions of nondiscrimination in three significant respects:

   a. The integration imperative is as central to Section 504 as it has been to all other civil rights acts. So long as state and local governments and their instrumentalities have undertaken to provide services to the public, Section 504 requires that such services be made available to handicapped persons in the most integrated fashion.
   b. Unlike Constitutional violations of equal protection, violations of Section 504 do not require proof of purposeful intent, but only proof of discriminatory effect.
   c. The statutory formulation of equal protection principles requires that all of those bound must act affirmatively to discharge their duties and to assure meaningful implementation of equal protection. Thus, strategies to overcome rehabilitation barriers should focus on access to services and on the legal rights of the applicant.

   In reference to access, a litigation strategy could focus on exclusion from particular rehabilitation services, arbitrary limitation of those services, and failure to guarantee due process in decisions as to eligibility for those services. For example, of the over 435,000 new active vocational rehabilitation cases in fiscal year 1977, only 41,900 were provided with any extended evaluation services (Laski, 1979; Mars, 1978). In regard to the legal rights of the applicant, Section 102 of the Rehabilitation Act of 1973 (as amended in 1974) requires an individualized written rehabilitation plan that entitles the applicant to a preliminary diagnostic study to determine rehabilitation potential; access to extended evaluation to determine rehabilitation potential; a certification of eligibility unless it can be determined beyond any reasonable doubt that the basic conditions of eligibility are not met; and, even after that determination, annual review in certain cases. In addition, the applicant can challenge any decision during the intake process (Laski, 1977).

3. *Community Services Strategy* The following case law examples provide strategies in reference to least restrictive alternatives and community alternatives to institutionalization (Laski, 1977):

   a. The right to least restrictive alternative was clearly stated by Chief Judge D. Bazelon in *Lake* v. *Cameron* over a decade ago and has since been adopted as a constitutional requirement in commitment cases and treatment and community services cases. In *Lessard* v. *Schmidt* the court held that the U.S. Constitution required the state to show that alternatives to institutionalization, such as day treatment, nursing home placement, referral to a mental health clinic, or placement in the custody of a friend or relative, were unsuitable options before commitment could be ordered.

b. In *Wyatt* v. *Stickney,* the court declared that residents have a right to "the least restrictive conditions necessary to achieve . . . habilitation or treatment." "No person," the court held, "shall be admitted to the institution unless a prior determination shall have been made that residence in the institution is the least restrictive habilitation setting feasible for that person" and "no mentally retarded persons shall be admitted to the institution if services and programs in the community can afford adequate habilitation to such persons."

c. In *New York Association for Retarded Children* v. *Rockefeller,* the court ordered that less restrictive settings be made available, and established a planning process to create sufficient services in the community to allow the reduction within 6 years of Willowbrook's [institution] population from 3,000 to 250. Similarly, in *Horacek* v. *Exon,* following the same least restrictive alternative corollary to due process, the court ordered the creation of sufficient services in the community to reduce the population of Beatrice State Home in Nebraska from 1200 to 250.

d. In *Halderman* v. *Pennhurst,* the court (basing its decision on the equal protection clause of the Fourteenth Amendment, Section 504 of the Rehabilitation Act of 1973, and the Constitutional due process clause) held that "the confinement and isolation of the retarded in the institution called Pennhurst is segregation in a facility that is clearly separate and not equal," and that, for each of its residents, Pennhurst is "unnecessarily separate" and hence, "discriminatory and unlawful" (Note 3).

4. *Best Technology Strategy* An essential element in the litigation cases discussed thus far has been the placing before the court of the best existing technology and stressing that it is used in complying with court orders. A well-established principle of law is that when a choice of technologies is presented, legal responsibility requires that the better technology be chosen as consistent with the state of the art. This requirement necessitates demonstrating that appropriate technology is available in the community to deal effectively with developmentally disabled persons, and that as new technologies are developed, comprehensive evaluations and cost-benefit analyses are conducted to document the fiscal and social implications of their application (Laski, 1977).

Legislative Strategies

A number of barriers currently impede the implementation of appropriate services to developmentally disabled adults. These barriers involve the issues of entitlements, mainstreaming, wages, technology, sheltered employment, and lack of coordination. The barriers, along with proposed legislative strategies to overcome them, are outlined below (Note 4).

1. *Entitlement* The courts have repeatedly affirmed the rights of handicapped persons to treatment and training, and Congress has mandated free and appropriate education for handicapped children. But handicapped adults generally lack rights or entitlement, especially in regard to employment. The primary issue is whether the entitlement to education and training now afforded handicapped children should be extended to handicapped adults, especially those who were denied education and training opportunities because they were not covered by the mandate. Possible remedies include:
   a. Mandate educational services for handicapped adults who were unable to benefit from mandated education for children.
   b. Increase the targeting (set-aside) of Vocational Education and Adult Education funds for handicapped youth and adults.
   c. Amend the CETA program to establish handicapped persons as a special group with earmarked funding, as opposed to the current system under which handicapped individuals are included in the generally eligible group.
   d. Clarify coverage of Section 504 with regard to employment rights.
2. *Mainstreaming* The issue of mainstreaming handicapped persons into the regular work force is complicated by several problems, including the resistance on the part of private employers toward hiring handicapped people, the inability of the labor market to supply jobs, and the lack of effective job placement programs. Possible remedies include:
   a. Expand competitive employment placement through increased support for job placement programs in workshops. Model programs, such as Projects with Industry, have demonstrated success.
   b. Expand Targeted Jobs Tax Credit Program utilization (incentives for employers) and provide technical assistance to private business and industry in barrier removal, improving accessibility, and accommodation.
   c. Develop demonstration projects to test feasibility of extending the trial work period for handicapped persons entering the competitive labor market from workshops.
   d. Revise Section 503 employment requirements for federal contractors to specify hiring goals and/or quotas.
3. *Wage Earnings* Handicapped people generally tend to be either unemployed or underemployed. The Fair Labor Standard Act provides for employment of handicapped workers at less than the statutory minimum if the worker is unable to meet minimum industry production standards. Three factors have contributed to the wage issue, including restrictions to wage payments imposed by the Fair Labor Standards Act governing work activities centers; inadequate attention to wage payment requirements by workshop managers or staff; and disincentives to higher wage earnings contained in the Social Security and Disability Insurance programs, which provide income support to a large proportion of workshop clients. Possible remedies to the wage issue include:

a. Amend Fair Labor Standards Act to require sheltered workshops to pay all employees hourly wages that are at least equal to the federal statutory minimum rate established under the Fair Labor Standards Act.
b. Provide wage subsidy to workshops to permit increasing all wages to statutory or poverty level.
c. Revise Fair Labor Standards Act to change to a single exemption certificate for sheltered employment, concentrating on requirement for payment of commensurate wages to all workers.

4. *Technology* The ineffectiveness of many workshops has been attributed to the lack of business and industrial technology. Improved methods and systems for operating workshops are available, but the technology is not widely distributed, nor do communities have the available resources to develop and support the techniques. Legislative options include:
a. Expand research utilization programs to support replication and distribution of proven technology in training, assessment, rehabilitation engineering, management, production systems, and job placement.
b. Establish a special program of technical assistance and management consultation to focus on upgrading workshop efficiency.
c. Develop information dissemination programs describing available technologies for workshops.
d. Promote volunteer assistance of business and industry through national organizations and trade associations.

5. *Sheltered Employment* We are now beginning to realize that training and employment services in sheltered workshops often involve a continuing long-term program of accommodating the social and vocational needs of severely handicapped persons. One critical question in this area is, "Is extended sheltered employment desirable and acceptable as an employment system for severely handicapped persons?" Funding for such employment is usually provided from Title XX funds, combined with state/local public and private financing. This issue is already being addressed in several states because of the steady increase in clients entering workshops and the lack of movement of clients out of workshops, thereby exhausting federal resources and creating a drain on state and local financial resources, as well as increasing service demands on community-based sheltered workshops. Options currently being discussed include:
a. Expand Extended Sheltered Employment Centers, funding the program from state tax dollars, with administration by a specially established state staff. The population employed would be those severely disabled persons evaluated and found to be not feasible for competitive employment. Minimum functional requirements would be optional.
b. Establish programs to provide technical assistance to states in utilizing Title XX funds in combination with other public and private funds to operate Extended Sheltered Employment programs.
c. Establish Extended Sheltered Employment workshop programs, but

restrict eligibility to those who can meet certain production standards. Serve the less productive handicapped person in day care or therapeutic activities programs.

6. *Coordination* Three federal agencies (U.S. Department of Labor, Health and Human Services, and Education) are responsible for funding training and employment services for handicapped individuals; yet none has the major responsibility for planning and coordination. The lack of specific planning responsibility in any state or federal program has resulted in the development of a fragmented and nonintegrated proliferation of work activities centers, developmental centers, and sheltered workshops. Legislative options to overcome this barrier include:
   a. Establish planning for sheltered workshops, training, and employment services for handicapped persons as a special component of the State Manpower Planning Commission (or its counterpart).
   b. Include training and employment services in the planning requirements for the State Developmental Disabilities Council.
   c. Assign lead planning responsibility to the State Rehabilitation Agency. Rehabilitation agencies are mandated to do facility planning by the 1978 amendments to the Rehabilitation Act.

Community Education Strategies

Negative attitudes and fears concerning developmentally disabled individuals frequently result from ignorance. Conversely, evidence shows that once exposed to a community-based program, skeptical individuals generally become more supportive of the program (Heal, Sigelman, and Switzky, 1978; Kastner, Reppucci, and Pezzoli, 1979; Lauber and Bangs, 1974; Sigelman, 1976; Willms, 1981). Two necessary components to a community education strategy thus become apparent: 1) dispell myths and stereotypes regarding developmentally disabled persons; and 2) sensitize people to what the community-based program is attempting to do.

1. *Dispelling Myths and Stereotypes* Society generally supports a number of inaccurate perceptions of developmentally disabled persons and programs dealing with them. These perceptions can frequently be overcome if accurate facts are presented in rational ways. Developing a community education program should begin with accurate information concerning the eight negative perceptions of handicapped persons and programs as listed in Table 6.2.

   While knowing the facts regarding each attitude is important, the manner in which they are presented to the people and the community-at-large is also critical. This may well involve a community education program such as outlined below.
2. *A Community Education Program* The need for an organized, comprehensive community education program is essential, given the documented relationship between public attitudes and the successful community integration of de-

Table 6.2. Common attitudes and facts regarding developmentally disabled persons

Attitude		Current state of knowledge	References
1. Developmentally disabled persons are childlike.	a.	Many are unidentifiable behaviorally from "normals."	Schulman (1980); Thompson (1977)
	b.	Many often succeed in social and interpersonal interactions.	Achenbach and Zigler (1968); President's Committee on Mental Retardation (1976)
	c.	Observed suggestibility is partially due to expectations of failure, which cause the person to depend on others' judgment.	Sternlicht (1977)
	d.	Affectionate behavior, mistrust, and/or fear may result from social deprivation.	Schulman (1980)
	e.	Mental and social age measurements do not consider the person's learning experience or functional skill level.	Schalock and Karan (1979); Zigler and Trickett (1978)
2. Group homes lower adjacent property value.	a.	Property values in areas with group homes neither increase nor decrease, as compared to matched control areas.	Jones and Jones (1976a, b); Wolpert (1978)
	b.	Proximity to group homes does not affect a property's market value, nor does the existence of group homes generate a higher degree of neighborhood property turnover.	Novak and Heal (1980)
3. Developmentally disabled persons are better off in institutions than they are in the community.	a.	Community programs can increase self-esteem, socialization and independence.	Brolin (1976); Kugel and Shearer (1976); Nirje (1969)
	b.	Home-reared developmentally disabled persons are generally superior intellectually and socially to institutionally-reared persons.	Kimble, Garmezy, and Zigler (1980); Zigler and Balla (1977)
	c.	Institutions involve regimentation, limited choices, and lack of privacy.	Blatt (1976); Blatt et al. (1977); Wolfensberger et al. (1972)
	d.	Institutional environments reinforce dependency, compliance, and introversion.	Robinson and Robinson (1976); Thompson (1977)
4. Developmentally disabled persons present a threat to the community.	a.	Frequency of sexual delinquency is not more evident among retarded adults.	Hart (1978)

	b. Mentally retarded persons do not have a higher incidence of delinquency or crime.	Brown and Courtless (1977); Friedman (1977); Menolascino (1977)
	c. Mental retardation bears no casual relationship to crime.	Allen (1968); Edgerton (1981)
5. Mental retardation is usually a hereditary condition and is not likely to occur in the typical family.	a. There are over 200 causes of mental retardation.	Menolascino (1977)
	b. Infection and intoxication may damage the fetus.	Swanson and Willis (1979)
	c. 10% to 85% of babies exposed to rubella in the womb exhibit abnormality.	Carter (1977)
	d. Damage to the developing central nervous system causes mental retardation.	Grossman (1977); Kimble et al. (1980)
	e. Postnatal infections and/or trauma may result in mental retardation.	Kugel and Shearer (1976)
	f. 70% –75% of mental retardation is socioculturally based.	Scheerenberger (1975); President's Committee on Mental Retardation (1976)
6. Developmentally disabled persons are incapable of becoming productive members of society.	a. Employment rates are estimated at: (1) 87% for mildly retarded males and 33% for mildly retarded females (earnings estimated at 87% of average);	Conley (1973); Brolin (1976)
	(2) 45% for moderately retarded males and 12% for moderately retarded females (earnings estimated at 19% of average).	Flynn (1981)
	b. An estimated 690,000 mentally retarded adults are without work; about 400,000 could be gainfully employed if appropriate services were available.	Whitehead (1979)
7. Developmentally disabled persons are incapable of learning.	a. Adaptive behavior skills in social and vocational areas may negate the presence of developmental disabilities.	Swanson and Willis (1979)
	b. Profoundly handicapped persons can develop self-help and simple communication skills.	Kolstoe (1972); Smith and Pollaway (1979)
	c. Developmentally disabled persons demonstrate a wide range of learning ability and products.	Kimble et al. (1980); Schulman (1980)

velopmentally disabled persons (Baker, Seltzer, and Seltzer, 1977; Kastner et al., 1979; Luckey and Newman, 1975; and Mamula and Newman, 1973). Although communities vary greatly in reference to the issues discussed in Table 6.2, fears and misunderstandings regarding community placement of developmentally disabled individuals need to be addressed via a systematic community education program. The parameters for such a program are featured in Table 6.3. These parameters include the audience, purpose, message, and delivery method. The model is patterned after that developed and evaluated by The Association for the Developmentally Disabled of Columbus, Ohio.

SUMMARY

Program administrators are well aware of barriers that prevent them from doing all they would like for developmentally disabled adults; frequently, however, they are unaware of what to do to overcome them. The dual message of the need to identify and remove barriers provided the focus of this chapter. The barriers discussed included obvious ones related to architecture, employment, housing, and funding; more subtle barriers including attitudes and public policy; and still other barriers that result from our own ignorance. The barrier removal techniques discussed, including legal, legislative, and community education strategies, have all been demonstrated to be effective in overcoming one or more of the multiple barriers administrators face.

DISCUSSION QUESTIONS

1. What are the five most significant barriers encountered by your organization? Rank order their significance.
2. In reference to the barrier ranked first (most significant) in Question 1, develop an action plan based on one or more of the strategies presented and then monitor the effects of the plan.
3. Existing federal legislation dealing with handicapped persons was summarized in Table 6.1. Which of those laws do you currently apply the most in pursuing your organization's objectives? Which additional ones might you be able to use?
4. One of the legal strategies frequently overlooked relates to "best technology." Analyze your organization's current technology, keeping in mind, "Is this organization subject to litigation for not using the best, most up-to-date, and cost-effective technology?"
5. Parameters for a community education program were outlined in Table 6.3. Use these parameters to develop a community education program associated with a desired program expansion.

Table 6.3. Parameters to a community education program

Audience	Purpose	Message	Method
1. Neighborhood residents	Disseminate accurate information about proposed plan for home. Identify support as well as opposition, including: a. Concerns b. Dispel myths c. Introduce residents and staff d. Advocate belief that people with developmental disabilities are valuable neighborhood members e. Alleviate neighborhood fear	Written description of: a. The people who will live in the home, including number and sex of clients, where clients are coming from and type of disability b. The program offered in the home c. Information about the staff who will be involved with the home d. A floor plan of the home e. Also, an information sheet about developmental disabilities	Door-to-door campaign, individually talking with neighbors and leaving written information; leaving information for those who are not home Follow-up contact with identified neighborhood support An open house is scheduled and neighbors invited
2. Community institutions	Disseminate information as well as generate support for proposal	Written description of the residents and purpose of the home as well as how interested individuals can support the proposal (e.g., letters/calls to city council members) Same message given to neighbors	Letters and follow-up telephone calls or personal contact Public speaking
3. Supporters	Mobilize support as well as disseminate information	Written description of the proposed program and of how individuals can support the proposal Information on how to show support; material on how to present information	Internal agency memo, letters, and telephone contacts
4. Governmental bodies	Disseminate information General political support	Written description of the proposed home, floor plan, the agency, and the program Same message given to neighbors	Letters followed by telephone call Invitations to visit existing residential facilities Invitations to open house

Table 6.3. *(continued)*

Audience	Purpose	Message	Method
		Funding information, floor plan, information on community education efforts, any requested information	Ask supporters to also speak
5. Media	Disseminate accurate information (See Table 6.2)	Written description of proposed plan	Press release following standard format; encourage person living in the home to speak
		information depending on media's needs	
	Promote positive image about developmental disabilities	Human interest story in local newspapers, television	Letters to the editor

Adapted from the Association for the Developmentally Disabled. 1981. Community Acceptance of Group Homes in Ohio. The Association for the Developmentally Disabled, Columbus, Ohio. Adapted with permission.

REFERENCE NOTES

1. This debate is discussed in more detail in the following publications:
   Balla, D. A. 1976. Relationship of institution size to quality of care: A review of the literature. Am. J. Ment. Defic. 81(2): 117–124.
   Blatt, B., Bogdan, R., Biklen, D., and Taylor, S. 1977. From institution to community: A conversion model. In: E. Sontog (ed.), Educational Programming for the Severely/Profoundly Handicapped. The Council for Exceptional Children, Reston, Va.
   Blatt, B. 1970. Exodus from Pandemonium: Human Abuse and the Reformation of Public Policy. Allyn and Bacon, Boston.
   Bogdan, R., and Taylor, S. 1976. The judged, not the judges: An insider's view of mental retardation. Am. Psychol. 31(1): 47–52.
   Center on Human Policy. 1979. The Community Imperative: A Refutation of All Arguments in Support of Institutionalizing Anybody Because of Mental Retardation. Syracuse University, New York.
   Dybwad, G. 1978. A Society Without Institutions: Presentation to the Presidential Alternatives Symposium. Paper presented to the Presidential Alternatives Symposium, University of Hartford, December 9, 1979, West Hartford, Conn.
   Ferleger, D. and Boyd, A. 1979. Anti-institutionalization: The promise of the Pennhurst case. Stanford Law Review 3:15–25.
   Luckey, R. E., and Newman, R. S. 1975. The president's panel recommendations—today. Ment. Retard. 13(3): 32–34.
   Muehlberger, C. 1974. The social-psychological experiences of adult former residents of a state school for mentally retarded. Ment. Retard. 12(6): 23–25.
   Murphy, J., and Datel, W. 1976. A cost benefit analysis of community versus institutional living. Hosp. Community Psychiatry, 27(3): 165–170.
   National Association for Retarded Citizens. 1973. The Right to Choose. National Association for Retarded Citizens, Arlington, Tex.
   Throne, J. M. 1979. Deinstitutionalization: Too wide a swath. Ment. Retard. 17(3): 171–175.
   Vail, D. 1967. Dehumanization and the Institutional Career. Charles C Thomas, Springfield, Ill.
   Zigler, E., and Balla, D. A. 1977. Impact of institutional experience on the behavior and development of retarded persons. Am. J. Ment. Defic. 82: 1–11.
2. U.S. Department of Education. 1980. Summary of Existing Legislation Relating to the Handicapped. Publication No. E-80-22014. Office of Special Education and Rehabilitative Services, Office of Handicapped Individuals, Washington, DC 20202.

3. In April, 1981, the U.S. Supreme Court reversed a federal appeals court ruling that residents of Pennyslvania's Pennhurst institution had a right to individual

evaluation and treatment in settings "least restrictive to personal liberty." The Court argued in a 6 to 3 decision that a federal "bill of rights" for mentally retarded persons does not entitle them to personally customized treatment or obligate states to place these people in community settings rather than in large public institutions. In the majority opinion, Justice William Rehnquist said that Congress did not intend in passing the 1975 Developmentally Disabled Assistance and Bill of Rights Act to mandate the provision of better services to developmentally disabled persons, but rather to encourage the provision of these services. It cannot be assumed that Congress would impose on participating states the massive financial obligation of providing these services. The Court also remanded to the federal court of appeals issues it had not addressed, namely federal Constitutional claims under Section 504 of the Rehabilitation Act.

4. This material is a summary of that presented in "Final Report: Training and Employment Services for Handicapped Individuals in Sheltered Workshops" (Whitehead, 1981).

7
STAFF DEVELOPMENT

The shortage of qualified staff requires a more careful assessment of the functions and competencies required for effective work with the retarded.

(Bilvosky and Matson, 1977)

No one would argue that there is a critical need for well trained persons to work with the developmentally disabled population. The rapid expansion of community-based programs during the last 10 years, combined with the high staff attrition in those programs, have placed administrators in a serious dilemma. Despite the need for program excellence, legislative or legal mandates cannot insure quality programs without a competent, reasonably stable administrative and service delivery staff. Four points should be kept in mind as you read this chapter: First, human service programs are labor intensive and labor dependent, with as much as 80% of an organization's budget devoted to staff salaries and fringe benefits. Second, a major staffing problem cited by community residential facility administrators (as discussed in Chapter 2) is trouble in recruiting, training, and retaining qualified staff (Bruininks et al., 1981). Third, staff-related factors, rather than lack of client ability, contribute substantially to the failure of community living (Novak and Heal, 1980). And fourth, services for developmentally disabled persons have traditionally been organized around a custodial treatment model emphasizing the care and physical well-being of the client. The recent trend toward rehabilitation, education, and normalization has significantly altered the needed skills of administrative and program personnel. The rapidly changing population, (re)habilitation techniques, divergent agencies providing services, and number of personnel involved are forcing a reconsideration of staff development needs. One change that is occurring is that discipline-oriented staffing is used less than in the past. Concurrently, there has been an increased emphasis on functionally based training, especially among paraprofessionals. What this means is that staff are trained in certain functions, rather than relying on specific disciplines (Carlin et al., 1981; Joint Commission on Accreditation of Hospitals, 1979). The implications of this emphasis on competency-based training, staff evaluation, and the development of career ladders is discussed later in the chapter in reference to a proposed staff training model.

The chapter begins with a general discussion of current staffing problems, including staff attrition and "burnout" in addition to reviewing several available staff training programs. A competency-based staff training model is then outlined that focuses on the development of specific competencies related to the assessment-training and case management-assistance processes. Use of the suggested training model can help to improve your staff performance significantly. However, you may still have additional staff development issues to solve. The chapter concludes, therefore, with a discussion of techniques to improve staff performance, centering on the areas of organizational design, staff-referenced technology, staff stress and burnout, and what I call a responsibility center approach to staff duties.

Regardless of the approach used for staff development, staff training activities must be related to an organization's goals, be systematically taught and monitored, be geared to entry-level paraprofessional personnel with little prior experience or appropriate education, and be upgraded continuously. Effective staff development is both time consuming and expensive. The investment is worth it, however, in improved staff performance and attitude.

CURRENT STAFFING DILEMMAS

Ask administrators to list their greatest problem, and the response will usually pertain to staff attrition, staff "burnout," recruiting qualified staff, and the difficulty in providing staff training. Each of these issues is discussed below.

Staff Attrition

High staff turnover has been documented for both public residential facilities and community-based programs (Baker, Seltzer, and Seltzer, 1977; George and Baumeister, 1981; Meyer, 1980; Sarata, 1975; Skarnulis, 1976; Zaharia and Baumeister, 1978a,b, 1979). High attrition is generally cited as the major factor in poor staff patterns and service delivery. Although attrition rates vary from program to program, it is not unusual to find annual turnover rates exceeding 70% (George and Baumeister, 1981; Skarnulis, 1976). The major factors contributing to this problem include ineffective orientation and integration methods: inadequate and widely varying salaries for similar types of work; and lack of training and support systems to deal with behavioral problems presented by some clients (George and Baumeister, 1981). The longitudinal nature of these problems is reflected in data reported in 1954 by McIntire, who found that high staff turnover in state schools was primarily related to low salary, inadequate qualifications of persons applying, and poor working conditions.

Staff "Burnout"

Staff attrition and staff "burnout" are somewhat different phenomena. "Burnout" in the human services professions has been defined in a number of ways, including a syndrome of: "physical and emotional exhaustion involving the development of negative self concept, job attitudes, and loss of concern and feelings for clients" (Pines and Maslack, 1978); a loss of care and concern for clients, including depersonalization and negative attitudes (Cherniss, 1980b); a separation or alienation from one's work (Berkeley Planning Associates, 1977); and "a progressive loss of idealism, energy, and purpose experienced by people in the helping professions as a result of the conditions of their work" (Edelwich and Brodsky, 1980). The major characteristic of burnout is a loss of care and commitment in response to job related factors. Staff burnout is found at all staff levels, including (Edelwich and Brodsky, 1980):

Front-line staff—who experience powerlessness, low status, polarization between clients and administrators, low pay, and considerable work.

Middle management—who undergo a constant balancing act between loyalties and commitments to those above and below them on the organizational chart; in addition they are subjected to a range of burnout phenomena including paperwork, heavy case loads, bureaucratic hassles, and staff polarization.

Top management—who face the serious frustration of being inadequately trained to perform all their required duties.

Unfortunately, burnout can be contagious. To quote Edelwich and Brodsky (1980, p. 25):

> If burn-out only affected individuals in isolation, it would be far less important and far less devastating in its impact than it is. Burn-out in human services agencies is like staph infection in hospitals; it gets around. It spreads from clients to staff, from one staff member to another, and (most crucially) from staff back to clients. Perhaps it ought to be called staff infection.

Some of the more important job related factors leading to staff burnout relate to poor communication (Gann, 1980), major organizational change, excessive paperwork and budgetary problems (Cherniss, 1980a,b; Lawrence and Lorch, 1969), unrealistic expectations of treatment and rehabilitation gains (Carlin et al., 1981), and overall frustration with the system (Halpern et al., 1980).

Given the complexity of staff burnout etiology and symptoms, it is not surprising that dozens of strategies have been proposed to alleviate or prevent burnout. These strategies are discussed in the final section of the chapter.

Staff Training Programs

The proliferation of programs for developmentally disabled persons has resulted in an equally rapid growth of training programs to meet staff training needs. Some of those that the author is most familiar with are outlined in Table 7.1. The table attempts neither to evaluate the efficacy of these programs nor to be an all-inclusive listing. National clearing houses that may be referred to for the latter include:

The National Inservice Network
Indiana University
2853 E. Tenth St./Cottage L
Bloomington, IN 47401

Table 7.1. Staff training programs and content areas

Area/Topic	References
1. Orientation to developmental disabilities:	
a. Facts	a. Lombardo, 1980; Mamula and Newman, 1973; Murphy, 1975; Provencal and Evans, 1977; Schinke and Landesman-Dwyer, 1981
b. Ideology	b. Lombardo, 1980; Murphy, 1975; Provencal and Evans, 1977; Meyer's Children's Rehabilitation Institute (MCRI), 1980
c. Services	c. LeVine and Zubrack, 1975; Mamula and Newman, 1973; Moise, 1980; Murphy, 1975; Soyka, 1979; Ulrey and Schnell, 1981
2. Residential/Client care:	
a. Physical	a. Mamula and Newman, 1973; Provencal and Evans, 1977; Reilly, 1976; MCRI, 1980
b. Medication	b. Provencal and Evans, 1977; MCRI, 1980
c. Nutrition	c. Bell, 1979; Yager, 1978
d. Routine health	d. Lippman, 1979; Mamula and Newman, 1973; Provencal and Evans, 1977; Yager, 1978
e. Self-help skills	e. Foxx and Azrin, 1976; Hart, 1978; Lippman, 1979; Murphy, 1975
f. Behavior management	f. Dickerson, 1977; Gardner, 1972; Lippman, 1979; Panyan and Patterson, 1974; Provencal and Evans, 1977; Waisman Center, 1976
3. Individualized Habilitation Plan:	
a. Assessment	a. Dickerson, 1977; Schinke and Landesman-Dwyer, 1981; MCRI, 1980; Waisman Center, 1976
b. Writing goals and objectives	b. Dickerson, 1977; Houts and Scott, 1975, 1976; Green, 1977a,b; Page et al., 1981; MCRI, 1980; Waisman Center, 1976
c. Prescriptive programs	c. Crosby, 1976; Dickerson, 1977; Green, 1977a,b; MCRI, 1980; Waisman Center, 1976
d. Recording	d. Dickerson, 1977; Goldstein, 1978; Green, 1977a, b; Waisman Center, 1976
e. Effective team work	e. Faison, 1980; Hawkins, 1978; Throne et al., 1977
4. Client training areas:	
a. Community living skills	a. Green, 1977a, b; Hale, 1979; Chapter 4 Reference Notes
b. Vocational training	b. Batsche, 1980; Blanc, 1976; Lippman, 1979; Weissman-Frisch, Crowell, and Inman, 1980; Chapter 4 Reference Notes
c. Community integration	c. Gardner and Cole, 1981a; Hale, 1979; Chapter 4 Reference Notes

National Resource Center
for Paraprofessionals
in Special Education
Center for Advanced Study in Education
Graduate School and University Center
City University of New York
33 W. 42nd St.
New York, NY 10036

American Society for Training and Development, Inc.
Washington Office
One Dupont Circle, Suite 400
Washington, DC 20036
202/659-1085

National Center for the Study of the Professions
1527 New Hampshire Ave., NW
Washington, DC 20036

Training programs such as those outlined in Table 7.1 are generally sophisticated and can be relied upon to reflect the state of the art; however, staff training programs frequently exhibit problems related to content validity (Lackey and Burke, 1980; Tynan, 1980), clearly defined anticipated outcomes (Cuff, 1977; Ebert, 1979) and lack of generalization probes (Budner, Arnold, and Goodman, 1971; Fredericks et al., 1977; and Weissman-Frisch, Crowell, and Inman, 1980). This author has also noted a failure to focus staff training programs on the behavioral skill requirements of the client's environment. For example, each of the environments related to residential/living, training, competitive employment, and independent living requires specific behavioral skills associated with successful adaptation and adjustment. When one considers the numerous environments affecting a developmentally disabled person, one begins to appreciate the multiple competencies required of staff to perform their job effectively. The staff development model in the next section addresses this problem.

A COMPETENCY-BASED STAFF TRAINING MODEL

Three lines of research provide the background to the model's development. First, data indicate that many community-based programs have behaviorally based entry criteria for clients, such as self-help skills and "appropriate" social behavior (Karan, 1981; Laski, 1977). Such data pose a serious dilemma for staff and clients alike: Either wait until the client somehow develops the necessary entry-level skills, or train staff to work with the clients in developing the appropriate skills. The second line of research is that disabled persons, including low-functioning clients, can live and work in less restrictive and more productive environments if appropriate support or assistance is provided. This assistance can be in the form of a facilitator (Schalock, Harper and Carver, 1981; Schalock and Spearman, 1981), benefactor (Edgerton, 1975), or prosthetic device (Weisgerber, Dahl, and Appleby, 1980). Third, the current emphasis on social ecology demonstrates that client growth and development frequently occurs by modifying the environment or changing staff behaviors (Price, 1979; Stucky and Newbrough, 1981; Watson, 1970; Weisgerber et al., 1980).

The above data suggest strongly that staff training programs should focus on developing competencies that will permit staff to:

1. Assess environmental characteristics and requirements
2. Assess the client's functional level in reference to those environmental requirements
3. Implement individualized remediation programs to overcome as many behavioral skill deficits as possible
4. Provide assistance to the client in the few critical steps or skills necessary to adapt successfully to less restrictive and more productive environments

The competency based staff training model suggested here (Figure 7.1) provides for the development of competencies in each of the above areas. Its essential features involve separating the process of assessment and training from case management and assistance; identifying within each process three levels of program staff and associated competencies; interfacing assessment/training and case management/assistance with other components of the service delivery system and generic services within the community; and depicting the relationship between levels of service needs, specialization of personnel, and probable percentage of the client population. In reference to the latter feature, it is estimated that 80% of the personnel who come in contact with developmentally disabled persons in service programs are paraprofessionals who are the least trained, lowest paid, and frequently least qualified to provide the services. It is hoped that implementing the proposed model will help overcome these difficulties. The conceptual basis, implementation strategies, and specific competencies involved in each feature of the model are discussed below.

Assessment/Training Process

The assessment-training process begins with an environmental analysis of the characteristics and behavior requirements of the client's present and subsequent living-training environments. The importance of an initial environmental analysis is obvious: Adequate performance means meeting the requirements of a person's envionment.

Environmental Analysis Indeed, evaluating environmental characteristics and behavioral requirements is the core ingredient of an ecological approach to assessment and training (Karan, 1981; Price, 1979). During the 1970s, Rudolph Moos (1974a,b) developed a number of inventories that allow one to evaluate

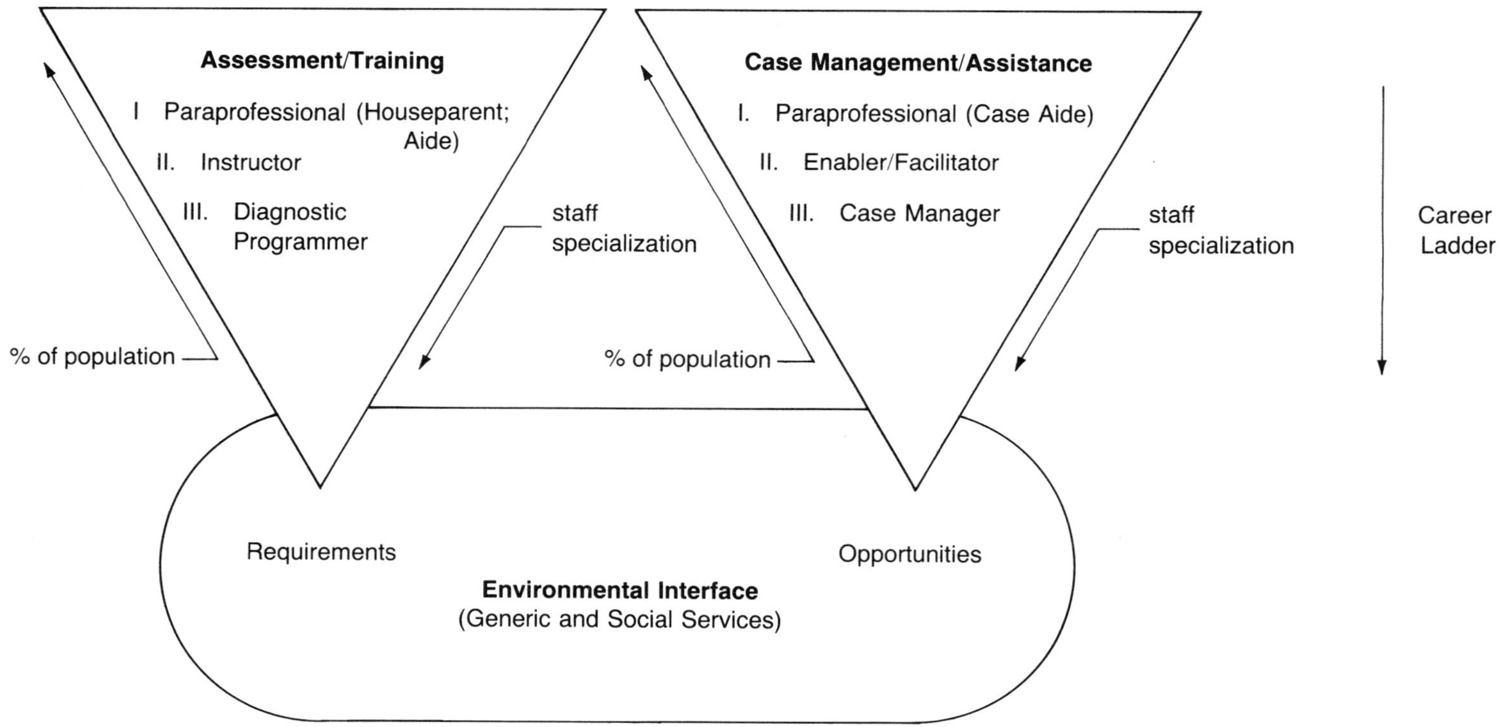

Figure 7.1. Competency-based staff training model.

various "personality" characteristics of treatment environments, including dimensions related to involvement, support, spontaneity, autonomy, practical orientation, personal problem orientation, anger and aggression, order and organization, program development, program clarity, and staff control. The inventory results can be used to match clients to particular environments, determine the attitudes of staff versus administrators and thereby reduce attitudinal discrepancies associated with staff burnout and attrition, or identify staff training needs. For example, in a recent study by Landesman-Dwyer, Sackett, and Kleinman (1980), it was reported that among staff in a number of Washington State group homes, less than 1% of the staff members' behavior fell into categories of praising, rewarding, defending, assisting, protecting, and/or sharing.

The other dimension of environmental analysis relates to determining the behavioral skills required of the client to function adequately within present and subsequent environments. In Chapter 3, Table 3.1, for example, outlined the relationship, based on the author's research to date, between living-training facilities and behavioral skills required within each of the 10 behavioral domains associated with increased independent living and 9 domains associated with vocational training and employment. The reader is cautioned that the required behavioral skills are probably environment specific, and therefore, the skills listed in Table 3.1 may not generalize across all environments. However, once the required skills are identified, then the client needs to be assessed as to the presence or absence of each skill.

Criterion-Referenced Assessment A recent development in measurement involves the use of criterion-referenced assessment techniques designed to yield data that both reflect within individual growth and are directly interpretable in terms of specified performance standards (Carver, 1974; Schalock and Karan, 1979). The current interest in criterion-referenced tests is the result of a series of factors, including increased questioning of the relevance of standardized assessments (Hoffman, 1962; Martuza, 1977; McClelland, 1973; Ysseldyke and Salvia, 1974), the growing instructional technology movement (Glaser, 1971; Mechner, 1965) and the increasing belief that most persons can achieve competency in functional behavioral areas (Block, 1971; Schalock and Harper, 1981a). Operationally, criterion-referenced assessment involves first a delineation of required behavioral skills; second, the development of standardized evaluation procedures; and third, the establishment of a "level of performance criterion" associated with each behavioral skill and resulting from the environmental analysis described above.

Prescriptive Remediation Remediation can focus on either the client or the environment. In reference to the latter, advances in the areas of environmental modification and rehabilitation engineering have significantly reduced the "mismatch" between disabled persons and their environment. Regarding the former, staff training programs should focus more on developing the staff competencies required to systematically remediate the clients' skill deficits and thereby increase the person's functional skills. Prescriptive remediation then emphasizes component skills and their integration into complex terminal behaviors, rather than the training of test-identified abilities that presumably underlie or cause skills to develop. Such an approach causes one to shift away from the currently dominant prediction orientation to one that stresses individualized skill acquisition and intervention planning. As Reynolds (1975) states:

> We are in a zero-demission era; consequently, programs require a decision orientation other than simple prediction; they need one that is oriented to individual rather than institutional payoff. In today's context, the measurement technologies ought to become integral parts of instruction, designed to make a difference in the lives of persons and not just a prediction about their lives (p. 15).

Operationally, the prescriptive remediation system includes the following elements.

1. Assessment of the presence or absence of each behavioral skill identified in the environmental analysis.
2. Establishment of the teaching objectives for each behavioral skill and of the relationship of the teaching materials and techniques to the same target behavior.
3. Implementation of an individualized program utilizing currently accepted behavioral/instructional technology. Figure 7.2 presents a suggested format for such implementation.

Staff Training Program The suggested approach to assessment and remediation outlined above places stringent requirements on staff who are involved in the assessment and training processes. As depicted in Figure 7.1, the staff training program involves developing specific competencies in three levels of assessment/staff training including:

Level I (Aide or Houseparent): Level I is a paraprofessional with some formal training in behavioral management. The individual at this level should be able to run an individualized prescriptive program that was written by either the instructor or the diagnostic programmer.

Level II (Instructor): The instructor should be able to both write and run individualized prescriptive programs.

Level III (Diagnostic Programmer): The diagnostic programmer should be able to evaluate the client on a criterion-referenced assessment instrument, complete the environmental analysis, write and monitor prescriptive programs, and run individualized programs.

The specific competencies required for each of the above three levels are listed in Table 7.2 and discussed more fully in Karan and Schalock (1982). According to the proposed model, staff training activities center around a 2-day intensive, individualized training session in which staff are shown how to perform each of their respective competencies, are allowed to practice the competencies, and are then evaluated as to which specific competencies have been acquired and those that

Name: ______________________ CLS ________ VT ________ Instructor: ______________________

Behavioral Skill: ______________________ Start date: ____________ Stop date: ____________

Primary Learning Channel: Auditory ________ Visual ________ Haptic ________ Recommendation: ______________________

Days Run: M T W Th F S S Location: Center ________ Residence ________ Other ________

Behavioral Objective	Teaching Strategy	Ratio and Reinforcer	Correction Procedure
			specify level of assistance

Figure 7.2. Prescriptive remediation format.

require more work. Subsequently, staff are evaluated on these same competencies as part of a systems review procedure (discussed in Chapter 9) in their actual job location. The evaluation data from systems review are then used to provide additional staff training for those persons who are still not demonstrating the necessary competencies. A recent unpublished study by the author found that 92% of the competencies demonstrated by 20 staff at the conclusion of a formal staff training session were maintained when evaluated on systems review 6 months later. Fredericks et al. (1977) report comparable skill generalization data using a similar staff training model.

Case Management/Assistance Process

The three staff levels suggested below for accomplishing the case management and assistance part of the staff training model are based on a number of studies done within the Mid-Nebraska Mental Retardation Services program over the last 10 years revealing that: 1) A significant proportion of case management (or social service) staff time is spent either on ''endless paperwork'' or in transporting clients to various appointments and sitting in waiting rooms; 2) The preceding activity does not require many skills short of patience and a drivers license; 3) Lower-functioning clients can be placed into less restrictive living and more productive vocational environments if some staff support and actual training (not just advice) are provided; and 4) The implementation of our agency's goals of making people more productive and less dependent requires the integration of agency-based training programs, agency-sponsored assistance in maintaining a client's placement into apartment living and/or competitive employment, and community-based generic services involved in living and working. In an effort, therefore, to use staff more productively—and thereby provide enhanced benefits to clients—we implemented the three levels of case management/assistance outlined below.

Level I (Aide): This person deals with case finding and paper-oriented procedures including evaluation, diagnosis, and certification. The person also monitors client progress and maintains records and information system requirements. Finally, the Level I person handles client maintenance functions such as appointments, errands, correspondence, and recertification.

Level II (Facilitator): This person provides assistance to clients placed from the training program, and thereby facilitates their adapting successfully to the increased environmental requirements. Although the assistance provided is client-specific, the general areas relate to community living, vocational placement, and community integration.

Level III (Case Manager): The case manager assures appropriate services and maximum client development through three major activities: 1) working with the diagnostic programmer in identifying the available placement options and specific behavioral skills required of those environments; 2) interfacing with other components of the service delivery system, including generic community services, to optimize client movement; and 3) procuring the agency-

Table 7.2. Competencies for Levels I, II, and III Assessment/Training Staff[a]

Level I (Paraprofessional)	*Level II* (Instructor)	*Level III* (Diagnostic programmer)
Knowledge	Classroom organization	Client assessment
1. Characteristics of client population 2. Interdisciplinary process 3. Rights of the client population	1. Uses learning centers 2. Adapts materials to student's needs 3. Manages time and resources	1. Analyzes client's occupational and independent living interests and aptitudes 2. Collaborates with other educators, specialists, parents and clients in developing an individualized plan 3. Uses diagnostic and prescriptive assessment techniques for planning intervention programs 4. Develops individual performance goals and behavioral objectives
Skills	Classroom management	Program planning and evaluation
1. Behavioral management a. arranges environment to maximize learning b. applies "ABC" behavioral analysis and change principles (1) antecedent conditions (2) behaviors (3) consequences	1. Utilizes behavior management techniques 2. Employs reinforcement techniques 3. Integrates all clients into training activities 4. Utilizes paraprofessionals productively 5. Recognizes variables affecting client behaviors	1. Analyzes local or regional job market and/employment trends 2. Analyzes available community living alternatives 3. Identifies and uses community resources in planning programs and services 4. Establishes program advisory committees 5. Identifies occupations and living environments to determine instructional content 6. Designs and implement a system for monitoring client progress 7. Obtains information following placement
2. Skill development a. uses task analysis b. encorporates principles of imitation training, generalization, discrimination and maintenance into precriptive programs c. measures client performance d. uses appropriate acceleration and deceleration consequences (rewards, negative consequences)	Curriculum 1. Utilizes and adapts local curriculum 2. Utilizes pre-vocational, vocational and independent living curriculum	

Attitudes	Instructional methods/materials	Implementing individual programs
1. Respect of person's individuality 2. Commitment to client's growth and development	1. Utilizes individualized instructional methods 2. Documents instruction on an ongoing basis 3. Uses multi-resources and materials 4. Modifies materials to client's functional level	1. Coordinates vocational and independent living with academic areas 2. Uses diagnostic and prescriptive assessment techniques for planning intervention programs 3. Uses instructional techniques that individualize instruction 4. Selects or modify instructional materials appropriate for different special needs learners 5. Plans and coordinates off-campus work and living instructions
	Prescriptive program writing	
	1. Understands developmental and behavior sequences and the characteristics of different developmentally disabled groups 2. States specific target behaviors or behavioral objectives based on either a "task" or "ABC" analysis 3. Completes all parts of prescriptive remediation format, including graphing of results	

[a]Adapted from Batsche (1980) and Phelps (1975).

and community-based services that the client requires (such as additional assessment, specialized intervention, housing, and transportation).

The three activities performed by the case manager require two levels of case management and two types of individualized programs. *Client-level* case management utilizes the individualized habilitation plan to insure client growth and development commensurate with moving into, through, and out of the agency's active training program. This is the traditional orientation and focus of case management. Increasingly, however, *systems-level* case management is becoming necessary. This level, utilizing the individualized transition plan, insures the interagency development and implementation of a sequential movement plan that guarantees the client's progression within an independence-productivity continuum. In the transition plan process, representatives from the person's current and future living-training environments work together to identify the potential environments, required skills, and appropriate training activities (Brown et al., 1981).

The specific competency areas associated with each of the three levels of case management assistance are outlined in Table 7.3. Staff training activities and competency probe procedures are the same as discussed previously for the assessment/training staff.

IMPROVING STAFF PERFORMANCE

Effective staff training helps to improve morale and performance. However, you may still face other staff-related issues that tend to reduce staff efficiency and, thereby, your organization's effectiveness. Four of these issues—the relationship between organization design and staff performance, utilization of staff-referenced technology, handling stress and staff burnout, and implementing a responsiblity center approach to staff duties—are discussed below.

Organizational Design and Staff Performance

Evidence (Cherniss, 1980a; Cherniss and Egnatios, 1978) increasingly suggests a close relation between an organization's design, staff motivation, and staff performance. Three aspects of an organization's design seem to exert the most influence on staff (Cherniss, 1980a). These include role structure, power structure, and normative structure.

Role Structure This refers to the manner in which duties are allocated among staff. Cherniss (1980), for example, reports that sustained staff motivation is fostered by high levels of the following organization design dimensions:

Variety—involves change and variety in responsibilities and procedures
Autonomy—permits independent thinking and acting.
Challenge—allows the worker to test his or her ability to achieve difficult tasks

Table 7.3. Competency areas for levels I, II, and III in case management/staff training

Level I: Paraprofessional (Aide)	Level II: Enabler/Facilitator[a]	Level III: Case Manager
Enrollment	Assists community living	Client-level case management
—Case-finding	—Medication	—Individualized Habilitation Plan (IHP) Development
—Certification	—Clothing repair/replacement	—IHP Implementation
Monitoring	—Meal planning/grocery shopping	—IHP Monitoring
—Maintaining records	—Home living/coping skills	Systems-level case management
—Information systems (computer) input	—Crisis intervention/emergency services	—Determine placement alternatives
—Client progress/movement	—Money usage	—Coordinate services (individualized transition plan)
Maintenance	—Time awareness and utilization	—Interface with generic services
—Appointments	Assists vocational placement	
—Errands	—Learning/coping strategies	
—Correspondence	—Job-related skills	
—Recertification	—Work performance	
	—Work behavior	
	—Job-seeking skills	
	Assists community integration	
	—Transportation	
	—Recreational facilities	
	—Community utilization	
	—Language generalization	
	—Interpersonal relations	

[a]Referenced to Community Living/Vocational Training areas.

Task-identity—allows the worker to work on a project from planning to completion; or to work with a case or client from referral to termination; or to be involved in many aspects of service provided to the client
Feedback—yields results that the worker can see
Participation—involves helping to plan future programs and to make administrative decisions affecting large parts of the organization
Information—involves keeping the worker informed about decisions, plans, and activities affecting the job
Learning—provides opportunities to learn new techniques and approaches
Contact—provides opportunities to informal contact with other workers

Power Structure Power structure refers to how decisions are made and authority allocated among the organization's members. All staff seem to want to be part of the decision-making process and tend to lose a sense of personal responsibility and involvement if prevented from playing a role in policymaking (Cherniss and Egnatios, 1978).

Normative Structure Normative structure defines the shared values, goals, beliefs, and norms governing staff behavior and performance. Philosophically, one can discuss normalization, integration, mainstreaming, dignity of risk, and the developmental model; the critical variable, however, is how those factors are operationalized in the organization's service programs and the staff's attitudes. Hasenfeld and English (1974) suggest that shared norms and values are especially important in human services because of the uncertainty created by soft technology, outcomes that are difficult to measure, and the strong moral commitment found among human service staff. Furthermore, Cherniss (1980a) reports that the following three aspects of normative structure influence staff attitudes, satisfaction, and motivation: 1) shared norms and beliefs regarding clients and treatment; 2) concern for staff welfare regarding pay, working conditions, support, recognition, and encouragement; and 3) articulation of a guiding philosophy. In this regard, staff should be involved in the development and implementation of the organization's philosophy, service programs, and management system.

Staff-Referenced Technology

Persons currently being served by developmental disability programs generally have significant physical, mental, and social training needs. At the same time, the program staff frequently are either poorly trained or exhibit considerable attrition and burnout. The dual issues of complex need on the part of clients and the need for sophisticated skills on the part of staff can often seem to pose overwhelming problems for administrators. Although the issues are multi-faceted, it is important to realize that technology is available that can be used for staff and client training activities.

Staff Training Computer assisted instruction (CAI) has been used for the last decade in education, medicine, industry, and the military. Its major advantages include individualized instruction and monitoring, reduced travel and training time, standardized and up-to-date materials, elimination of transfer of training problems ("the workshop syndrome"), and better evaluation of the training activities (Dyer, 1972; Freidman, 1973; Hickey, 1976; Keith, 1979; Keith, Lipson, and Jones, 1980; McGuire, Solomon, and Bashook, 1976).

The essential elements of the CAI system include a central processing unit, storage, terminals, and communication. These elements can be assembled in many different configurations, as reflected in the following currently available systems (Hickey, 1976):

Plato IV—consists of a typewriter keyset and a display unit that shows computer-generated graphic information. Magnetic disks contain lessons.

IBM System 1500—features a terminal designed for instruction, combining an electronic display, computer-selected slides, audio, light pen, and keyboard.

Time Sharing Service (TSS)—gives a large number of users access to a single, large computer. More than 100 companies now offer TSS commercially. To date, TSS has been used primarily by business, industry, and the military; increasingly, however, it is being used in human services for staff training and development.

Piggyback Systems—adds a CAI component to already existing large computers such as those required for an organization's management information needs.

"In-House" System—provides multiple terminals connected by telephone wire, cable, or a satellite. Because of the cost of communications, it might be more economical to install a small, special-purpose training computer at each site.

CAI is attractive, but requires time, programming competencies, and an initial orientation. Technology is advancing rapidly in this area. Before making a commitment to one system, or expending large sums of money, talk with various computer representatives, as well as with other agencies that use computers. Outline your staff training needs and go from there. A vital factor in using CAI is that the equipment be suited to your needs.

Client Training Developing a valid individualized habilitation plan is time consuming, labor intensive, costly, and, unfortunately, frequently unrelated to assessment and training data. Therefore, one of the most important staff-referenced technologies is the use of computerization to interface assessment data with individualized habilitation plan development and prescriptive training activities. The necessary steps involved in this process include:

1. Evaluate the client as to the presence or absence of specific skills dealt with in the training program.
2. Input the information and generate a client profile summarizing the person's behavioral strengths and weaknesses.
3. On the basis of the profile and client-referenced objectives, generate a list of

appropriate training areas. This list could constitute the client's individualized habilitation plan.

4. On the basis of stored prescriptive programs, list the specific training steps and activities required of each objective of the plan.
5. Have staff train the client using the suggested prescriptive programs, recording the specific data as training occurs.
6. Summarize client progress and generate "Habilitation Plan Progress Reports" as deemed necessary.

Once the above system is operational, then the staff can also utilize the computer's memory system to identify additional training needs or intervention programs. For example, the Plato IV system has the capacity to demonstrate range of motion activities, feeding procedures, language stimulation programs, and positioning activities. Drug-behavior monitoring and the parameters of behavior modification programs can also be computerized for ready access.

Handling Stress and Staff Burnout

In recent years, hundreds of publications have dealt with stress, stress management, and the relationship between stress and staff burnout. Of course not all stress comes from the world of work; however, work contributes its share through job-related conflicts and organizational factors.

Stress and the Agency Conflicts are stressful to people. A conflict is characterized by the appearance of two or more motives that cannot be resolved simultaneously. Some are philosophical (deinstitutionalization vs. institutionalization, independence vs. dependence, risk vs. safety); some are job-specific (administration vs. line staff, psychometric vs. edumetric, specialist vs. generalist, centralized vs. regionalized); and some are person-specific (job vs. family, money vs. status, professional vs. personal). Unfortunately, once conflict develops between organizational members, each side tends to ascribe stereotypical characteristics to the other, which further supports and maintains the conflict (Hampton, Summer, and Webber, 1973). Thus, each side exaggerates the differences so that actual overlap and potential resolution are underestimated.

Stress also results from job-related factors such as unidirectional communication flow; unpredictable or changing relationships; infrequent interactions; discrepancy between a person's needs, expectations, and job role demands; and uncertainty about job performance appraisal (Hampton et al., 1973). Cherniss (1980b) has recently suggested that job-related stress leads to the staff burnout phenomenon discussed earlier in the chapter. The initial stress response is manifested primarily as emotional exhaustion that mobilizes coping efforts. If these are unsuccessful in reducing the stress, then the person will use defensive reactions such as depersonalization and withdrawal. The net result is a motivational deficit that leads to impaired performance.

Job dissatisfaction does not necessarily cause staff burnout, however. On the basis of currently available literature, it appears that the following variables are most often associated with staff burnout:

Personality characteristics including a strong need for achievement and control (Edelwich and Brodsky, 1980; Freudenberger and Richelsen, 1980).

Demographic factors including younger, newer, and more highly educated (Gann, 1980).

Organizational factors including lack of communication (Gann, 1980), major reorganizations, change of top leadership, budgetary problems, rapid growth, and general disruptions (Cherniss, 1980; Lawrence and Lorch, 1969).

Stress Reduction Techniques Although specific relaxation exercises are often proposed to ease stress, they do not address the heart of the problem. A more appropriate focus for this chapter is to suggest techniques you can use to reduce organizational conflict, and change those organizational factors associated with stress and staff burnout. Some of the strategies proposed emphasize *individualized techniques,* such as lowering one's goals, taking time off, pursuing outside interests, and developing more effective stress reduction methods (Cherniss, 1980b, 1981; Edelwich and Brodsky, 1980; and Frendenberger and Richelsen, 1980). Other strategies focus on *organizational change,* including improving work conditions (Pines and Maslack, 1978), providing better feedback, staff training, and career ladders (Horjesi, 1979), and developing formal orientation programs for new staff designed to foster realistic expectations (Edelwich and Brodsky, 1980; Gartner, 1979).

Reducing Organizational Conflict Turner (1969) suggests that the key to all conflict resolution is "the repair of previous injury and protection against future injury." You will be involved in conflict resolution dealing with both intergroup and organizationally-based conflicts. Before outlining possible resolution techniques for these two types of conflict, some advice from Walton and Dutton (1969), which is that: managers should set a proper example for handling conflict by confronting and inviting differences, listening with understanding rather than evaluation, clarifying the nature of the issue, recognizing and accepting feelings, suggesting a procedure for resolving differences, and coping with threats to reasonable agreement. With this advice as a background, specific conflict resolution techniques are outlined in Table 7.4.

Dealing with Staff Burnout Techniques for reducing job-related stress and staff burnout are listed below:

Provide adequate salary, supervision, training, and working conditions (McIntire, 1954).

Respect and respond to staff motivators including good pay, importance of job, respect, steady work, and chance for promotion (Scheerenberger, 1975).

Reduce the large discrepancy between job demands and resources by providing program orientation and skills training (George and Baumeister, 1981).

Table 7.4. Conflict resolution techniques

Focus of conflict	Possible resolution techniques	References
Intergroup tension	1. Negotiation by group members	Blake and Manton, 1971
	2. Exchange of persons	Peterson and Duffany, 1976
	3. Handing the conflict to judges	
	4. Have subcommittee develop superordinate goals	
	5. Intergroup therapy	
Organizationally based	1. Develop a coalition	Zaleznik, 1970
	2. Bargaining between the parties involved	Leavitt, 1972 Hampton et al., 1973
	3. Personal absorption of stress/conflict	Cherniss, 1978
	4. Restructure system by decoupling and buffering, unifying work flow, or modifying role demands	Hampton et al., 1973 Lawrence and Lorch, 1969
	5. Introduce transcendent objectives	Sherif, 1958

Improve staff management by providing job descriptions, staff respite services, open communication channels, and objective performance evaluations.

Provide backup support when necessary, and especially for severe behavioral disturbances (George and Baumeister, 1981).

Introduce staff training immediately after employment. Facilities that experience high turnover rates usually lose the bulk of new entrants before these workers have passed the probationary period (Zaharia and Baumeister, 1979).

One additional technique—implementing career ladders for paraprofessional staff—warrants additional discussion. Paraprofessionals are typically persons involved in direct care services who do not have a baccalaureate degree and who serve in a position for which a professional person has ultimate responsibility (Gartner, 1979). Paraprofessionalism as a distinct movement developed during the 1960s as a result of the federal mandate for social welfare programs to use community service aides who were from poor or low-income groups (Carlin et al., 1981). Although human services had been employing nonprofessionals for many years, this legislation led to the development of training programs directed specifically at this group.

> The most profound impact of paraprofessionals upon the network of social services appeared in the area of personnel administration. As a result of inadequate inservice training and dead-end jobs, paraprofessionals focused attention upon agency personnel practices which were recognized by many as archaic and unresponsive to the needs of all levels of workers. Rallying around the concepts of career ladders and career lattices, professionals and paraprofessionals alike began to recognize the need to create career opportunities within agencies and between agencies for all levels of staff (Austin, 1978, p. 16).

In 1971, the Canadian National Institute on Mental Retardation developed one of the first training models for all levels of staff dealing with developmentally disabled persons. At that time it identified key issues as: the need for national training standards, definition of levels of training with diplomas at all levels, and career ladders as an outgrowth of training plans. The Canadian model is based on four levels of education starting with one-year, community college programs and escalating to graduate school on the final level; it has had a marked influence on paraprofessional training programs in the U.S. (Gartner, 1979).

Responsibility Center Approach

Operations or systems design is an essential management tool that facilitates planning, monitoring, and evaluating of program activities to increase the probability of achieving the organization's goals and objectives (Alkin, 1972; Rivett, 1968; Suchman, 1972). The systems approach focuses on input, process, and output; it assumes that each discrete element of the service delivery system affects each of the other parts; and it stresses answers to questions such as "who, what, when, where, why, and how."

	INPUT	PROCESS	OUTPUT
Client Training →	Assessment (Behavioral Skills) →	Remediation/ Reassessment →	Behavioral Skill Acquisition and Client Movement
Case Management →	Intake (Certification and IPP Development) →	Client Monitoring (Recertification and IPP Implementation) →	Placement and Support Services
Financial →	Budget →	Cost Accounting →	—Units of Service —Cost per Unit

Figure 7.3. Functional flow analysis.

While most human services organizations can readily provide impressive printed statements regarding their philosophy and goals, far fewer can offer a clearly articulated chart of how their programs work or of who is responsible for providing specific services with anticipated outcomes. Such a chart requires a systems approach to management that analyzes how the organization flows in relation to its three critical components: client training, case management, and finances. This concept, referred to here as functional flow analysis, is outlined in Figure 7.3. Specific responsibilities are identified for each critical component during the input, process, and output phases of the organization's operation. Therefore, staff recruitment, training, and monitoring can focus on the corresponding staffing needs and expected outcomes.

SUMMARY

Most programs for developmentally disabled individuals are currently experiencing a shortage of qualified staff. This chapter suggested that part of the reason is that to date we have not done a very good job either at determining what we want the staff to do or deciding what specific skills and competencies are required to work with developmentally disabled persons across a number of different environments. The chapter began by discussing the current situation in reference to staff attrition, staff burnout, and currently available staff training programs. Thereafter, a proposed competency based staff training model was described that outlines the different levels of staff competencies required to assist clients in dealing effectively with the behavioral skill requirements of their living-training environments. A staff training program used to develop their competencies, as well as a suggested competency probe technique, was also presented. The chapter concluded with a discussion of four additional staff-related issues including organizational design and staff performance, staff-referenced technology, staff stress and burnout, and the use of a responsibility center approach to staff duties.

DISCUSSION QUESTIONS

1. Edelwich and Brodsky in *Burn Out: Stages of Disillusionment in the Helping Professions* (1980) describe a 12-point planning board exercise that, with minor modifications, can be given to anyone in the helping fields as a way of identifying significant sources of frustration and potential burnout. In this exercise, a person is asked to rank the following items in importance and to comment on their relevance to his or her situation:

   Not enough money
   Too many hours
   Career dead-end
   Too much paperwork
   Not sufficiently trained for job
   Not appreciated by clients
   Not appreciated by supervisor
   No support for important decisions
   Powerlessness
   System not responsive to clients' needs
   Bad office politics

   In addition, a blank piece of paper called a "Wild Card" is given out, on which the person is asked to record any other major source of frustration that he or she faces. The items that turn up repeatedly as Wild Cards (for example, sexism, too much travel, no social life, isolation from peers) can be added to the standard list. Use this technique to assess current staff on present and potential sources of burnout.
2. Evaluate the basis on which staff-client ratios are developed within your organization. You may wish to use one of the following techniques to then estimate your staff requirements (Carlin et al., 1981):
   a. *Staff/Population Ratio:*
   Staff = Population × Designated Ratio of Health Professionals.
   "How many personnel are needed?"
   b. *Service Targets:*
   Staff = Population × Services/Per Person Productivity.
   "How many personnel are needed if there are definite standards for service provision and staff productivity?"
   c. *Health Needs:*
   Staff = Population Needing Care × Average Number of Conditions/

Person/Year × Average Number of Given Kind of Service/Person/ Condition/Year × Average Time/Service ÷ Average Workload of Practitioner.
"What kind of health manpower is needed to provide *optimal* health care?"

d. *Economic Demand:*
Staff = Amount of $ Resources Available for Health Personnel.
"What financial resources are available to pay for health services?"

e. *Supply Predictions:*
Staff = Current Supply + New Entrants − Occupational Losses.
"How can the supply of health manpower be predicted?"

3. How would you characterize your staff training program? Does it cover those areas outlined in Table 7.1? Does it attempt to demonstrate content validity, define anticipated outcomes, or complete generalization probes? How would you evaluate its strengths and weaknesses?
4. Part of the staff training model presented requires an analysis of environments significantly affecting the clients. One part of the analysis is to use an inventory (such as that developed by Moos, 1974a,b) to generate an "environmental profile." Generate an environmental profile, then analyze it in reference to strengths, weaknesses, and implications for client behavior. A similar analysis should be made of environmental requirements regarding necessary and appropriate behavioral skills. Once this analysis is completed, relate its results to your assessment, remediation, and case management processes. Are they congruent?
5. Design a staff training module that could be incorporated into a computer assisted staff training program. What are your major staff or client training needs that could be computerized?

Section III

MANAGING, MONITORING, AND EVALUATING SERVICES

Whereas Part I stressed what to do, and Part II, how to do it, Part III will outline specific techniques to manage, monitor and evaluate your organization's activities, services, and products. Mastering these techniques involves expenditure of time, effort, money, and expertise. But the expenditure is justified, for as Chapter 10 points out, good management and monitoring yield valid program evaluation data. As was stated early in this book, good measurement and monitoring also result in much needed programmatic reportability and accountability.

Chapter 8 emphasizes eight management skills the author has found to be characteristic of competent managers. Chapter 9 focuses on monitoring your organization and the critical variables and processes involved in what is referred to as an "organizational review." Chapter 10 deals with a topic whose importance cannot be over emphasized—client and program evaluation strategies. The message that these three chapters repeat consistently is that programs for developmentally disabled persons must do a better job at managing, monitoring, and evaluating their activities in order to achieve their goals and objectives.

8

MANAGEMENT SKILLS

Managers do many things and play many roles including. . .that of figurehead, liaison, leader, monitor, disseminator, spokesman, entrepreneur, disturbance handler, resource allocator and negotiator.

(Mintzberg, 1973)

As a human service program administrator, you are no doubt frequently asked how you became a manager. Although you would probably like to answer, ''through formal training,'' you are more likely to respond, ''through staff attrition,''. . .''the process of elimination,''. . .''a background in behavioral sciences,''. . .or ''because no one else would take the job.'' Yet, program administrators are expected to be both leaders and good administrators who manage an effective and efficient organization. The skills required to do that are phenomenal. Reading this chapter will not automatically make you a better manager. What the chapter does do is enumerate some of the critical skills and processes involved in management, and encourage you to pursue additional training where appropriate. The chapter's guiding philosophy is that managers become incompetent when they exceed their skill or understanding level. To prevent the Peter Principle from becoming personal, the chapter focuses on those management skills that ideally should generalize across the organizational functions you are most responsible for — implementing, monitoring, and evaluating.

EFFECTIVE LEADERSHIP

Managers must be experts in business and in human relations, because the primary responsibility of a manager is to run an effective and efficient organization. Leadership and managership, in the author's opinion, are two very different phenomena, requiring different skills, competencies, and foci. A phenomenal leader can be a miserable manager; the converse is equally true. Effective leadership requires a complex combination of behaviors, including (French, 1974):

1. *Personal qualities* such as technical competence, role satisfaction, problem-solving abilities, adjustment, task orientation.
2. *Attitudes toward subordinates* that include asserting leadership, displaying confidence in staff, encouraging staff participation, being approachable and friendly, helping subordinates to be more effective, being emotionally supportive, rewarding or recognizing good work, evaluating staff on mutually established performance standards.

3. *Approaching tasks* in a manner that utilizes current technology, plans both short- and long-range goals and contingencies, and interfaces all levels of the organization.

Thomas Peters (1978) suggests that skillful leaders consciously and meticulously bring people together to stimulate and forge desired behavior and to minimize undesired behavior or failure. In this regard, he lists a number of setting variables that can induce and support behavior consistent with the leader's expectations. These setting variables include being present at critical meetings and thereby serving as a model and guide; changing meeting location to underscore the importance of a person or organization; controlling the agenda, which reflects priorities, expectations, and desired behavior; inviting the participation or support of persons who will bring status, responsibility, and accountability to the organization; directing issues and discussions through critical phases of development and change, including problem awareness, possible solutions, experimentation with new behaviors and reinforcing newly acquired attitudes and behaviors; and setting specific goals, objectives, and time lines.

Leadership is essential during the development and implementation stages; however, the organization's needs change once it becomes operational and begins to focus on stability, accountability, staff development, program sophistication, and orderly change. While leadership remains important once the organization becomes operational, this author feels that operating needs can best be met through a group of eight core management skills, of which leadership is one. These skills include understanding people, leading people, decision making, organizing for accountability, setting goals and objectives, working with boards and political groups, facilitating planned change, and recognizing one's limitations. Each of these management skills is discussed below with guidelines and implementation suggestions.

EIGHT MANAGEMENT SKILLS

Understanding People

While generalizing about human actions is difficult and risky at best, most people are motivated by certain needs, all have expectations, some are defensive, and all want to be satisfied with their work.

Individual Motivation Maslow's (1970) hierarchy of needs is a good way to conceptualize the relationship between motivation and personality. Important needs in this hierarchy include:

Physiological—the need for food, water, oxygen, elimination, sleep, relaxation, and sexual and muscular activity.

Security—avoidance of threat and harm, as manifested in desires for job security, fair treatment, and predictability.

Belonging—the need for affiliation, affection, nurturance, and cooperation.

Esteem—the need for feelings of competence, autonomy, independence, dominance, achievement, recognition, attention, appreciation, prestige, and status.

Integration/Wholeness—the need for a consistent picture of one's self and one's world, to avoid inconsistencies, to resolve conflict, to feel fairly and justly treated, and to make order out of disorder.

Growth—the need for self-fulfillment and the realization of one's potential.

Individual Expectations People within organizations are not passive to the above needs; rather they develop plans aimed at fulfilling or meeting them. These plans or expectations are part of what Schein (1970) calls the "individual's psychological contract" with the organization in which the person expects certain rewards in return for meeting the organization's expectations. Managers fulfill their part of the "contract" through personnel policies, management styles, and organizational structure.

Job Satisfiers and Dissatisfiers Herzberg and his colleagues (Herzberg, Mausner, and Snyderman, 1959) have discussed the importance of various factors involved in job satisfaction. In descending order, these factors include security, intrinsic job interest, opportunity for advancement, appreciation from management, wages, supervision, social aspects of jobs, working conditions, communication, and benefits. Based on these and other data, Herzberg et al. (1959) developed a motivation-hygiene theory of worker satisfaction and dissatisfaction as follows:

The Motivators—which when present increase satisfaction; when absent, these factors do not lead to dissatisfaction. Those factors found to increase job satisfaction and motivation include achievement, recognition for achievement, work itself, responsibility, and advancement.

The Hygiene Factors—which when absent increase worker dissatisfaction with their job; when present, these factors serve to prevent job dissatisfaction. They include company policy and administration, technical supervision, salary, working conditions, and interpersonal relations.

Relationship between Satisfaction and Performance Research suggests that focusing solely on external factors associated with worker satisfaction will not result in high productivity (French, 1974). Rather, the level of performance may be a causal factor in job satisfaction, with intrinsic feelings of accomplishment and extrinsic rewards (pay, promotion, status) as reinforcing variables. The relationship between satisfaction and performance that a manager might expect, therefore, is: Performance + Intrinsic/Extrinsic Rewards ⟶ Satisfaction (Lawler and Lyman, 1967).

Leading People

Leading people requires skills, techniques, and a willingness to act on the assumptions you have about people. This section begins by looking at two different sets of assumptions managers can make about their employees.

Assumptions about People Douglas McGregor in *The Human Side of Enterprise* (1960) contrasts two different sets of assumptions one can make about human behavior. One set encompasses *Theory X*, the other, *Theory Y*. Theory X, or the traditional view of direction and control, makes one or more of the following assumptions:

The average person has an inherent dislike of work and will avoid it if possible.
Most people must be coerced, controlled, directed, and threatened to work at their best.
The average person prefers to be directed, wishes to avoid responsibility, has little ambition, and wants security above all else.

Theory Y, or the integration of individual and organizational goals, assumes:

It is fun to work.
People will exercise self-direction and self-control if committed to an organization's goals.
Commitment to goals and objectives is related to the rewards associated with achievement.
Under proper conditions, persons will both seek and accept responsibility.
Many employees have imagination, ingenuity, and creativity.
The potential of most persons is only partially realized and utilized.

Maximizing People William Ouchi, in his recent book *Theory Z* (Ouchi, 1981), extends McGregor's concepts to the organizational level and suggests that the 1980s will require a "Model Z Organization" that emphasizes long-range planning, consensus decision making and strong, mutual worker-employer loyalty. This concept is consistent with a 1981 report prepared by the Long Range Planning Committee of the United Way of America that states:

> Management philosophies will have to change along with the work environment. Management credibility, authority and legitimacy will be increasingly derived from the consent (and the cooperation) of the managed. Workers will demand a bigger say in deciding how they do their jobs, the conditions they work under and the rewards they get. In the future, organization charts will more likely resemble spider's webs than pyramids. Workers may more nearly resemble small entrepreneurs within organizations than subordinates who only follow orders (p. 19).

Therefore, maximizing people will involve using management principles, including (French, 1974): emphasizing both people and production, and thereby creating a climate of reciprocal influence; allowing an atmosphere that permits job latitude, recognition, warmth and support, implicit and explicit performance standards, and open communication differences; and providing administrative and personnel policies, effective staff training, and emphasis on fair play and integrity.

Decision Making

Decisions are not hard to make—nor problems hard to solve—if you have all the facts and can deal effectively with people. Depending on your management style, decisions may be made by yourself or collectively. The process of decision making ideally includes diagnosis, evaluating all the alternatives, and choosing the best alternative based on the available facts. In the real world, however, the manager's actual decision process is probably characterized by one or more of the following (Alexis and Wilson, 1967): First, search or information-gathering strategies are used that are directly related to the "cognitive strain" imposed by time, information retention, and recall; second, since problem-solving behavior is adaptive, a manager starts with a tentative solution, searches for information, modifies the initial solution, and continues such activity until there is some balance between expected and realized behaviors; and third, a manager makes decisions based largely on his or her personality, preference, or aversion for risk.

Because of the above problems, a wise manager uses groups of a workable size for much of the organization's decision making. Groups are generally superior in problem-solving situations because the group process provides a self-correcting mechanism and furnishes support and competition among group members. This advantage exists only under certain conditions, however, including (Berelson and Steiner, 1964):

1. There is little expression of personal needs.
2. There is a pleasant and cooperative atmosphere.
3. The group's problem-solving activity is understandable, orderly, and focused on one issue at a time.
4. Facts are available and used.
5. The chairperson assists the group and moves it in the direction of a decision.

As a manager you will frequently be the chairperson who directs the group's decision making. A good chairperson is informed, organized, supportive, decisive, and able to handle conflict and controversy within the group and still reach a decision. Table 8.1 suggests (with tongue in cheek) techniques that should not be used in your role as a decision maker.

Organizing for Accountability

A theme repeated throughout this book is that human service programs are increasingly expected to be accountable; therefore, regardless of whether you are planning, developing, administering, or changing a program, keep the following "accountability rules" in mind:

1. *Know what's happening*. A person is held responsible for a particular outcome regardless of the type of authority he or she exercises.
2. *Use a responsibility center approach*. People who are not clear about their job duties are either ineffective or overextended.
3. *Measure it*. If you can't measure it, it may be of no consequence. Hence, don't be afraid of data; rather, be scientific and empirical in reference to defining operationally critical subject and program variables, relating intervention techniques to outcome, and sharing the results of your organization's efforts. These concepts are developed fully in Chapters 9 and 10.

Table 8.1 Thirteen ways to not make a decision

1. Find a scapegoat and ride him or her.
2. Profess not to have *the* answer. That absolves you from having *any* answer.
3. Say that we must not move too rapidly. That avoids the necessity of getting things started.
4. For every proposal, set up an opposite and conclude that the "middle ground" (no motion whatever) represents the wisest course of action.
5. Say that the problem cannot be separated from other problems. Therefore, no problem can be solved until all other problems have been solved.
6. Rationalize the status quo: There is much to be said for it.
7. State all the reasons why "it" cannot be done. Carry the problem into other fields; show that it exists everywhere; hence everyone will just have to live with it.
8. Move away from the problem into endless discussion of various ways to study it, or introduce analogies and discuss them rather than the problem.
9. Retreat into general objectives on which everyone can agree. From this higher ground you will either see that the problem has solved itself, or you will forget it.
10. Appoint a committee or task force and weigh the pros and cons (these must *always* be weighed).
11. Say, "That is not on the agenda; we'll take it up later." This may be extended ad infinitum.
12. Conclude that we have all clarified our thinking on the problem, even though no one has thought of any way to solve it.
13. Point out that some of the greatest minds have struggled with this problem, implying that it does us credit even to have thought of it.

Adapted from Paul B. Diederich, Senior Research Associate, Educational Testing Service, Princeton, New Jersey. (Personal Communication)

4. *Use a management information system*. And use it for its intended purpose—to improve your organization's measurability, reportability, accountability, and "manageability" (see Chapter 5).
5. *Focus on output measures*. The critical output from human service programs should be client-referenced. Even though the central problem today in client and program evaluation is the inadequacy of the output measures used (Sorensen and Grove, 1977), there are techniques available (see Chapter 10) for measuring the full range of benefits derived from rehabilitation, including reduction of functional limitations in activities of daily living and improved social and psychological well-being. It was a sad commentary to recently hear an administrator say, "The only way persons leave my program is to die."
6. *Give the program time*. Once you establish a system, give it time to operate so as to provide meaningful data. All too often, administrators respond to a crisis or problem by completely changing the system. This type of reactive management is counterproductive and ultimately results in the organization losing focus, direction, goals, and stamina. By the same token, do not be afraid to modify your approach if the data justify a change.
7. *Define accountability*. Table 8.2 outlines for the various types of accountability who is accountable to whom and for what. The table also lists data sources to use to answer accountability questions.

Setting Goals and Objectives

Managers do not do well in a "fuzzy" world of subjectivity and randomness. Hence, a number of techniques using the by-products of operations research, have

Table 8.2 Summary of accountability types, questions, and data sources

Accountability types	Accountability questions			Data sources to use to examine status of relationship
	"Who is accountable"	"To whom"	"For what"	
Goal accountability	Agency/consortium boards Management team	Client/public	Goal and objective selection	Goal attainment scaling Funding source Interagency agreements
Program accountability	Agency/consortium management	Agency/consortium boards	Training programs Appropriate objectives Appropriate standards	Skill acquisition and client movement indexes Individualized Habilitation Plan objectives
Outcome accountability	Program staff Consortium/agency management	Management	Outcomes consistent with goals Outcomes usable for reporting and change purposes	Service performance indicators Anticipated benefits Collaboration levels

Adapted from Allein (1973).

evolved to facilitate becoming more objective and systematic. The techniques include zero-based budgeting, performance evaluation review techniques, critical path method, management by objectives, goal attainment scaling, and planning program budget systems. Many of the above are private-industry based, and have not adapted well in human sevices. Goal writing and management by objectives, however, have been used successfully in human services and are the major focus of this section. Specific monitoring and evaluation techniques related to achieving your goals and objectives are presented in Chapters 9 and 10.

Goal Writing R. F. Mager in *Preparing Instructional Objectives* (1962) presents a workable, five-step process that managers can use to move from the "fuzzy" world to a more objective one. The five steps include:

Write down the goal.
Jot down in words and phrases the performances that denote that the goal is achieved.
Sort out the jottings. Delete duplications and unwanted items. Repeat the first two steps for any remaining abstractions (fuzzies) considered important.
Write a complete statement for each performance describing the nature, quality, or amount you will consider acceptable.
Test the statements with the question, "If someone achieved or demonstrated each of these performances, would I be willing to say he or she has achieved the goal?" When the answer is yes, the analysis is finished.

Management by Objectives (MBO) MBOs are typically used to manage, evaluate, and develop the performance of employees. A manager and subordinate using this approach periodically set and review the subordinate's goals (Ordiorne, 1965, 1976). The MBO approach is being used increasingly in governmental and human service programs (Brody, 1973; Humble, 1970; Levinson, 1970) to: measure and judge performance; relate individual performance to organizational goals; clarify the job to be done and the expectations of accomplishment; increase competence and growth of the subordinate; enhance communications between superior and subordinate; serve as a basis for judgments about salary and promotions; stimulate motivation; serve as a device for organizational control and integration. (MBOs as performance appraisal techniques are discussed in Chapter 9.)

Working with Boards and Political Groups

The probability is great that as a program administrator you will work with one or more boards of directors and various political groups. A few words, although not definitive, about the skills necessary to work with each are in order:

Working with Boards Your organization cannot operate without a board of directors. The composition of the board is usually set by legal or funding requirements. The board's primary responsibilities include policy determination, procedure review, participation in significant personnel matters, and performance audit (Brown, 1976). Responsibilities might also involve management succession, resource allocation, and developing administrative structure.

Some characteristics and potential weakness of boards are summarized by Weissman (1973):

> The agenda for board meetings is sent in advance along with considerable amounts of material to be read prior to the meeting. This appears to be a real board of directors; yet, it is all style and form, with little substance. . . A high-powered board generally hires a high-powered executive who knows how to keep the board happy and run the agency his own way. He gives the board just the right amount of the right information.
>
> Some boards are dominated by a small clique called the executive committee. The board acquiesces to whatever the executive committee decides because friends of the executive committee have been briefed in advance. In most situations the board and the executive are hand in glove. The board hires the executive to take care of the agency. In so doing, the board relinquishes most of its responsibility (p. 73).

Working with a board requires fostering open communication and maintaining a delicate balance between the organization's staff and the board. Part of the delicate balance is recognizing and appreciating the strengths and contributions of each. For example, board members have expertise, influence, objectivity, knowledge, and the ability to affect organizational change. Staff have professional expertise, knowledge of the organization, and the ability to bridge the gaps between the board and organization (Conrad and Glenn, 1976). Strong boards and strong staffs usually go together; but that process requires the open communication and delicate balance mentioned above.

One of your most important tasks as administrator is to work with and educate your board. In that regard, Conrad and Glenn (1976) suggest the following rule of thumb: If there are effective committee meetings going on, then board meetings need occur only four to six times a year. These board meetings should fulfill a number of purposes including:

To review organizational objectives
To make policy decisions
To hear committee reports
To maintain organizational control and give guidance to committees
To legitimatize, communicate, coordinate, organize, and inspire board members toward greater service

Do not forget that there are ways to "turn off" board members, including (Conrad and Glenn, 1976):

Forget that the board members are volunteers, that they like positive strokes, and that they have the same feelings and emotions that you do.
Exclude them from opinions, advice, or decisions.
Fail either to provide them with meeting notices and agendas, to keep scheduled meetings, to respond promptly to phone calls, or to provide requested information.
Embarrass them through inaccurate or insufficient data.
Antagonize them by attempting to manipulate or minimizing their role.

Dealing with boards requires considerable skills. Some final guidelines to keep in mind:

1. Board members should be well educated and kept up-to-date regarding the organization's philosophy, goals, objectives, procedures, and budgetary process.
2. Board duties, responsibilities, and functions must be clearly understood. A general principle: Boards have the right to determine what should be accomplished, but not the right to determine how it is to be accomplished (Weissman, 1973).
3. Board members should have opportunities for observing programs and talking with staff and clients.
4. There should be a formal procedure that permits staff to bring matters to the board during noncrisis situations. This will prevent circumvention of the system or of normal communication channels.
5. Potential for conflict, stalemate, and delay is reduced through communication, reasonableness, and mature problem-solving techniques.

Working with Political Groups You may not be a politician, but you need to have political savvy and lobbying abilities. In reference to political savvy, remember that politics is defined as the art of compromise. Avoid potential pitfalls by understanding your opposition, maintaining your friends, taking care with words, and charting your own course (Smith, 1979).

In reference to lobbying, Greenwald in *Group Power: Lobbying and Public Policy* (1977) defines lobbyists as "salesmen for their groups; but they sell information and ideas instead of toothpaste." According to Greenwald, lobbyists (such as yourself) must deal with policy, strategy, and tactics. Each of these involves communication methods and lobbying skills, including:

Direct Methods—presenting arguments and/or facts directly to decision makers
Indirect Methods—using group members, citizens, or the media
Constituent Action—marshalling constituents toward specific individuals or groups
Alliances—magnifying impact of grass roots lobbying by multiplying numbers

Facilitating Planned Change

Organizations change when new ideas or concepts are introduced or when they are under pressure to change (Beckhard and Harris, 1977; Beer, 1980). The stimulus for planned change can come from within or without the organization. Externally, stimuli can come from research findings, changes in public policy, funding sources, licensing-certification agencies, or demands from the organization's heterogeneous constituency. Internally, stimuli can come from staff suggestions, program evaluation, high attrition, program stagnation, or lack of significant client development and movement.

Many opportunities for planned change flounder or fail because management ignores the need for change or the readiness and motivation to change. A crisis often results. Although these crises can provide the motivation to change, the author's experience has been that such reactive change is much less effective, efficient, and viable than that which is planned. Hence, the focus of this section is on planned change.

Planned change should be based on data that justify the change and also provide the direction for it. There is considerable evidence suggesting that organizational members are willing to change if they are provided information about the reasons for it (Beer, 1980; Lawler and Rhode, 1976). However, the data must be perceived as relevant, accurate, and important to significant persons within the organization (Nadler, 1977).

One way to begin the change process is to use the following three-phase, problem-solving strategy. Using the strategy may help you overcome the frequently heard statement, "we cannot change the system."

1. *Problem Identification* The first phase involves three steps designed to identify implementation barriers, to rank and select specific barriers, and to measure the occurrence of the barriers identified.
   a. *Step 1—Identification of Barriers*. List all possible or potential barriers that would diminish the goals and objectives of the planned change.
   b. *Step 2—Selection of Barriers*. Specify (define in behavioral terminology for measurement), select and rank order the barriers to the planned change. Two effective techniques for accomplishing Steps 1 and 2 include the Delphi (Morrison, 1976; Turoff, 1970) and Nominal Group techniques (Delberq, Van De Ven, and Gustafson, 1975; Gustafson et al., 1973).
   c. *Step 3—Measurement of Barriers*. This step involves the collection of baseline data. The frequency of target barriers is critical if the planned change is to occur. In counting target barriers, it is frequently found that they are less of a problem than anticipated.

2. *Problem Analysis* The second phase involves an analysis of the antecedents, interrogatories (see below) and consequences surrounding and maintaining the perceived barrier. Remember that barriers involve behavior; and that behavior is embedded in an *antecedents-behavior-consequence* sequence. You are in a good position to overcome a barrier once you analyze the antecedent events that trigger it, determine the interrogatories (who, what, where, when) that "maintain" the barrier, and analyze the consequences that prolong it.
3. *Problem Solving* The third phase focuses on an action plan that details steps, time lines, and responsible persons involved in the planned change. Once a solution is proposed, then a variety of change strategies can be implemented. The responsibility for this implementation is ultimately yours; but there are a number of options available to you, including (Beer, 1980; Greiner, 1967):

Top Down—implementing the change through decree, technological improvements, replacement, or modifying internal aspects of the organization.

Bottom Up—implementing the change without much input from management and through techniques such as training all levels of staff or conducting a pilot study and generalizing to the entire organization if successful.

Shared Responsibility—wherein management defines the problem and jointly develops a solution through task groups composed of staff, consultants, and board members.

How does one evaluate the effectiveness of the change approach used? A number of criteria have been proposed (Beer, 1980) and involve demonstrating that the change:

Comes closer than any other choice in satisfying the most people
Is faster than other options
Results in immediate and long-term performance improvement
Is least disruptive to the organization
Is internalized by people throughout the organization
Facilitates future change because of a successful effort
Is supported by critical organization members and reflected in changed policies and procedures
Conforms to the *Zeitgeist* or mood of the time

Recognizing Your Limitations

A statement made earlier in the chapter bears repeating: Managers become incompetent when they exceed their skill or understanding level. Since most managers are not trained formally to do what is expected of them, it is not surprising that they sometimes feel incompetent, frustrated, and even ineffective. One way to prevent your "Peter Principle Waterloo" is to use the supplemental resource management team discussed in Chapter 1.

A second technique is to use outside consultants when you need to expand capability rapidly, have a need for specialized expertise or facilities not provided by the supplemental team, or if you need the intangibles of objectivity and expertness (Parry and Ribbing, 1976). If you cannot bring experts in, you might go to them. Note, for example, the phenomenal increase in management skill short courses. Their numbers alone indicate that such courses may be effective. An alternative explanation for the growth in short courses, however, is that managers are becoming increasingly frustrated and perceive themselves as needing some quick answers! Unfortunately, there are none.

SUMMARY

Managing people and an organization requires a number of skills in addition to simply being a good person or a good leader. Managers must assume a variety of roles, including that of business person, expert, public relations specialist, psychologist, and scapegoat. The chapter stressed that management and leadership skills are different: Leadership is essential during an organization's planning, development, and implementation phases; management skills are critical during the organization's stabilization and change phases. The management skills discussed included understanding people, leading people, decision making, organizing for accountability, setting goals and objectives, working with boards and political groups, facilitating planned change, and recognizing one's limitations.

DISCUSSION QUESTIONS

1. Managers typically perform a number of roles, including planner, policy maker, organizational representative, controller of internal relations, purveyor of punishments and rewards, arbitrator or mediator, ideologist, father figure (counselor), and scapegoat. Rank order each of these roles from the most important to you to the least important to you; then indicate the percentage of your available energy you would *choose* to invest in each. Second, rank order these roles again from the most to the least important, based on the percentage of energy you *actually* invest in each. Discuss the differences and possible techniques you can use to reduce any discrepancies.
2. Use the same technique as that outlined in #1 to have staff rank Herzberg's motivators and hygienic factors, as discussed in the chapter. Use "satisfaction" as the basis for the rankings. What implications are there for your organization's personnel policies and management approach?
3. Develop specific results of using Theory X versus Theory Y (see chapter) in the assumptions you make about people. Analyze these examples to determine which theory you actually use.
4. Evaluate your management styles against the "accountability rules" (Table 8.2) outlined in the chapter. How accountable is your organization?
5. What data would be most indicative of the need for planned change? Are these data available; if not, could they be? Consider the last change that occurred in your organization. Was it based on data? Was it planned? Was it effective?

9

MONITORING

> *There are few rewards to being a good manager in a time of retrenchment. Necessity in this instance, however, may be a virtue. Minimizing loss, damage control and laying a foundation for future regeneration can be activities that bring their own reward.*
>
> *(Callahan, 1981; p. 699)*

Monitoring an organization's activities is the only way to ensure an effective, efficient service delivery program. The monitoring approach proposed in this chapter is similar to that used for the last 9 years in the Mid-Nebraska Mental Retardation Services program. The model outlined is based on the assumption that monitoring is most feasible when it is an integral part of the service delivery system, and most effective when it is a continuous *internal* process of feedback and planned change. The approach suggested is, therefore, different from external program audits such as those conducted for accreditation or licensure; these generally evaluate a program's compliance with a set of standards typically unrelated to effectiveness or efficiency outcome measures.

RATIONALE

The focus of monitoring the process and products of your organization is on continuous information gathering to provide feedback to management. As such, it is an essential management tool that generates information that can be used both for organizational improvement and program evaluation. Some of you may be apprehensive about data, monitoring, and evaluation. Because of my commitment to the axiom that "good decisions require good information," I have attempted to follow a suggestion made by Weiss (1972):

> . . . the system provides information that the audience has defined as relevant to their values and their needs. It enables them to make decisions and take actions on the basis of the kind of information that they value. It is important to keep the basic system as simple as possible so that the data clearly show what each audience wants to know. (p. 5).

This author noted previously that the developmental disabilities movement is a large-scale social experiment whose efficacy is still being determined. As a social experiment, it must recognize the dynamic nature of social movements, both in terms of the fleeting and perishable nature of attitudes and opinions, and the constantly changing nature of human value structures and social priorities. In light of the need to demonstrate efficacy and flexibility, programs for developmentally disabled persons must both monitor and evaluate their processes and outcomes. In addition, an underlying assumption is that these programs should not be managed solely by budgets and client data generated to satisfy external funding sources. Such practices are not only insufficient for effective management and program improvement, but also reduce the program's responsiveness to its constituency.

Two prerequisite conditions are necessary for the effective monitoring of a service delivery program's operations and services. These include a management information system and a monitoring-review procedure. Although the parameters of a management information system were presented in Chapter 5, their relationship to the monitoring process warrants further discussion. (The monitoring-review procedure is outlined later in the chapter.) A management information system quantifies selected service elements and thereby allows monitoring of the organization's responsiveness, effectiveness, and general operation. Elements of such a system could include service utilization and certain performance measures such as appropriateness and extensiveness. By monitoring utilization data, a human service program can determine which segments of the community are using services. Appropriateness measures (such as average length in treatment, planned versus actual time receiving services, anticipated progress versus actual progress, and receipt of services related to the clients' disability) establish and maintain standards for service usage and continuity of care. Extensiveness measures that detail the amount and type of services offered by all member agencies indicate whether service gaps or duplications exist; they also suggest the point at which referral networks or cooperative programs among member or outside agencies should be developed.

The chapter begins with a discussion of four critical variables to monitor and some of the monitoring approaches available for each. By now, you are familiar with three of these variables—resources, technology, and staffing. This chapter introduces a fourth, critical performance indicators. An organizational review model and process are then outlined, with program changes resulting from their use summarized. Throughout the chapter, the reader should keep the purpose of monitoring in mind: to ensure a quality program that is efficient and effective.

CRITICAL VARIABLES TO MONITOR

Monitoring Resources

An organization's resources consist of money, facilities, and interagency collaboration. These resources are typically evaluated externally through financial audits or licensing, certification, and accreditation surveys. They can also be monitored internally as outlined below.

1. *Financial Monitoring* Government agencies have historically used fiduciary accounting systems that require income and expenses to be recorded and

ideally equated (Gleim, 1977). To date, this approach has met the requirements of specific funding sources, government regulatory bodies, and the general public (Jenkins, 1977). However, fiduciary accounting systems will not meet the requirements of the impending performance audits. These will include not only financial and compliance audits, but also audits for economy, efficiency, and achievement of desired results (Comptroller General, 1974; Steinberg, Miller, and Menzel, 1981). Current approaches to cost-outcome analysis are referenced in Note 1, and discussed more fully in Chapter 10.

A number of ratios obtained from an organization's fiscal statements can also provide important financial monitoring. Some of these ratios include (Ryan, 1979):

Current: ratio of current assets to liabilities
Acid-test: ratio of quick assets (cash plus accounts receivable) to current liabilities
Debt-asset: ratio of total liabilities to total assets
Equity-asset: ratio of fund balance to total assets
Accounts receivable: ratio of revenue to average accounts receivable

2. *Facility Monitoring* A number of evaluation instruments are available for monitoring facility characteristics (McLain, et al., 1979; Note 2). The best known of these instruments is the Program Analysis of Service System (PASS-3), developed by Wolfensberger and Glenn (Note 3). PASS-3 can be used to assess a service system's characteristics including attitudes, staff capabilities, environment, funding, and administrative practices (Janicki, 1981). Factor analytic studies of PASS-3 have identified six factors, including four that are most relevant to facility monitoring (Eyman, De Maine, and Lei, 1979; Mayeda, 1979):

Normalization—including autonomy and rights, intensity of relevant programming labels and age-appropriate forms of dress, social over-protection, routine activities and rhythms, possessions, rights, sexual behavior, facilities, environmental design and appointments, interaction, socially integrative activities, age-appropriate personal appearance, individualization, culturally appropriate personal appearance, physical over-protection, culturally appropriate labels and forms of address, and staff development
General Environment—including model coherency, program-neighborhood harmony, deviant client and other juxtaposition, building-neighborhood harmony, .deviancy program juxtaposition, congregation and assimilation potential, and facility and location names
Location and Accessibility—involving access, local proximity, physical resources, and regional proximity
Comfort and Physical Setting—consisting of environmental beauty, physical comfort, internal design and appointment, and deviant staff juxtaposition.

3. *Interagency Monitoring* Interagency monitoring should focus on the anticipated benefits and outcomes resulting from the collaboration. As discussed previously, these include:

   Improved quality of care, training, and normalized living
   Reduced duplication of services
   Increased availability and accessibility of services
   Reduced administrative and direct service costs through shared services
   Improved manpower utilization
   Increased influence in the public policy arena

   Specific techniques to monitor the above anticipated outcomes should be incorporated into the original interagency agreement. Additional monitoring techniques can be found in Baum et al. (1982), Magrab and Elder (1979), and below, under "Monitoring Critical Performance Indicators."

Monitoring Technology

Monitoring technologies related to clients, staff, and management assures proper programmatic implementation and increases the probability of desired outcomes.

1. *Monitoring Client Technology* Utilizing the best technology available may either become a legal strategy to overcome barriers or a factor in litigation against human services. In that respect, monitoring the technology used with clients must go beyond the current requirements of the person's individualized habilitation plan, which is a *process document* that does not stress *outcomes*. Note the following plan requirements as discussed by Yaron and Walker (1979). A client's individualized habilitation plan must:

   Be in writing
   Be developed jointly by the institution's or agency's representative, the resident and, where appropriate, the resident's parent or guardian
   Include a statement of long-term habilitation goals and short-term objectives relating to the attainment of those goals
   Have specific objectives, stated in sequence and expressed in terms of behaviors or measurable indicators of progress
   Describe how the objectives will be achieved and barriers that might interfere with the achievement of the objectives
   State objective criteria and an evaluation procedure and schedule for determining whether the objectives are being achieved
   Provide for a coordinator responsible for implementing the plan
   Describe clearly the specific services to be provided
   Identify which agency will provide the service
   Describe the personnel and their qualifications to provide the services
   State when the services will begin and how long they will be provided
   State the role and objectives of all parties involved in implementing the plan

Be reviewed annually
Allow parent or guardian the opportunity to review the plan and participate in its revision

One might wonder how all of the above requirements relate to monitoring client technology. Take, for example, the fifth requirement that states that the plan must describe how the objectives will be achieved and the barriers that might interfere with the achievement of the objectives. It is the next step (which unfortunately is not a requirement) that is critical: *How will the barriers be overcome to reduce the mismatch (that is, handicap) between the person and the environment?* That process relates to technology, and *that* is what should be monitored. In monitoring individualized habilitation plans, the author looks for barrier resolution techniques, including: Developing client skills through currently available behavioral techniques; providing sensory, motor, and cognitive prosthetics to reduce the mismatch; and modifying the environment to accommodate the client or providing for the client to remain in a less restrictive environment.

2. *Monitoring Staff Technology* Monitoring staff technology is not the same as monitoring staff competencies, the latter of which is discussed in the next section. Rather, staff technology refers to how staff are trained and the technology they use with clients. Staff training, for example, should employ current techniques that have demonstrated content validity and that result in measurable competencies, and should be followed by competency probes. In addition, staff should use:

   Assessment techniques—that are reliable, valid, and result in functional behavioral skill profiles reflecting performance on environmentally required behaviors

   Remediation strategies—that incorporate the best behavioral technology available and result in quantifiable information

   Barrier resolution strategies—that implement skill development, prosthetics, or environmental manipulation strategies

   A management information system—that provides relevant, useful, understandable, and valid data

Monitoring Staff Competencies

Staff evaluations can be unpleasant for a host of reasons, including the notions on the administrator's part that he or she is playing God (McGregor, 1957) or is hurting others (Levinson, 1970). My feeling is that competent, well-trained people do not need to fear evaluations, especially if they know the criteria. Evaluations can furthermore be one of the most productive ways to increase staff effectiveness, efficiency, and motivation. A number of performance appraisal techniques have historically been used, with merit ratings and management by objectives (MBO) probably the most popular.

Merit rating techniques can involve:

1. *Rating scale*—such as Likert-type ratings (1 to 5; 1 to 7) on characteristics including knowledge, quantity and quality of work, abilities to learn new duties, initiative, cooperation, judgment, and common sense (Miller, 1959; Teffin, 1959)
2. *Rank order method*—in which a supervisor ranks all staff across a number of traits from best to poorest (French, 1974)
3. *Forced distribution method*—wherein staff are distributed along one or more scales, with fixed percentages at each end (French, 1974)
4. *Paired comparisons*—in which for each trait rated, each subordinate is compared with every other one (Oberg, 1972).

MBO was introduced in Chapter 8 in reference to the management skill of setting goals and objectives. As a staff-monitoring technique, MBO involves five process steps, including: 1) discussion between supervisor and employee regarding job description; 2) establishment of short-term performance targets; 3) periodic meetings to discuss progress toward targets; 4) establishment of check points to measure progress; and 5) final evaluation of objectives reached within the defined period (Levinson, 1970).

Unfortunately, there are some serious problems with managment by objectives, including imposing objectives without joint diagnosis or discussion, or providing insufficient acknowledgement of interdependency between jobs (French and Bell, 1973; McGregor, 1957; Ordiorine, 1976). In light of these problems, French and Bell (1973) recommend the following ingredients to what they refer to as ''collaborative management by objectives'':

Real subordinate participation in goal setting as opposed to unilateral and autocratic approaches.

A team approach in reviewing targets and achievements.

Superior-subordinate relationships characterized by joint efforts and mutual assistance.

Recognition of a person's personal needs and career goals, and attempting to make these complementary to the organization's goals.

Merit ratings and MBO can be effective performance-appraisal techniques. Staff monitoring should also focus on the *specific* staff competencies required to implement the organization's service delivery system. Monitoring these competencies is discussed later in the chapter in conjunction with implementing the organizational review model.

Monitoring Critical Performance Indicators

A good manager is aware of a number of indicators reflecting the organization's health and welfare. More specificially, a group of six critical performance indicators provide information about the underlying processes by which the organization's efforts are translated into outcomes. These indicators include (Sorensen and Grove, 1977; Suchman, 1967):

1. *Availability*—amount and type of service provided
2. *Awareness*—knowledge of user population and of other agencies; existence, range, and conditions for which services are appropriate
3. *Accessibility*—ease of reaching service and whether or not service can be obtained by appropriate groups
4. *Extensiveness*—quantity of services rendered in relation to extent of need
5. *Appropriateness*—proper use and quality of service(s) for presenting problem(s) and needs
6. *Acceptability*—user satisfaction with services based on congruence between service needs and services/program provided

Monitoring these critical performance indicators necessitates your focusing on outcome data such as that presented in Table 9.1. These data should be readily available, since they are part of your management information system (see Chapter 5).

ORGANIZATIONAL REVIEW MODEL

The previous section outlined four critical variables to monitor to increase the organization's efficiency and effectiveness, including resources, technology, staff, and performance indicators. The remainder of the chapter describes an organizational review model that structures the monitoring process. The review model encompasses four aspects including purpose, components, functional flow analysis, and organization review variables.

Purpose of Organizational Review

The review's primary purpose will most likely involve monitoring one or more of the four critical variables discussed previously. Organizations may select different variables to review. The importance of clearly articulating a purpose should not be underestimated, however, for it establishes the focus and framework for all subsequent aspects of the review.

Critical Organizational Components

Critical organizational components monitored during your organizational review should include client assessment/training, case management/assistance, cost accounting, and a management information system. Once these critical components are identified, then it is necessary to see how the organization actually flows in reference to the components. This necessitates completing the analysis outlined in the next step.

Table 9.1. Suggested outcome measures to use in monitoring service performance indicators

Indicator	Suggested outcome measures
Availability	List of services; number of units of service; number of persons served.
Awareness	Percentage of user group aware of organization's services; patterns of referrals; centralized client referral system; documentation of outreach/public information activities.
Accessibility	Availability of person to physically reach the service outlet; availability of city/county transportation system; sloping curbs to accommodate wheelchairs; barrier-free buildings where services are provided; average travel time; hours of service available by day of week.
Extensiveness	Functioning range of client population; services provided to all developmentally disabled persons; some clients receiving direct training/programmatic services and some receiving follow-along/support services; and number and rate of ''catchment'' area resident's use of services.
Appropriateness	Correspondence between diagnosis/functional level and services received; range of training activities and living-training environments associated with the client's increased independence and productivity; indication that an environmental assessment (such as PASS-3) has been used to evaluate the organization's normalization aspects and quality of life variables.
Acceptability	Number of complaints; number of vacancies; number of referrals from friend/family members associated with current clients; financial support from local political bodies/social organizations.

Functional Flow Analysis

The systems approach to service delivery has been advocated throughout this book as the most efficient way to plan, implement, and monitor services. The systems approach assumes that each discrete element of the service delivery system affects each of the other parts; therefore, the system stresses interrogatories such as "who, what, when, where, and how." The proposed organizational review technique employs a responsibility center approach to staff utilization that specifies for each critical organizational component the major responsibilities in regard to the input, process, and output dimensions of a service delivery program. This concept is referred to as functional flow analysis and is diagrammed in Figure 9.1.

Organizational Review Variables

As depicted in Figure 9.1, functional flow analysis results in a list of staff competencies or critical performance indicators that can be monitored during the organizational review process. The particular variables monitored will depend on the organization's goals and the review's purpose. Over the last few years, for example, the author has monitored within the same organization program implementation, staff competencies, standards necessary for accreditation, and critical normalization indicators. Some of the variables monitored on one or more of these reviews are listed in Table 9.2. It is important to stress here that the variables reviewed are specific to the organization and the review's purpose. The monitoring process, however, should be standardized as outlined in the next section.

Responsibility Center	**Input**	**Process**	**Output**
Client Assessment/ Training	Assessment →	—Training → —Reassessment	Behavioral Skill Acquisition
Case Management/ Assistance	—Intake → —Certification —IHP Development	—IHP Implementation → —Service Procurement —Assistance Training —Advocacy —Follow-Along	—IHP Objectives Achieved —Client Movement
Cost Accounting	—Budget → —Responsibility Centers	—Units of Service →	—Cost per Unit —Performance Audit —Operationalizes Critical Performance Indicators
Management Information System	—Data Entry →	—Data Storage → —Data Analysis	—Data/Report Output

Figure 9.1. Functional flow analysis as related to program monitoring. (IHP = individualized habilitation plan.)

Table 9.2. Sample performance indicators involved in an organizational review

Review focus	Responsibility center	Performance indicators
Client's living facility	Case management/assistance (or program director)	1. Safety and sanitation (e.g., flammable materials stored, written emergency procedure, annual fire marshal's report) 2. Community utilization records 3. Quality of life (physical comfort, environmental beauty, individualization, social interaction)
Client and staff records	Management information system	1. Personnel files (application, staff training record, performance appraisal results, health and vacation records) 2. Committee records (behavioral management, health and sanitation, research, safety) 3. Client medication records (including behavioral/chemical intervention programs)
Data accuracy	Management information system	1. Demographic variables such as age, IQ, entry date, referral source, movement patterns, primary and secondary disabilities 2. Fiscal variables related to units of service received and cost per unit 3. Behavioral skill data including baseline level, skills achieved through systematic programming and reassessment data
Staff competencies	Assessment/training and case management/assistance	See Tables 7.2 and 7.3.

ORGANIZATIONAL REVIEW PROCESS

The organizational review process is made easier if one remembers that monitoring, as stated earlier, is most feasible when it is an integral part of the organization's activities, and most effective when it is a continuous process of feedback and planned change. Accordingly, the review process involves the following six steps: 1) operationalize the variables (input, process, or outcome) to be monitored; 2) link the selected variables to data within the management information system; 3) define when and how data will be gathered and the party or entity from which it will be obtained; 4) establish judgement criteria for acceptance or rejection of evidence in relation to each variable; 5) conduct the activities (on-site) specified in steps 3 and 4; and 6) interpret the data and specify the action or correction strategy if needed.

Two examples from the Mid-Nebraska program reflect how an organizational (or "systems") review can be implemented. One example relates to evaluating 65 assessment and training staff on the competencies listed in Table 7.2. The competencies were those identified as necessary to implement the suggested programmatic approach to client assessment and prescriptive teaching. The 65 staff had completed a staff training program that focused on the development of these competencies. The review in question occurred 6 months after the training and involved observing each staff working individually with a client, then rating the staff person (using a 3-point Likert Scale) on each competency. Results indicated that staff did not demonstrate acceptable competencies in the use of alternate communication strategies, establishing pass/fail criteria on the basis of baseline data, using reinforcement sampling techniques, and employing appropriate correction procedures. These deficiencies were corrected first, by contracting with a consultant to teach staff sign language, and second, by using the inservice coordinator to provide additional training in the three other deficiency areas observed. These differences were not observed during a subsequent systems review.

The second example involved a significant training component change. The entry-level training component to the Mid-Nebraska Program was referred to as "Basic Skills." It was initiated in 1972 and involved assessing and remediating deficits in the behavioral domains of sensorimotor functioning, visual-auditory processing, language, symbolic operations, social-emotional development, and work skills (see Schalock, Ross, and Ross, 1976). Initially, the skill acquisition data (one critical performance indicator; see Chapter 10) was impressive, with clients gaining skills and progressing to the other two training components (community living skills and vocational training). However, skill acquisition indices decreased significantly beginning in 1977, as lower functioning clients began entering the system. In fact, on 6-month repeated assessments, some clients actually lost skills (see Schalock and Karan, 1979, for the specific data). As a result, the utility and continuation of Basic Skills was seriously questioned by the management team. The decision was made to disband Basic Skills, to do "downward" extensions on the assessment and training materials associated with Community Living and Vocational Training, and to integrate the Basic Skills clients into these two training components. Basic Skills training was no longer cost-effective.

These two examples demonstrate, it is hoped, the utility and flexibility of a systematic organizational review. The author's experience with organizational review across a number of organizations suggests strongly that it is probably management's most productive, cost-effective, and creative activity.

SUMMARY

Monitoring an organization's activities, staff, and output need not be futile or unpleasant. However, if it is to be productive, it needs to be an integral part of the organization and a continuous process of feedback and planned change. As such, monitoring or "reviewing" an organization is significantly different from audits, licensure, certification, or accreditation activities. The organizational review process outlined in the chapter begins by selecting the critical variables to be reviewed. These can be client-, staff-, or organization-referenced. Once selected, each variable needs to be related to the organizational component responsible for its elicitation. This step is augmented by the third process step, which analyzes the organization's functional flow in reference to input, process, and output variables. Functional flow analysis results in a list of staff competencies and critical performance indicators that can be monitored during the organizational review process. Although this process is organization- and purpose-specific, a number of standardized procedural steps are involved. These steps were discussed along with two examples of how the review technique has been employed.

DISCUSSION QUESTIONS

1. Outline how your organization is currently monitoring finances and facilities. Are any of the fiscal ratios presented currently being used; if not, what prevents their implementation? What are your critical financial and facility performance indicators?
2. The PASS-3 inventory can be used to evaluate environmental normalization and personality characteristics of various environments. Use either the actual instrument, or the brief descriptions given in this chapter, to monitor the normalizing qualities of your living-training programs and the attitudes of your staff. Are you surprised by the results? What planned change strategies are obvious?
3. If you are involved in interagency collaboration, use the proposed service performance indicators to determine if the collaboration has actually improved or increased the service delivery system. If not, what needs to be changed?
4. Evaluate critically the approach to (and content of) your individualized habilitation plans. A point was made in the chapter that these plans are

typically *process* rather than *output* oriented. Is this true of yours? In addition, review the sections in Chapter 6 on barrier removal strategies. Are barrier removal techniques presented, and do they represent "best technology?"

5. Outline the procedural steps and methodology involved in completing an organizational review. Steps should include at least those outlined under "Organizational Review Model." Complete the review process.

REFERENCE NOTES

1. Current approaches to cost-outcome analysis can be found in:

Attkisson, C. C., Hargreaves, W. A., Horowitz, M. J., and Sorensen, J. E. (eds.). 1978. Evaluation of Human Service Programs. Academic Press, New York.

Bolton, A. 1974. Measuring the costs and benefits of alternative services for the mentally retarded. In: Program Budgeting and the Mentally Retarded. Perspective Series, Vol. I. National Association of Coordinators of State Programs for the Mentally Retarded, Arlington, Va.

Carter, D., and Newman, F. 1975. A Client-Oriented System of Mental Health Service Delivery and Program Management: A Workbook and Guide. Department of Public Welfare, Commonwealth of Pennsylvania, Harrisburg, Pa.

Gilbert, J. P., Light, R. J., and Mosteller, F. 1975. Assessing social innovations: An empirical base for policy. In: R. Zeckhauser (ed.), Benefit-Cost and Policy Analysis. Aldine Publishing Co., New York.

Sorensen, J. E., and Grove, H. D. 1977. Cost-outcome and cost-effectiveness analysis: Emerging non-profit performance evaluation techniques. The Accounting Review 52(3): 658–675.

Stromsdorfer, E. W. 1972. Review and Synthesis of Cost-Effectiveness Studies of Vocational and Technical Education. Ohio State University Press, Columbus, Ohio.

2. Major evaluation tools and checklists are presented in: S. J. Taylor (ed.). 1980. A Guide to Monitoring Residential Settings. DD Rights Center of the Mental Health Law Project and the Center on Human Policy, Syracuse University, Utica, New York. These evaluation tools and checklists are summarized in:

A Normalization and Development Instrument: A Rating Instrument to Evaluate the Quality of Services to Individuals with Developmental Special Needs. Ann Flynn and Sandra K. Weiss, ANDI, P. O. Box 60964, Sacramento, CA 95860.

Monitoring Service Quality: A Manual for Voluntary Associations. John O'Brien, Georgia Association for Retarded Citizens, 1575 Phoenix Blvd., Atlanta, GA 30349.

Observing Community Residences and *Observing in Institutions*. Steven J. Taylor and Robert Bogdan, Center on Human Policy, 216 Ostrom Ave., Syracuse, NY 13210.

PASS 3: A Method for the Quantitative Evaluation of Human Services. Wolf Wolfensberger and Linda Glenn, National Institute on Mental Retardation, York University, 4700 Keele St., Downsview (Toronto), Ont. M3J 1P3 Canada.

Residential Programming for Mentally Retarded Persons: Developmental Programming in the Residential Facility. National Association for Retarded Citizens, 2709 Avenue E East, Arlington, TX 76011.

Take Steps to Look and Learn: A Guide for Observing Residential Facilities. Pennsylvania Association for Retarded Citizens, 1500 N. Second St., Harrisburg, PA 17102.

3. The author is indebted to M. P. Janicki from whose work (1981) much of the PASS-3 discussion material was taken.

10

EVALUATION STRATEGIES

The ideal organization would be self-evaluating. It would continuously monitor its own activities so as to determine whether it was meeting its goals or even whether these goals should continue to prevail.

(Wildavsky, 1972)

The demand for accountability and outcome evaluation of (re)habilitation services has grown steadily during the last few years. Program administrators, however, are not generally enthusiastic about evaluation, since many perceive it as an externally imposed requirement for which there is neither adequate preparation nor sufficient funding, while others feel that evaluation methods are insensitive to their program's complexities or client characteristics. Many rehabilitation agencies, in addition, have only one center, do not consider themselves as part of a continuum of services, and thereby typically use their own approaches to assessment, training, and program evaluation. This situation makes agency or systems-level comparison impossible. It furthermore explains why some states, in their attempt to improve program quality, require accreditation as a prerequisite to financial participation.

Accreditation focuses on process variables and quality assurance; however, at this time it does not address outcome measure in terms of the benefits clients receive from the services being rendered. The critical question of whether a client's handicapping condition is being diminished through the provision of services goes unanswered, albeit the accreditation standards presume this will be the case if the stated requirements are met. The fact remains that the nationally recognized accreditation standards only present a model from which to work and not a formula for guaranteed successful rehabilitation programs. These standards concentrate on the reportability issues related to legal, regulatory, financial, organizational, and quality of life issues, as opposed to the technological impact on the individual's disability, the method by which technology is used to diminish the handicapping condition, and the measurable outcome from the services received.

This chapter makes a case for effective and ongoing client and program evaluation. My orientation and bias is that program evaluation is most feasible when it is an integral part of the organization's service delivery system, and most beneficial when it is used as a management tool to improve the program's effectiveness, efficiency, and environmental impact.

The chapter begins with discussion of "the why and what of evaluation." Thereafter, the prerequisites to program evaluation are described. The prerequisites may seem formidable at first; however, you will probably find that most of them have already been incorporated in your program, though they may not be currently recognized as evaluation variables. Following the description of prerequisites, a program evaluation model is then presented, including examples of how to use it in evaluating a service delivery program, in generating management hypotheses, and as a basis for cost-effectiveness analysis. The chapter concludes with some "dos and don'ts" of program evaluation and a suggested approach to cost-effective analysis.

THE WHY AND WHAT OF EVALUATION

The "why" of program evaluation is easier to answer than the "what." In answer to "why," program evaluation should be done to improve the program's effectiveness, efficiency and environmental impact. In this regard,

> . . . program evaluation must be viewed as an integral aspect of organizational design and development that promotes external accountability to citizens, consumers, and funders. Evaluation also must function as a linkage mechanism for the systematic integration of human services. . . [It] is primarily a process that occurs within on-going organizational management, decision making, and planning (Attkisson and Broskowski, 1978, p. 204).

The "what" is dependent on a number of factors, including the organization's philosophy, goals, objectives, heterogeneous constituency, and evaluation needs. A number of measures can be used that generalize across the above factors and thereby provide some guidelines as to what program evaluation should encompass. These measures are summarized in Table 10.1, with additional measures and approaches presented in Reference Note 1.

PREREQUISITES TO PROGRAM EVALUATION

Program evaluation prerequisites include a number of factors discussed in previous chapters. This was by design, as the intent has been to demonstrate that an organization's planning, implementing, and monitoring processes are intrinsic to its service delivery and program evaluation activities. If you accomplish the first aspect, you should be able to do the second, and so on. Figure 10.1 diagrams the relationship among the various evaluation prerequisites. Each is discussed, below, and is accompanied by pertinent references that outline or discuss specific implementation strategies.

Client Referenced Variables

Programs for developmentally disabled persons can easily identify their target population, since the population is defined in Public Law 95-602. It is more difficult, however, to determine objectively a person's functional or behavioral skill level, and to relate that determination to program services and evaluation

Table 10.1. Program evaluation measures

Author	Measure's focus	Definition of measure	Type of data required[a]
Posavac and Carey (1980)	Process	The extents to which the program was implemented as designed and serves the target population	Number of clients served Representativeness of clients Staff-client contact Staff work load
	Outcome	Assessment of outcomes achieved by the program	Client change scores Number of goals obtained Number of management by objectives achieved Peer-review results
	Efficiency	The extent to which the program achieves its success at a reasonable cost and/or whether the program achieves a better level of success than other programs costing the same	Cost analyses Cost-benefit analysis Cost-effectiveness analysis
Sorensen and Grove (1977)	Efficiency	Compares resource inputs to specified process or output variables	Service unit costs Staff contacts Direct and indirect cost figures Client outcome measures
	Effectiveness	Compares accomplishment to goals	Client outcome measures Client demographic descriptors Client follow-along measures (employed, living, etc.) Deinstitutionalization and reinstitutionalization rates
	Outcome/Benefits/ Impacts	Identifies social or economic benefit	Changes in earnings Welfare payments Change in level of social functioning after treatment Institutionalization and deinstitutionalization prevalence rates

Table 10.1 *(continued)*

Author	Measure's focus	Definition of measure	Type of data required[a]
Suchman (1967)	Effort (input)	Information about the amount and distribution of resources into program	Income and expense records Allocation of staff time Numbers and types of clients Interrelation among dollars, staff, and clients
	Performance (output)	Information about the outcomes and effectiveness of program effort	Client acceptance of services offered Improvement in client status Changes in incidence or prevalence of problems Interagency linkages and client referrals Level of service availability and accessibility achieved over long-term
	Adequacy (output/need)	Information about effort and performance relative to measures of community need or demand	Mandated services provided Appropriateness of services being received Awareness of availability of services Client utilization rates Citizen's survey results
	Efficiency (output/input)	Information about how effort is organized to get greatest performance and adequacy	Units of service cost Cost-outcome data Cost-effectiveness comparisons Data comparing different organizational methods in costs and effectiveness
	Process (outcome = function of effort)	Information about the underlying processes by which effort is translated into outcome	Selection of service comparisons[a] Assignment of subjects to services Selection of subjects (including informed consent) Description of sample Description of services provided Selection of predictor variables Selection of outcome measures

[a]From Hargreaves and Attkisson (1978).

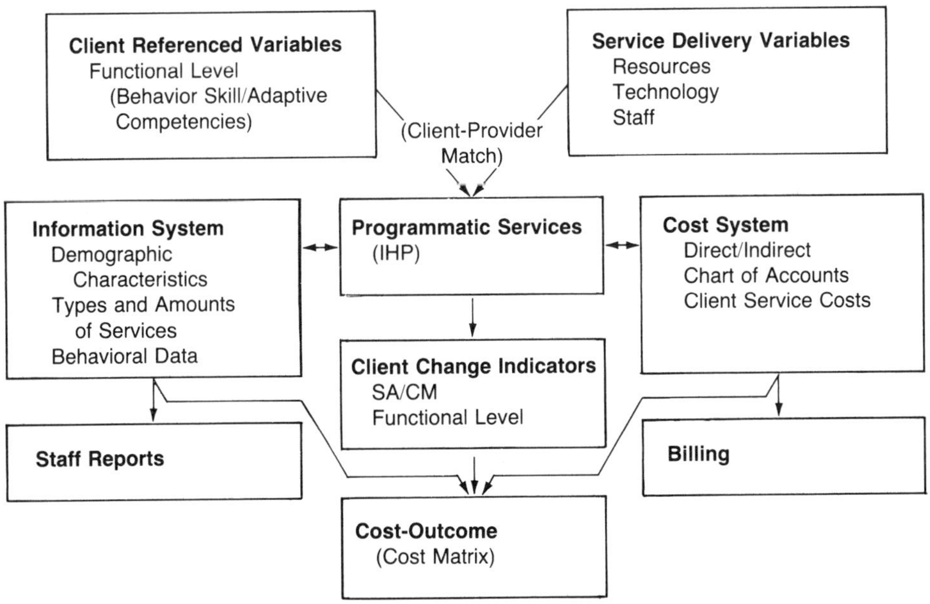

Figure 10.1. Client/program evaluation prerequisites.

activities. Either of the two approaches outlined below can be used to determine a person's functional level.

1. *Level of Functioning Scales* A number of rating scales have been developed to measure a client's overall ability to function in the community. The scales typically involve a 5- to 9- point rating that permits staff to evaluate a person from "dysfunctional" to "functioning independently and not needing services." Discussion of the scales' standardization and use can be found in Carter and Newman (1976), Luborsky and Backrach (1974), and Sorensen and Grove (1977).
2. *Adaptive Behaviors* Chapter 4 discussed a number of behavioral scales that evaluate a person's skill level on behaviors related to developmental programming, vocational training, and community living skills. The following criteria should be used when choosing an adaptive behavioral scale (Carver, 1974; Douchette, 1979):

   Content validity Do the scale items actually measure what they are supposed to measure (adaptive behavior, vocational skills, and so forth)?
   Administration Time and staff competencies involved.
   Interpretability Meaning of resulting scores (are normative comparisons available?)
   Utility Can the assessment data be used for individualized habilitation plan development and as a basis for systematic programming?
   Test construction Have acceptable test development principles been used including item analysis, field testing, replications, and standardization?

Reliability Are scale scores consistent among raters and across measurement times?
Validity Is scale sensitive to individual growth with demonstrated content and criterion validity?

Service Delivery Variables

The organization's resources, technology, and staff capability represent the second program evaluation prerequisite. These variables reflect the organization's programmatic services and living-training progressions; therefore, they can be related to the skill acquisition and client movement indices discussed later in the chapter. The variables can also be used to develop a "client-provider match" that interfaces a person's living-training needs with available and appropriate services (Sutherland, 1977).

Programmatic Services

Programmatic services relate to client intervention, training, or treatment. Their purpose is to promote growth and development. The vehicle established to implement and monitor those needed services is the individualized habilitation plan (IHP), that should result in:

The integration of interdisciplinary services.
A systematic procedure for setting a timed sequence of intermediate objectives and long-term goals, and for relating these sequential objectives and goals to the client's level of functioning (Carter and Newman, 1976).
A current functional profile reflecting skills gained from the original baseline evaluation.
An indication of client development, disposition of goals and objectives, and the quantity of programmatic services received (Yaron and Walker, 1979).

Given that individualized habilitation plans are written according to mandated guidelines and should result in the four products listed above, the next question to ask is, "Can IHPs be used for client and program evaluation?" I think not, at least without modification. This statement might surprise you, especially in light of PL 95-602 (Section 112), which specifies that a state-level evaluation system for developmentally disabled individuals shall

> (1) provide objective measures of the developmental progress of persons with developmental disabilities using data obtained from individualized habilitation plans or other comparable individual data; and (2) provide a method of evaluating programs providing services for persons with developmental disabilities.

Using the IHP for client and/or program evaluation would place program administrators in a "Catch-22" position. On the one hand, the plan must relate to the client's needs; on the other hand, the subjectivity resulting from the first requirement negates the objectivity and comparability requirements of acceptable data analysis. This author therefore suggests that IHP data are most appropriately conceptualized as *intervening* variables in program evaluation efforts, rather than as *dependent* variables. This opinion is based on the "current state of the art" regarding plan development, implementation, and monitoring; the process nature of the plan as discussed in the previous chapter; and the need for program evaluation to focus on both process *and* outcome measures. As an intervening variable, the plan can be used in program evaluation to relate programmatic services received, including technologies and interdisciplinary staff involvement, to the outcome variables discussed in the next section.

Outcome Variables

Client-referenced outcome variables embody an organization's philosophy, goals, and objectives; they can also summarize (that is, "evaluate") the outcome of the organization's programmatic services. Outcome variables can be operationalized in one or more of the following behaviorally based data areas:

Behavioral skills required through systematic, prescriptive programming
Change scores on the standarized assessment instrument used (Note 2)
Movement or placement into more independent or vocationally productive environments

Information System

Relating programmatic services to the outcome variables selected will require a management information system such as that outlined in Chapter 5. In reference to program evaluation, the information system should provide data regarding:

1. *Client demographic characteristics* such as age, primary/secondary disabilities, referral source, program entry and movement within program progressions, dates, and placement information (facility, date, duration)
2. *Type and amount of service received* including units (hours) of prescriptive programming, interdisciplinary therapies (occupational therapy, physical therapy, speech, etc.), and generic services (home health, medical, dental, etc.)
3. *Behavioral data* including behavioral skills acquired through systematic, prescriptive programming and/or change scores on a standardized assessment instrument

Cost System

The concept of responsibility center budgeting and accounting was introduced in Chapter 9 under "Monitoring Finances." In reference to program evaluation, the cost system should provide data that: summarize direct and indirect service costs (Carter and Newman, 1976; Posavac and Carey, 1980; Schalock and Harper,

1982); estimate direct and indirect service costs per hour (unit) of service delivered (Carter and George, 1973; Sorenson and Phipps, 1972; Underhill and Newman, 1974); aggregate units of service received (from management information system) with cost per unit to generate "service X cost figure" (Note 3).

A PROGRAM EVALUATION MODEL

Both program evaluation and human service delivery are rapidly developing disciplines. Given their "emerging status," it makes sense *that current efforts at program evaluation should be formative or process oriented.* Such a level of evaluation focuses on continuous program assessment and feedback for the dual purposes of improving program performance and facilitating the administrative processes of planning, implementing, and monitoring (Schalock and Harper, 1983).

The process model of evaluation depicted in Figure 10.2 has its roots in operation and systems research. It assumes that program evaluation will be most feasible when it is an integral part of the service delivery system, and most effective when it provides for a continuous process of feedback and readjustment of activities. As reflected in the model, evaluation involves all stages of the system, with specific input, process, and output components. Relevant aspects of each component are discussed next.

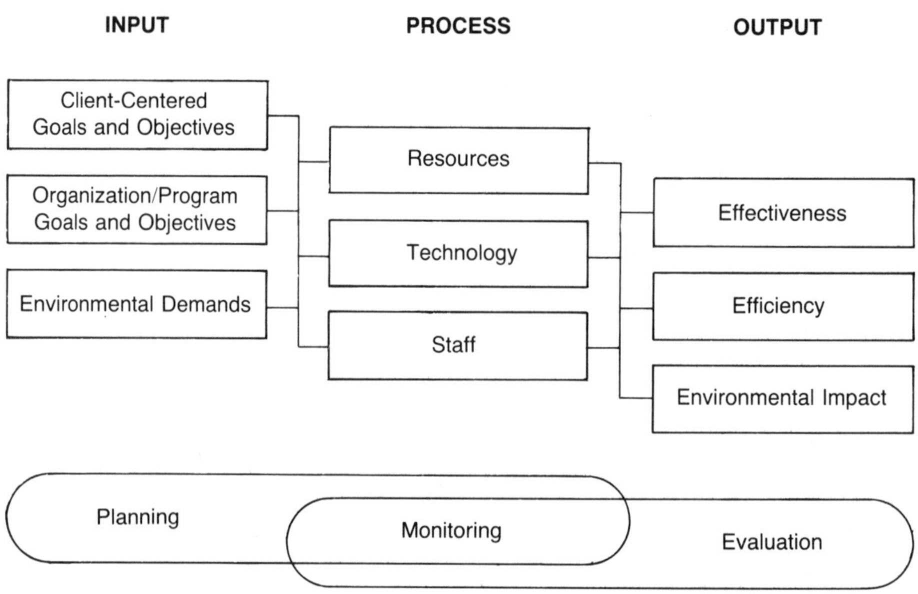

Figure 10.2. Program evaluation model.

Input

Chapters 2 and 3 discussed the input side to an organization, including client needs, environmental demands, and the organization's goals, objectives, and desired outcomes. Once operationalized, these become the input data for the evaluation model. Examples include:

Client-centered goals and objectives such as increasing behavioral competency level; moving into less restrictive and more productive environments; or obtaining individualized habilitation plan objectives.

Organization/program goals and objectives such as developing systematic programs dealing with community living skills, vocational training, respite care, and prevention; developing sequential living-training facilities; and/or placing clients into more independent living and/or vocationally productive environments.

Environmental demands such as providing alternatives to institutionalization; preventing or reducing the high incidence of cultural-familial retardation; and/or increasing effectiveness and efficiency through interagency collaboration.

Process

An organization's process variables, including resources, technology, and staff, are part of the evaluation model because they are intervening variables that can be related objectively to the obtained programmatic outcomes; conversely, they can be manipulated to modify those outcomes. For example, this author (Schalock and Harper, 1982) recently published data comparing skill acquisition indices (discussed later in the chapter) for 126 clients involved in three comparable community living skills training programs. Analysis of the data indicated that the indices were significantly different among the three programs and that low indices were positively correlated with training location (center-based versus community-based), units of prescriptive programming delivered, amount of money spent on training materials, and demonstrated staff competencies.

Output

One of the major problems in evaluating human services involves the difficulty in quantifying outcome measures. One solution to this problem is to focus on *nonmonetary* output measures reflecting the organization's effectiveness, efficiency, and environmental impact. Definitions and examples of each measure include:

1. *Effectiveness* Effectiveness measures compare accomplishment to goals and can include one or more of the following:
   Number of behavioral skills gained

Increased functional level score
Number of clients placed into independent housing or competitive employment
Number of IHP objectives obtained
Number of sequential living-training options provided
Changes on goal-attainment scale measures

2. *Efficiency* These measures compare resource input to specific process or output variables. They can include:
   Acquisition-movement indices (ratio of change to possible change)
   Acquisition-movement ratios (ratio of cost to change)
   Cost-analytic ratios (relating costs to nonmonetary outcomes)
   Cost-effectiveness ratios (comparison of cost-outcome to program cost)
   Cost benefit analysis (comparison of cost to ensuing monetary benefits)
3. *Environmental Impact* The focus here is on providing data evaluating the impact or effect the program has had on the larger environment. Examples include:

   Prevention (screening for phenylketonuria; lead poisoning; early intervention)
   Economic impact of successful rehabilitation
   Deinstitutionalization rates and results

PROGRAM EVALUATION EXAMPLES

Once the evaluation prerequisites and evaluation model are in place, you can enter the "world of program evaluation." Two recent formative evaluations done by the author are summarized in this section. The two outcome measures used reflect skills gained and client movement. The procedure for computing a skill acquisition index (SAI) involves reassessing the client's skill level on the standardized assessment instrument. This is done by diagnostic programmers who are trained on the assessment instruments and demonstrate the necessary assessment-programming competencies at the conclusion of their formal training and again during the organizational review process described in Chapter 9.

A SAI, which is the ratio of the number of skills gained for a specific time period to the number of skills in the domain, is then computed for each behavioral domain (see Table 10.2) according to the following formula:

$$\text{SAI} = \frac{\text{Number of Skills Gained/ Time Period}}{\text{Number of Skills in the Domain}}$$

For example, according to Table 10.2, if a client gained two behavioral skills in the Personal Maintenance Domain of Community Living skills training, the SAI would be 2/25 or 0.08. SAIs are computed yearly within the Mid-Nebraska Mental Retardation Services program for each client per behavioral domain.

Table 10.2. Skill acquisition indices used in formative evaluation

Community Living Skills Study			Vocational Training Study		
	Skill Acquisition Index[a]			Skill Acquisition Index[a]	
Domain	Center-based training	Living environment training	Domain	Successful job retention	Unsuccessful job retention
1. Personal maintenance (25)[b]	0.10	0.19[c]	1. Self-help skills (12)[b]	0.08	0.00[d]
2. Dressing and clothing care (21)	0.08	0.15[c]	2. Personal/Interpersonal behavior (12)	0.15	0.05[d]
3. Eating and food management (22)	0.13	0.12	3. Information processing (19)	0.13	0.04[d]
4. Social behavior (17)	0.03	0.11[c]	4. Learning/Coping strategies (10)	0.21	0.10[d]
5. Expressive skills (10)	0.02	0.02	5. Prevocational skills (15)	0.10	0.09
6. Home living (24)	0.02	0.09[c]	6. Job-related skills (22)	0.13	0.09
7. Money skills (13)	0.05	0.05	7. Work performance (45)	0.13	0.04[d]
8. Time awareness and utilization (12)	0.04	0.12[c]	8. Work behavior (22)	0.09	0.04
9. Recreation and leisure skills (11)	0.07	0.06	9. Job-seeking skills (6)	0.24	0.21
10. Community awareness and utilization (19)	0.06	0.17[c]			

[a]Mean SAIs.
[b]Number of behavioral skills per domain.
[c]$p<0.05$ (matched sample t-test).
[d]$p<0.05$ (t-test for paired comparisons).

One use of SAI data involved testing the following management hypothesis: SAIs would be larger for clients trained on community living skills within their actual living environment than if they were trained on the same skill areas within an adult developmental center. The hypothesis was tested recently in a matched sample study in which SAIs for 20 clients (10 pairs) were compared after 1 year of training in their actual living environments or the adult developmental center. Clients were matched on the basis of Wechsler Adult Intelligence Scale (WAIS) Full Scale IQ, age, gender, their current living environment (group home or staffed apartment), length of time in community living skills (CLS) training, and most recent CLS skill profile. There were 10 females and 10 males. One member of each pair received training in his or her living environment; the other, within the adult development center (10 individual, prescriptive programs run daily in either environment). SAIs after 1 year on the 10 community living skills domains are presented in Table 10.2. SAIs averaged 1½ to 3 times larger when training occurred in the client's natural environment; in addition, significant mean differences were obtained on 6 of the 10 domains.

A second use of SAI data involved 45 (25 females, 20 males) clients placed into competitive employment over a 2-year period. SAIs were computed and compared among those who had retained their jobs for 6 months or longer, and those who did not. The SAI data presented in Table 10.2 have been used to justify increased prescriptive programming in those low SAI areas associated with unsuccessful job retention, and to expand the on-the-job assistance given to clients by an enabler-facilitator.

The second outcome measure used was a client movement index (CMI), whose computation requires a progression of living-training alternatives such as those discussed in Chapter 3. The index, which is a ratio of the number of clients moving one step or further up the community living or vocational training-placement progression to the number of clients in that respective training component, is computed as follows:

$$\text{CMI} = \frac{\text{Number of Clients Moving up the Progression}}{\text{Total Number of Full-Time Clients}}$$

CMIs have been computed yearly within the Mid-Nebraska program progressions for both the community integration and vocational training-placement continua. Movement within the community integration continuum is from group home to staffed apartment to independent housing; for vocational training-placement, movement is from training into part- or full-time employment. CMIs for the seven area programs within the Mid-Nebraska system are presented in Table 10.3. These data, along with a recently published longitudinal study (Schalock, Harper, and Carver, 1981), have resulted in three programmatic changes. One change involves developing more transitional placement options (especially transitional living arrangements in adult foster homes) between the group home and staffed apartment; second, providing for a redefined instructor position (referred to

Table 10.3. Comparative vocational and community living client movement indices

	Client movement indices — vocational				Client movement indices — community living			
Area program[a]	1978	1979	1980	1981	1978	1979	1980	1981
I	0.69[b]	0.38	0.13	0.13	0.04	0.12	0.08	0.19
II	0.31	0.27	0.15	0.04	0.29	0.74	0.56	0.03
III	0.61	0.33	0.17	0.00	0.50	0.46	0.29	0.46
IV	0.14	0.14	0.48	0.05	0.13	0.00	0.21	0.42
V	0.67	0.11	0.00	0.00	0.50	0.27	0.14	0.18
VI	0.44	0.13	0.00	0.06	0.24	0.14	0.17	0.28
VII	0.07	0.07	0.07	0.00	0.00	0.30	0.26	0.00
Average	0.42 ± 0.10[c]	0.20 ± 0.05	0.14 ± 0.07	0.04 ± 0.02	0.24 ± 0.08	0.29 ± 0.10	0.24 ± 0.06	0.22 ± 0.07

[a]Represents the seven adult programs within Mid-Nebraska Mental Retardation Services. Each has an area director who is responsible for facilities, fiscal management, local public relations, staff hiring and firing, and program supervision. Assessment and training approaches are standardized within the seven programs (cf. Schalock and Harper, 1981a). Areas can be equated to comparable agencies within a larger service delivery system.

[b]Mean CMIs.

[c]Standard error of the mean.

as an enabler-facilitator) who works with the clients in their current living or work environment; and third, implementing a three-phase approach to vocational training, including extended employment, sheltered workshop, and center industry (prime manufacturing).

SOME DO'S AND DON'TS OF PROGRAM EVALUATION

While the program evaluation model just presented represents only one approach to the topic, it is hoped that it and other material presented in the chapter have served to underscore the feasibility and importance of evaluation. Numerous evaluation approaches are possible; a recent computer search of the literature on program evaluation, for example, listed 750 individual citations. Regardless of the program evaluation model or technique used, there are a number of important evaluation issues that an awareness of will help to ensure successful program evaluation. These issues are summarized below under important "do's" and "don'ts."

Do's

1. *Do consider program evaluation a management tool.* Evaluation should be a problem-solving enterprise that facilitates and improves decision making, program performance, communication, controlling and reappraising (Alkin, 1972; Suchman, 1972; Zusman and Wurster, 1975). Its focus and intent should be the improvement of services. Specific examples of such use include: client outcomes in rehabilitation (Walls and Tseng, 1976); decision making in rehabilitation agencies (Spaniol, 1977); client change indicators (Schalock and Harper, 1982).
2. *Do systematically plan the evaluation.* The following items should be delineated before embarking on an evaluation effort (Posavac and Carey, 1980): program goals; definition and goals of evaluation effort; evaluation audience; type of evaluation desired (formative or summative); role of the evaluator; measurement method and required evaluation prerequisites; reporting format.
3. *Do expect resistance.* Resistance to program evaluation can come from a number of sources and revolves generally around fears and accusations that evaluation will inhibit innovation, will lead to program termination, will abuse information and client confidentiality, will drain program money, and/or will have little impact (Posavac and Carey, 1980; Zusman and Wurster, 1975). Some of these concerns are based on genuine motives; others on misunderstanding or ignorance. All need to be addressed and resolved in the early planning stages of your program evaluation efforts.
4. *Do choose among possible outcome measures.* All human service programs have multiple outcomes. Decisions will consequently need to be made regarding: First, which measures to use (possible options were outlined in Table 10.1 and Figure 10.2). Second, when to measure the program's effect. Sorensen

and Grove (1977) suggest that output measures should be obtained at multiple points in time. If the time period is too short, changes may not be observable; if too long, important data for decision making may be missed. A general rule might be quarterly for periodic assessment and annually for more detailed assessment or reassessment. Third, what level of behavior to measure. For example, an appropriate outcome measure for severely or profoundly handicapped persons might be eye contact, simple verbalizations, object labeling, or developing self-help skills; for higher functioning persons, appropriate measures might relate to independent living or competitive employment.

5. *Do honor the constraints of simplicity, economy, and utility.*

Don'ts

1. *Don't confuse formative and summative evaluation.* Formative or process evaluation focuses primarily on accessing and improving programmatic services (Epstein and Tripodi, 1977; Rossi, 1979; Tripodi, Fellin, and Epstein, 1978). Summative evaluation focuses on programmatic impact (Rossi, 1979) or generalizing the results of program evaluation to other comparable situations for the primary purpose of providing inputs for policy decisions (Epstein and Tripodi, 1977; Tripodi et al., 1978). Most current program evaluation efforts are, appropriately, at the formative or process level. That situation will probably change as human services improve their measurability, reportability, and accountability.
2. *Don't use change scores without careful study.* A common evaluation procedure is to relate the amount of service received to how much the client changes ("the change score"). The usual technique is to subtract pretest from posttest scores, label the difference "improvement," and correlate the improvement score(s) with programmatic or service delivery variables. This is an attractive, logical, and easily understood procedure; however, there are inherent problems in it. The two most dangerous problems relate to the large amount of error variance contained in change scores, and a measurement phenomenon referred to as the "regression effect" (Nunnally and Durham, 1975; Posavac and Carey, 1980). This latter effect is typically found in repeated measurements in which people who score above the mean on the first evaluation frequently score below the mean on the second. One way to circumvent these two problems is to use residual change scores that are deviations of scores on the second occasion from those predicted by regression analysis determined on the basis of the first occasion (Cronbach and Furby, 1970; Lord, 1963; Nunnally and Durham, 1975; Posavac and Carey, 1980).

   An analogous change score technique is to use the number of IHP objectives achieved. However, using data in this way poses a number of threats to internal validity, the most significant threats relate to ongoing maturation of the client; extraneous influences including quality of staff interaction, opportunities for independent activities, and miscellaneous, non-controlled environmental variables; agency differences in regard to resources, technology, staff, and formalized IHP process; and differential selection and levels of clients (Yaron and Walker, 1979). Each of these threats to internal validity makes generalization and evaluation statements questionable.

3. *Don't use research designs inappropriately*. A number of research designs have recently been proposed for program evaluation efforts. Some of the more useful ones include:

    Time-series or interrupted time series analyses that involve collecting data over a number of time periods (Campbell and Stanley, 1963; Caporaso, 1973; Gottman and Glass, 1978; Tripodi and Harrington, 1979)

    Experimental-control designs that attempt to control threats to internal and external validity through traditional designs or modified ones such as Solomon four-group design (Mahoney, 1978)

    Nonequivalent control-group design that combines a pre-/posttest design with an experimental-control group (Posavac and Carey, 1980)

    A number of research guidelines are important to follow regardless of the research design used. These include: a) the results of the program should be observable; b) in any comparison of populations, treatment and comparison samples must be created by random or systematic allocation of individuals to groups; c) improvement or change scores of a specific target group must be supported by comparison with similar groups; d) evaluation instruments must be assessed for reliability, validity, and appropriateness for the target group (for example, do not use verbally loaded instruments with nonverbal clientele); and e) realize that observed differences are frequently modest and "slam-bang" effects are few.

4. *Don't attempt cost-outcome analyses prematurely*. Figure 10.1 outlined the necessary prerequisites to cost-outcome analysis. In general, these prerequisites require interfacing programmatic services, specific, measurable client outcomes, and individual client costs. Assuming these are done, then cost effectiveness emerges as the last of five sequential steps (Sorensen and Grove, 1977), including: a) identify the objective to be achieved; b) specify optional or alternative service programs to be used; c) determine cost of each program including cost per unit of service and units received; d) assess the effect or outcome of the program intervention on the target group; and e) determine cost effectiveness or cost-outcome analysis by combining cost and outcome information. Although we are just beginning to approach this level of sophisticated program evaluation, a suggested approach to cost-effective analysis is presented below.

A SUGGESTED APPROACH TO COST-EFFECTIVE ANALYSIS

Effectiveness measures are those that assess how well a program is achieving its objectives. The initial step in developing cost-effective analysis is to rethink what is "profit" in nonprofit organizations such as rehabilitation agencies. To quote Sorensen and Grove (1977):

> In profit-oriented organizations the amount of profit may be used as a measure of both efficiency and effectiveness. But this profit index approach to effectiveness is not applicable or appropriate for most human service organizations. This single, all encompassing measure. . .facilitates comparisons among varying organizational units. No such comprehensive measure exits for non-profit organizations; to date, there are few good ways of estimating whether additional inputs (or resources) will produce commensurate outputs. The central problem is the inadequacy of output measures, and assessing outcomes more accurately is the first step in remedying this deficiency (p. 659).

Profit, then, as suggested above by Sorensen and Grove, is used to measure a for-profit organization's efficiency and effectiveness. Such organizations show a profit when they sell products for more than they cost to produce—that is, they show return on investment. This can happen only in a market place relatively free of fiscal and regulatory restraints. Rehabilitation programs, which are usually controlled by third-party purchase of service and/or annual appropriations, cannot show a profit or, indeed, a loss. Return on investment can be shown by rehabilitation programs, however, by focusing on diminishing clients' handicapping conditions and moving rehabilitation clients into less restrictive and more productive environments. Cost-effective analysis then involves determining the effectiveness and cost of the diminution and/or movement.

The emerging measurement methodologies that involve effort accomplishment are consistent with this suggested approach to cost-effectiveness analysis. These methods stress linking monetary input to nonmonetary output measures. The advantage is that client benefits do not have to be monetized (translated into dollars), only the costs (Rossi, 1979). The importance of this approach is stressed by Levin (1975) who states:

> When the effectiveness of programs in achieving a particular goal (rather than their monetary values) is linked to cost, the approach is considered to be cost-effectiveness analysis rather than cost-benefit analysis. . . . In this context, cost-effectiveness analysis enables us to examine the costs of alternative programs for achieving particular types of outcomes, but prevents us from comparing the costs directly, with benefits. . . . [This] enables us to rank potential program choices according to the magnitude of their efforts relative to their costs. . . . (p. 92)

A number of steps are involved in implementing cost-effectiveness analysis. Three of the more important ones are outlined below.

Establish Objectives, Methods, and Outcome Measures

A rehabilitation program's goals can be translated into objectives that are clearly delineated, measurable, and tied to client progress rather than agency needs. Valid program evaluation, including fulfilling requirements of the proposed performance audit, is dependent upon how closely these objectives relate to the programmatic services provided and to the outcome measures obtained. The two outcome indices

(SAI and CMI) presented earlier represent one approach. Other outcome measures might include placements, reduced waiting lists, deinstitutionalization rates, increased social/personal functioning, and/or increased earnings.

Implement a Management Information System (MIS)

The agency-level information system should provide client change and service indicators such as client's level of functioning, type of services received, amount of services, who delivered the service, and direct/indirect service costs (Carter and Newman, 1976; Sutherland, 1977). Systems-level information system components should focus on client demographics such as available living-training placements and tracking client movement through sequential living-training programmatic progressions.

Monitor the Program

Agency- and systems-level monitoring is an essential step in implementing cost-effectiveness analysis, since it assures that programs reach appropriate target populations and that services delivered are consistent with program design specifications (Attkisson and Broskowski, 1978). Monitoring can also be expected to increase program accountability (Rossi, 1979); supplement impact assessment since "the failure of programs is often due to faulty or non-implementation of interventions rather than ineffectiveness of the treatments" (Rossi and Wright, 1977); provide data to help decide whether or not to continue ongoing programs (Ciarlo, 1977); and provide standardized data (Sutherland, 1977).

Determine Cost-Effectiveness

Cost-effective analysis is possible if the three steps outlined previously are done correctly. Rehabilitation programs will thereby be able to generate behavioral change and client movement units to which time and costs can be attached. This will then permit one or more of the following cost-effectiveness analyses, listed in ascending levels of sophistication based on the program's ability to do causality or group-comparison evaluation studies (Epstein and Tripodi, 1977).

1. *Skill Acquisition Cost* This cost-effectiveness measure focuses on agency-level evaluation and summarizes the cost involved in clients acquiring skills. It is admittedly a weak measure, but requires increased programming and monitoring sophistication. It might thereby be an appropriate first step for some agencies. The measure would not be comparable across agencies, but would allow individual agencies to use whichever assessment and remediation system they prefer.
2. *Client Movement Cost* This level of analysis focuses on how far along the available continuum a client has progressed, relating the movement to costs

incurred and time required. It represents an appropriate level of analysis for larger programs that have living-training options available, for encouraging the development of integrated service delivery systems such as consortia, or for monitoring and evaluating the cost-effectiveness of larger programs. Examples of comparable analyses in the mental health field can be found in Carter and Newman (1976) or Sorensen and Grove (1977).

3. *Cost-Effectiveness Comparisons* This level of analysis would permit comparing or ranking of programs according to the cost involved in reaching their goals and objectives, although it is important to stress that only those programs with similar objectives should be compared.

A FINAL WORD ON EVALUATION

This author recognizes that the formative evaluation approach summarized in this chapter has limited transferability either for single agencies or for agencies within a service delivery network that are not integrated into a service delivery system. Developing comparable effectiveness measures for monitoring and evaluation purposes in these cases can proceed in one of two directions. One is to standardize programmatic services across agencies within the service delivery network. The major advantage to this option is that it would permit developing a "chart of accounts approach" to program monitoring and program evaluation. The chart of accounts would also permit developing management hypotheses regarding outcome measures obtained and generating behavioral change units to which costs and funds can be tied. The major disadvantage is that individual programs or agencies might resist efforts to standardize their programs, thereby limiting their creativity and leading potentially to stagnation. A second direction would require all funded programs to at a minimum define clearly their goals and objectives; translate these goals and objectives into behaviorally-based outcome measures; implement a systematic, data-based approach to assessment and training, with the specific approach determined by the agency; and assess periodically how far a client has progressed within the available living-training progressions. The advantage to this approach is that it would allow single agencies to monitor and evaluate whether their preferred assessment and training method results in behavioral skill acquisition. Regardless of the "system" used, the client should be developing skills commensurate with the program's internal goals and objectives. External, or systems-level monitoring and evaluation, would focus on client movement and evaluate the larger program's effectiveness by determining how far clients have progressed within the available living-training progressions.

This author realizes moreover, that the proposed cost-effectiveness analysis does not involve cost-benefit measures that typically focus on monetary outcomes of rehabilitation services, but requires certain economic assumptions about translating program inputs and outputs into monetary figures. The requirements and assumptions regarding cost-benefit analysis are increasingly being questioned, however. Noble (1977) cautions, for example, against using cost-benefit figures for priority setting in rehabilitation programs, because of the inadequate analytic and conceptual models, the insufficiency of existing data, and the extreme sensitivity of cost-benefit results to the untested assumptions underlying their computation. The reader is also cautioned that the suggested approaches to cost-effectiveness analysis will not permit comparing which programs or projects produce *better* returns, since the benefits are not converted to the same denominator. One can only compare the relative efficiency of programs with same or similar goals. Nor will this approach permit demonstrating cause-effect relationships.

A number of special issues within rehabilitation services must be resolved before valid cause-effect and program comparison studies can be done. These issues include time patterns, different populations, multiple outcomes, and random assignment of clients to treatment groups. Causality and group comparison evaluations may emerge as service delivery systems and program evaluation efforts become more sophisticated; however, bear in mind that:

> . . . while highly sophisticated research designs may be required in program evaluation, the traditional and usually expensive and complex approaches are not likely to be the ones used by programmatic practitioners and administrators (Sorensen and Grove, 1977, p. 665).

SUMMARY

While program evaluation may not be fun, it can result in a more effective and efficient organization. After making a case for the "why" of evaluation, this chapter focused on how the process should be conducted. Program evaluation is impossible without certain "prerequisites" in place. These include program-based phenomena such as client-referenced and service delivery variables, programmatic services, management information and cost systems, and a clear understanding and measurement of client-referenced outcomes. Once the prerequisites are in order, then program evaluation can proceed. Since both program evaluation and human services are still evolving, it was suggested that current evaluation efforts should be process-oriented, focusing on continuous program assessment and feedback for the dual purposes of improving program performance and facilitating planning, implementing, and monitoring.

A process model of program evaluation was outlined, with examples of its use summarized. The model has its roots in operations and systems research and stresses that evaluation should involve the input, process, and output components of a system. The chapter concluded with some "do's and don'ts" in program evaluation and a suggested approach to cost-effective analysis.

DISCUSSION QUESTIONS

1. Evaluate the current status within your organization of each evaluation prerequisite. Check closely, for there may be more there than you think; they may be either camouflaged or "filed away."
2. Develop measurable indices within your organization of the three input variables depicted in Figure 10.2, then develop output measures that can be used to evaluate whether each input has been processed. Is there a close correspondence between the input and output? If not, why and what can be done to improve the congruence?
3. Review your last effort at program evaluation. Was it process- or outcome-oriented; did it result in one or more of the output measures listed in Figure 10.2?
4. Poll your staff as to the advantages and disadvantages of program evaluation. Do their comments reflect some of the attitudes of resistance discussed in the chapter? After reading this chapter, what are appropriate responses that you can give to each of their concerns?
5. Outline a program evaluation study that is possible within your organization. Components of the study should be methodology (subjects, apparatus, and procedure), anticipated results, and how those results can be used to improve the organization's performance, effectiveness, and/or efficiency.

REFERENCE NOTES

1. Other evaluation measures and approaches include weighted closure systems (Walls and Tseng, 1976); formative versus summative evaluation techniques (Epstein and Tripodi, 1977); optional outcome measures to use for evaluation (Finarelli, 1979; Rowitz, 1979); and appropriate research designs to use in program evaluation (Campbell and Stanley, 1963; Mahoney, 1978; Tripodi and Harrington, 1979; Weiss, 1972).
2. The reader should be aware of possible regression effects that occur when change scores are used (Carter and Newman, 1976; Nunnally and Durham, 1975). Residual change scores partially correct the problem (Posavac and Carey, 1980).
3. Detailed discussion of the problems related to valid cost and cost-output measures can be found in Conley (1975), Kiresuk (1979), McMahan (1979), Noble (1977), Nunnally and Durham (1975), Rothenberg (1975), Rowitz (1979), Sorensen and Grove (1977), Spaniol (1977), Stromsdorfer (1972), Struthers (1977), Suchman (1972), Touché-Ross Report (1980), Walls and Tseng (1976), and Zusman and Wurster (1975).

Section IV

THE FUTURE

This final section deals with the future of human service delivery systems, and especially those programs dealing with developmentally disabled adults. Alvin Toffler, in his recent book *The Third Wave*, suggests that we are currently experiencing "the death of industrialism and the rise of a new civilization." The implications of this "new civilization" for services to developmentally disabled individuals are significant. First, the world that Toffler envisions relies on a wider technological base than at present, with information and information processing becoming central activities. Second, says Toffler, much of the work now done in offices and factories will be accomplished in homes and electronic cottages. Third, managers will increasingly become managers of information. And fourth, thinking will be less influenced by analogies based on machines, and shaped more by concepts like process, feedback, and disequilibrium (Toffler, 1980). Human services and, more specifically, programs for the developmentally disabled must prepare for this new civilization, and such is the theme of this section.

11

Developmentally Disabled People in the 21st Century

If we knew where to look, we would find the future in our midst. The elements that will shape our lives in the next generation are already with us; the hardware and software of the future, the systems of values, technologies and business—all are among us in different stages of ripeness.

(Roeber, 1973; p. 5)

The following six predictions regarding the future suggest more specifically how technological and social changes may influence society's approach to developmentally disabled citizens.

1. Role expectations will continue to change, with a corresponding decline in role fixity and a wider acceptance of nonstereotyped social behaviors (McHale, 1980). This change will result in an altering of the current training focus that fits clients into existing structures and demands that they conform to our preestablished role expectations (Karan and Schalock, 1982). People now viewed as clients, patients, or residents will be provided with the skills and support that are "necessary for a society of diversity, rather than of conformity" (Rappaport, 1977). As summarized by Kittrie (1971) in *The Right to Be Different:* "A realistic and pluralistic society must recognize . . . that unless it is willing to pay the price for total conformity, it must learn to tolerate its deviants."
2. Increased free time, improved standards of living, and a shift to family-centered activities should provide both a more favorable lifestyle for disabled persons and a decreased incidence of socio-familial retardation. This latter trend will also influence staff utilization. Drucker (1977) suggests, for example, that the major personnel issue of the 1980s will be the vast number of people desiring only part-time work.
3. The decline of the productive work role as a prime status support in the larger society will also change the work-orientation of many "developmental" programs. The routine and repetitive jobs on which many developmentally disabled clients have been traditionally trained may well disappear or be relegated to a secondary role (McHale, 1980).
4. Considerable dialogue will redefine and reformulate the meaning, purpose, and function of human beings in society. The central question may be, "Is a

developmentally disabled person less worthy because he is less able?" This dialogue will force new constituency coalitions necessary to achieve desired goals and objectives. The traditional single-interest group will become increasingly difficult, counterproductive, and nonexistent (Haywood).

5. New technology will permit the use of sensory, cognitive, and motor prosthetics and augment the client's learning and performance levels. Similarly, the communications revolution will allow interactive television, thereby reducing the dependency on staff availability, personal contact costs, transportation, and physical facilities.
6. Money and resources will be tight, which will require different service configurations (such as consortia), better data-based management procedures, and integration of the public and private sectors.

Regardless of the accuracy of the above predictions, one thing is certain: The future will require changes in human service delivery systems. This chapter shares with you four major changes that I anticipate occurring in the human service delivery area in the next 20 years. Each change discussed is realistic and feasible, and, in many respects, has already begun. Between now and the year 2000, I predict that human services will become more systematic, comprehensive, technological, and ecological.

BECOMING SYSTEMATIC

Human service programs will become more systematic, both because of financial and political necessity, and as a product of their own growth and development. The author's experiences over the last 10 years have indicated that service delivery programs evolve through two phases that reflect increased clarity and systematization. In Phase I, the major focus is on funds, facilities, clients, and staffing. Phase II focuses on implementing management and program systems that are geared to the goals of developing and documenting client gains in independence and productivity. Each phase is briefly outlined below using the Mid-Nebraska Mental Retardation Services program as an example.

Phase I: Developing the Original Program

Originally, each of the seven geographical area programs within the Mid-Nebraska program had an adult component patterned after a sheltered workshop model in which the workshop and its contract activities were used to teach academics, competitive employment, independent living, recreation, and socialization skills. In addition, as is true of most sheltered workshops, each adult component had its share of birthday parties, bowling trips, ceramics and coveting of clients. Twenty-two group living homes were also a part of the adult component, although they were not used for any systematic training. After using this model for about 4 years, the program began to experience numerous problems, including:

1. We were beginning to develop a waiting list. Initially the waiting list was interpreted as meaning one of two things: Either we were so good that everybody wanted our services, or, more reasonably, there were no exits from our programs. Upon close examination, we discovered that there was indeed a lack of movement out of our program, but that this was not so much a result of client inability as it was a result of staff fear that clients would not make it in the "real world."
2. The sheltered workshop was the single center used to teach everything from academics, to skills for competitive employment, community living, recreation, and socialization. This not only confused the client, since he or she was receiving mixed messages, but also the staff, who frequently wondered, "Where do we start with this client and where do we go?"
3. Most of our clients who made the attempt to move into the community returned because they could not adjust adequately to community living. Why? We discovered that most of the placement failures were due to social and behavioral problems, and more specifically, deficits in community living skills. What we had overlooked in our original competitive employment-oriented program was the most important aspect of community integration—the development and maintenance of behavioral skills related to community living.
4. Group homes were becoming mini-institutions. Some individuals love buildings more than what transpires within them. We were initially guilty of perpetuating that phenomenon, for we stressed the "sidewalk appeal" of the residences, and were pleased at how normalizing they looked on the outside. Critical examination indicated, however, that because of the confusion generated from unclear goal-oriented objectives, our group homes were rapidly becoming community-based institutions in which clients were expected to cope with "institution-like settings" and were responding with "institution-like behaviors" (Sternlicht, Schalock, and Harper, 1979).

The collective impact of these problems resulted in sparse placement, with the net effect being a high-cost, low-yield program. At this point, it became clear that we had completed only the first phase of what had to be a multi-phase venture. The second phase, we decided, would require the design of management-program technology that would maximize both the client's and agency's goals of making persons less dependent and more productive.

Phase II: Developing a Systematic Approach

The management-program model chosen to implement the dual goals of training toward independent community living (independence) and competitive employment (productivity) was the systems approach. In the private sector, this management approach is well known (Borst and Montana, 1977). What may be unique about our using this approach in human services was that it included interfacing and monitoring the three critical components of a service delivery system: financial, client training, and case management. (The critical steps involved in implementing this systematic approach were outlined in the organizational review model presented in Chapter 9.)

Many human service programs today are in Phase I, but want to progress to Phase II. This trend toward implementing a systems approach geared to measurable outcomes will continue. When in place, a systems approach should result in one or more of the following significant improvements:

Increased numbers of persons who move through the training program into environments characterized by increased independence and productivity.

Formative program evaluation data suggesting needed refinements or changes in assessment/remediation procedures, outcome measures, staff competencies, and needed interagency programs.

Cost-outcome data that will result in more efficient and effective service delivery programs.

Available and appropriate programmatic services for other functionally deficient persons including those currently within large institutions, public schools, and nursing homes.

BECOMING COMPREHENSIVE

Developing comprehensive services is obviously a multi-phased operation. The process begins in Phases I and II outlined previously, and results in a systematic service delivery approach geared toward measurable outcomes. But the evolutionary process does not end there; Phase II automatically leads to a third phase, characterized by refinements in programmatic technology, expanded training-placement options, and effective interagency coordination and service delivery. Following is a discussion of two somewhat different Phase III activities involving increased comprehensiveness. One activity deals with increasing service coordination through the use of common language systems; the second relates to providing services to a currently underserved population—geriatric developmentally disabled persons.

Common Language and Measurement Systems

One of the most persistent and difficult problems that a service delivery program faces is the lack of interagency coordination. For example, federal programs provide for a host of program plans for clients ("IPP, IHP, IEP, IWRP, ITP, and IPTP"), with the only common denominator being the words "individualized" and "plan" (IP). The author has found that comprehensiveness (that is, effective interagency coordination and service delivery) can be increased if between the "I" and "P" one inserts a *common language and measurement system*. Two examples of how a common language can facilitate interservice coordination are discussed below. One example illustrates behavioral-chemical interfacing; the second, interagency integration.

Interfacing Drug Givers and Takers "Drug abuse," meaning the overuse of prescribed drugs and the underuse of delivered services, is common among developmentally disabled persons. Unfortunately, psychotropic medication is often used as a substitute for services, an alarming condition when one considers that high dosages of either psychotropic or anticonvulsant medication can impair learning, cognitive performance, and adaptive behavior (Dekaban and Lehman, 1975; Gadow, 1981; Stores, 1975). In addition, current drug treatment evaluation and monitoring practices are generally inadequate (Kaufman and Katz-Garris, 1979; Tu, 1979). Clearly, there must be an improved interface between the person who prescribes, the agency person who transmits information to the prescribing physician, and the staff who monitor the drug's effect(s). We successfully dealt with the problem in our Mid-Nebraska program by implementing a behavioral-chemical intervention procedure.

The procedure was initiated in response to the following typical scenario: Clients were frequently taking multiple drugs usually prescribed by different physicians unaware of one another's prescriptions; program personnel were unaware of the initial reason for the prescription, the desired effects, or the possible contraindications; and physicians were not providing meaningful data regarding desired effects and potential contraindications.

The procedure used to implement the intervention policy employed a standard programming sheet used for all training activities within the Mid-Nebraska program (see Figure 7.2). This was important, since staff were familiar with this format and consequently needed only minimal inservice training in recording and monitoring drug effects and communicating material on the programming sheet to physicians. The actual procedural steps either for initiating chemical intervention or reducing dosage/changing medication are outlined in Schalock and Gadwood (1979).

Two possible outcomes of this procedure are shown in Figure 11.1. The baseline data reflected high-frequency head banging behavior. The behavioral intervention employed a standard DRO approach to extinction. Example #1 in the figure reflects what happens at the 30-day review if the behavioral program appears effective—the program is continued and no chemical intervention is used. Example #2 represents the converse. This approach has been successfully used for monitoring drug effects on specific behaviors; reducing the dosage prescribed for behavioral control; sensitizing the staff to their role in drug administration and monitoring; and improving the interface between program staff and generic medical/mental health personnel.

Interfacing Service Delivery Components Comprehensiveness also involves interfacing community-based programs with public schools, private vendors, and ICFMR/DDs such as nursing homes and state residential facilities. The general concept is that if schools, private vendors, institutions, and other community-based programs can agree upon a common list of behavioral skills and training approaches, then the schools and institutions can begin the training of these skills, with the community-based programs continuing the training upon the client's entrance. The advantages of such interfacing include at least the following:

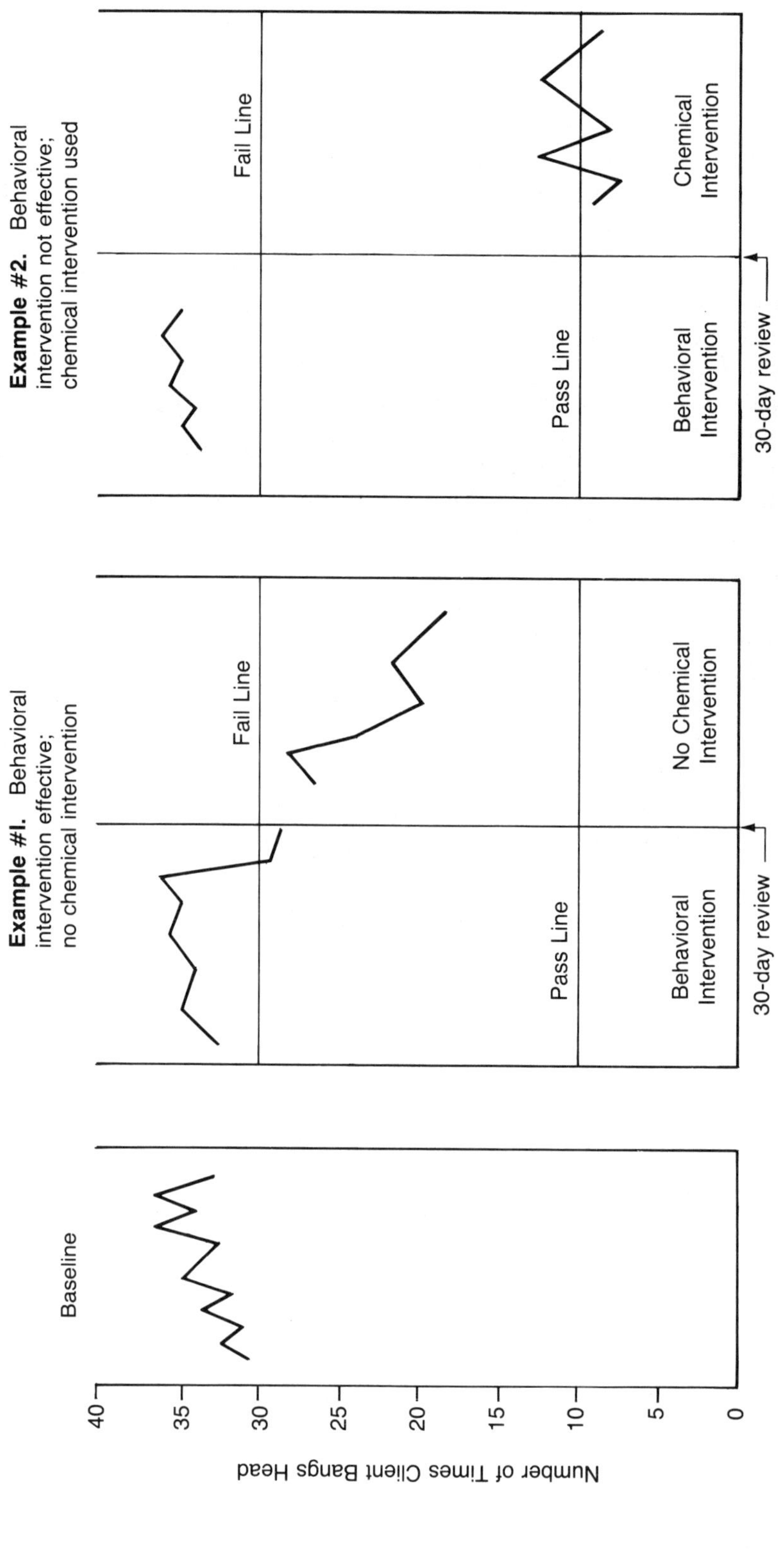

Figure 11.1. Graphic representation of possible effects of behavioral-chemical intervention strategy.

The client receives a consistent message regarding training, since the efforts begun in school or the institution are continued after enrollment in the community-based program.

There should be less cost involved in training due to the reduced need for retaining and/or extended training to facilitate the generalization of skills.

There will be program measurability, reportability, and accountability because of the data-based nature of the criterion-referenced assessment and prescriptive teaching remediation approaches used.

The mixed messages resulting from professional jargon and public law/accreditation standards are partly to blame for the lack to date of interfacing service delivery components. For example, diffuse terms such as normalization, mainstreaming, dignity of risk, least restrictive alternatives, developmental model, developmental domains, dehumanization, adaptive behavior, individual plan, and interdisciplinary team are critical terms regarding the *approach* that should be used; unfortunately, the above terms are not usually translated into clear, concise, meaningful training *goals*. There is no lack of clarity regarding even the behavioral domains with which developmentally disabilities and special education programs should deal. Table 11.1, for example, outlines the major behavioral domains that service delivery programs must attend to in order to comply either with public law or accreditation standards. The lack of agreement reflected explains why one frequently finds confusion about which behavioral skills to teach and which assessment-training approach to use. As another example, considerable literature has questioned the appropriateness of the developmental model and the fact that many special education curricula are simply watered down versions of regular classroom curricula (Childs, 1979; Hirshoren and Burton, 1979; Switzky et al., 1979). The result of employing an inappropriate training model is that we may be training rote skills that are neither meaningful nor appropriate to the development of those coping behaviors associated with increased productivity, independence, and community acceptance (Schalock, 1981).

The author has recently been involved in an interface project that reflects how a common list of behavioral skills and training approaches can be used as catalysts to promote interfacing a community-based mental retardation program with the Nebraska State Developmental Center. The project was initiated out of the shared belief that deinstitutionalization efforts are more productive and successful if there is agreement and joint effort on client-referenced goals and specific skill areas. The process used as a base the 164 behaviors assessed and remediated as part of the community living skills training program (see Chapter 4); then "downward" extensions were done in each of the 10 domains to incorporate behaviors appropriate to the lower functioning clients still residing in the State Developmental Center. Once the additional behaviors were identified, they were incorporated into the standardized assessment instrument and suggested remediation strategies were developed. This community integration system is now the focus of assessment and training within both programs. The common data will permit the implementation of

Table 11.1. Comparison of behavioral domains required by public law or accreditation standards

Domain/Description[a]	Public Law/Standards			
	PL 94-142[b]	DD[c]	ACMR/DD[d]	ICF/MR[e]
Cognitive:				
Academic	X			
Learning and problem-solving abilities		X		
Cognitive development			X	
Perceptual skills				X
Social-Emotional:				
Social adaptation	X			
Maladaptive behaviors		X		
Socialization		X		
Emotional development		X		
Social development			X	
Emotional stability				X
Social skills				X
Affective development			X	
Vocational:				
Prevocational skills	X			
Vocational skills	X			
Work habits and adjustment		X		
Independent Living:				
Self-help skills	X			X
Independent living skills		X		
Adaptive behaviors (IL Skills)			X	
Self-direction				X
Effective use of (leisure) time				X
Physical:				
Physical development		X		
Physical development and health			X	
Sensory Motor:				
Sensorimotor development			X	
Sensorimotor skills				X
Communication:				
Communication		X		
Communication development			X	
Communication skills				X

[a]As listed in respective public law or standards.

[b]PL 94-142—Education for All Handicapped Children Act of 1975.

[c]PL 95-602—Developmental Disabilities Assistance and Bill of Rights Act of 1975.

[d]ACMR/DD—Standards for Services for Developmentally Disabled Individuals: Accreditation Council for Services for Mentally Retarded and Other Developmentally Disabled Persons (1977).

[e]Final Interpretative Guidelines for the Application of the Regulations of Institutions of Mentally Retarded or Persons with Related Conditions (45 CFR 249.13—1977).

meaningful transitional program plans (Brown et al., 1981) and a shared computerized assessment and remediation system.

Interfacing service delivery components can also be facilitated by using interagency mechanisms (as discussed in Chapter 5) or a community broker network recently proposed by Linvill (1980). Conceptually, the network has four specific functions, including: the ability to survey the needs and resources of the consumers and to develop new institutional relationships to fulfill these changing needs; stimulating the development of new delivery mechanisms; developing and expanding new brokerage institutions; and implementing new agreements among the support and delivery institutions. Regardless of the vehicle used, interfacing service delivery components will integrate clients with the living-training environments that are most appropriate to their needs, functional level, and general desire for increased independence, productivity, and community integration.

Dealing with Geriatric Disabled Persons

The elderly disabled population is receiving greater emphasis now than in the past, when the major service delivery effort was on developmentally disabled youth. In reading this section, keep three points in mind: First, since aging is one thing that we all share, aging in itself cannot be regarded as a "problem"; our society, however, has made it one. Second, the geriatric developmentally disabled population is just as afflicted as the "normal" population by our culture's general attitudes toward aging. These attitudes are defined as "gerontophobia" characterized by denying the development of old age; segregating those who are elderly into retirement villages and nursing homes; and employing a "downstream," (see Chapter 2) long-term medical care service model that has resulted in elderly warehouses, dehumanization, neglect, and a general attitude that old age represents a pathological state. Third, there is a new liberation movement fighting "ageism" in this country that promises to be the civil rights movement of the 1980s and is reflected in significant:

Legislative changes such as the Older Americans Act Amendments of 1979 (Public Law 95–478). The focus of federal and state legislation is to ensure that all older persons have access to comprehensive, coordinated aging services that will fulfill one or more of the following goals: 1) secure, maintain, or enhance independence and dignity in a home or community environment; 2) remove individual and social obstacles to economic and personal independence; and 3) prevent or delay inappropriate institutional care or dependency.

Social changes reflected in alternative living arrangements (home care, day care, and congregate living), elderly advocates, intergenerational activities, and doing away with the "boxes of life," the last of which means pursuing recreation and leisure.

Table 11.2. Average behavioral skill levels[a] of geriatric clients residing in three different environments

Environment	I Personal maintenance (25)[b]	II Dressing & clothing care (21)	III Eating & food management (22)	IV Social behavior (17)	V Expressive skills (10)
Community-based program (N=13)	7.5[c]	12.8	6.7	12.1	7.9
ICF/MR (N=17)	4.1	7.2	3.5	10.6	5.7
State developmental center (N=10)	1.0	2.2	1.8	9.6	3.1

[a]As assessed on the *Community Living Skills Quick Screening Test* (Schalock and Gadwood, 1980).
[b]Number of skills in the domain.
[c]Mean score.

Conceptual changes regarding health care and its delivery. The trend is to focus on holistic health delivered within the person's community living environment whose goal is wellness in all of life's major areas—mental, physical, spiritual, and environmental.

We know little about the geriatric developmentally disabled population. In part this is because of the "kittens versus cats" emphasis mentioned earlier in the book, but also because of the "gerontophobia" attitude discussed above. However, we are beginning to gather some information that will help develop appropriate service delivery programs. The remainder of this section focuses on those data and service delivery programs (Note 1).

Programmatic and Service Needs Estimates vary widely regarding the number of geriatric developmentally disabled persons and their programmatic and service needs. A limited survey recently completed by this author suggests something about programmatic needs. The survey involved assessing the behavioral skill level of 40 geriatric (age 55 and older) developmentally disabled persons residing in three different environments—a community based mental retardation program, a community-based ICF/MR, and the State Developmental Center. These 40 persons were evaluated on the 10 behavioral domains of the *Community Living Skills Quick Screening Test* (Schalock and Gadwood, 1980). The average number of skills demonstrated for each group across the 10 domains is presented in Table 11.2. Note two trends in the tabled data: first, the generally low functional level across the domains; and second, the differences among persons residing within the three environments.

A recent conference (Hamilton and Segal, 1975) on gerontological aspects of mental retardation reached consensus on the following service needs for this population:

Environment	VI Home living (21)	VII Money management (13)	VIII Time awareness & utilization (12)	IX Recreation & leisure skills (11)	X Community awareness & utilization (19)
Community-based program (N=13)	5.7	4.5	8.5	6.2	5.5
ICF/MR (N=17)	2.2	1.3	4.5	3.7	3.8
State developmental center (N=10)	0	0.1	1.7	2.6	0.7

Health-related services (medical and dental care, physical therapy, visual care, podiatry, nutrition)
Social and emotional needs
Housing programs
Vocational services
Recreational and leisure time activities
Information and referral services
Transportation
Financial assistance
Advocacy, protective services
Support for families of the elderly (day care, family counseling, respite care)

Programmatic Goals The above-referenced programmatic and service needs suggest at least four realistic programmatic goals for the geriatric developmentally disabled persons. These goals, with accompanying objectives, are outlined below:

1. *Increase independence,* by achieving self-help skills to prevent, reduce, or eliminate dependency. The utilization of sensory, motor, and cognitive prosthetics (as discussed in Chapter 4) will help achieve this goal.
2. *Increase productivity,* by achieving or maintaining optimal self-sufficiency and reasonably productive use of leisure time.
3. *Reduce deterioration,* by achieving or maintaining psychomotor skills, communication, leisure-time activities, and social behaviors. Do not overlook the need for increased sensory stimulation in this process.
4. *Prevent inappropriate institutionalization,* by providing community-based support services; preventing neglect, abuse, or exploitation; and promoting social acceptance via increased community living skills.

It will not be easy to accomplish the above goals. There will be numerous barriers to identify and overcome (see Chapter 6). We can be bolstered by an awareness that the need is great, however, and spurred by the words, "Ageism has its roots in a society that has lost its compassion" (anonymous).

BECOMING TECHNOLOGICAL

An enhanced technology, plus the resources and human capability at our disposal, will provide the framework for service delivery systems in the late 20th and early 21st centuries. How we choose to use this technology is critical; not to use it is folly. The available and emerging technology should permit us to reduce the mismatch between individuals and their environments; to change significantly our current approach to staff and client training; and to apply a bio-behavioral approach to behavioral change. Simultaneously, biochemical advances will improve general health and undoubtedly reduce the incidence of severe and profound disabling conditions. Some of the more important biomedical advances anticipated include (Plog, 1980):

Detection of diseases in the embryo.
Capacity for precise, large-scale genetic counseling.
Understanding of pharmacology and its effects on intelligence, learning, and behavior.
Automatic health-screening diagnostic clinics.
Immunization against various bacterial and viral diseases.
Availability of drugs that increase learning and perceptual processes.
Repairing damaged central nervous system tissue.

These biomedical advances will directly interface the three anticipated technological changes discussed below.

Reducing the Mismatch

Earlier chapters discussed the notion that handicapism is due in part to the mismatch between persons and their environment. The disabling condition can be lessened by utilizing available technology to develop skills, provide prosthetics, and modify the environment. In this way, technology will narrow the gap between developing knowledge and capabilities in the developmental disabilities field (McHale, 1980). Specific examples include:

1. *Behavioral Skills* Progress in this area will occur as a result of the merging of two current trends. First, there will be better agreement as to the specific behavioral skills assessed and trained across living-training environments, which will maximize skill development, generalization, and maintenance. Second, the over 1,000 specific principles and techniques applicable to behavioral change will be computerized for ready access and use (Lynch, Kiernan, and Stark, 1981). The merging of these two trends will permit automated interfacing of a client's skill matrix with suggested prescriptive programming.
2. *Providing Prosthetics* Most people think of prosthetics as artificial arms and legs. Both are important for movement, but neither focus on sensory, informational, and cognitive prosthetics. Future prosthetics will include mechan-

ical sensory devices (Adelson, 1980); mental operations calculators that permit performing more complex cognitive tasks without requiring extensive prerequisite skills (McHale, 1980; Smeets, 1981); attachable television and telephone receivers that can be used for instruction, directions, and problem solving; and sophisticated artificial sensorimotor devices facilitating perceptual motor functioning. The reader can keep abreast of developments in these areas through publications listed in Reference Note 2.

3. *Environmental Modification* Environments can be modified physically or mentally; both modifications will occur in the future. Physically, the trend toward increased accessibility and usability of living, work, and recreational facilities will continue. For example, the Architectural and Transportation Barriers Compliance Board, in the *The Federal Register* (January 16, 1981; Volume 46, No. 11, pp. 4270–4304) issued its minimum guidelines and requirements for standards for accessibility and usability of federal and federally funded buildings and facilities by physically handicapped persons. The guidelines and requirements were issued pursuant to the Rehabilitation, Comprehensive Services, and Developmental Disabilities Amendments of 1978. They provide a basis for the issuance of consistent and improved accessibility and usability standards issued by the four federal standard setting agencies (the General Services Administration, the U.S. Department of Housing and Urban Development, the U.S. Department of Defense and the U.S. Postal Service) under the Architectural Barriers Act of 1968, as amended. The guidelines are available in printed booklet form (Note 3).

   Environments can also be modified psychologically. We will, in the future, do a better job at analyzing the realistic requirements of the various living-training environments within the service delivery network, and will then relate our training to those specific skill areas. Analogously, we will increasingly ask the question, "Who has the problem?" (Karan and Schalock, 1983), and in that way become more flexible in our expectations and demands.

Staff and Client Training

One of the most exciting technological changes that will occur in human services relates to staff and client training techniques. In the future, expect:

Computer-assisted instruction that can be used for developing staff competencies, diagnosing clients medically and behaviorally, and processing information regarding individualized program plan development, implementation, monitoring, and evaluation.

Voice-actuated computer access and use that allows either staff or clients to access the computer verbally, and thereby reduce the need to interact through a keyboard and monitor.

Interactional television that provides information on available services, work tasks, simulated job training, training/educational programs, nutritional/child care programs, legal counseling, and shopping (Nanus, 1980).

Client skill matrices based on assessment data that are matched to living-training environments and appropriate skill development programs. This interface will permit diagnostic programmers to maximize a client's skill development and movement within program progressions through the use of valid behaviorally based criterion-indexed movement norms.

Miniaturized communication devices that are carried on the person, keeping the individual constantly in contact with home, training area, or job (Linstone, 1980).

Telecommunication systems allowing staff to participate in case conferences, client counseling sessions, and conventions.

Applying Bio-behavioral Techniques

Future technology will increase our understanding of behavioral pharmacology, and provide human services with a powerful tool for modifying a person's cognitive, emotional, and behavioral functioning. Although many of the ethical and practical issues are yet to be resolved, we must begin to gear up for the rapidly approaching bio-behavioral era. Applying available bio-behavioral technology raises a philosophical question, "to what end?" In the author's opinion, the best answer to that question is contained, in part, in Abraham Maslow's book *Toward a Psychology of Being* (Maslow, 1962). In Maslow's conception, human needs can be divided into two categories, including deficiency needs (food, water) and individual growth needs (need for belonging, love, esteem, and self-actualization). Thus, according to Maslow, application of bio-behavioral technology will depend on human needs. Linvill (1980) and Lynch et al. (1981) extend Maslow's conception and suggest that when a society is primarily preoccupied with basic needs, there is a tendency to stress efficiency, productivity, and the puritan work ethic, and a tendency to minimize individual freedoms, aesthetic values, environmental quality, and quality of life factors. Conversely, when a society's basic needs are satisfied, value is placed on the development of the individual's growth needs, individual freedom and responsibility, and acceptance of individual differences. Technology can be used to expand the handicapped person's skills, environment, and, indeed, holistic health; unfortunately, the converse is also true.

BECOMING ECOLOGICAL

We are currently in an ecological as well as a systems-technical revolution. Both revolutions attack the assumption that the whole can be understood by studying the parts in isolation. As stated by the philosopher Ervin Laszlo (quoted in Toffler, 1980): " . . . we are part of an interconnected system of nature, and unless informed generalists make it their business to develop systematic theories of the patterns of interconnection, our short-range projects and limited controlabilities may lead to our own destruction."

An ecological theme recurring throughout this book is the need to interface developmentally disabled persons and programs with their local environment. To do otherwise is to overlook the meaning and significance of normalization, integration, mainstreaming, and holistic health. I am convinced that the ecological revolution will continue and intensify. Its effects on the service delivery system are outlined below.

Interfacing Living-Training Environments

There will be a continued integration and coordination of the vast array of facilities and programs involved in the worlds of living, work, and play. The interfacing catalysts will be a common language system (involving common skills and training technology) and an integrated service delivery network. The results of this interfacing are attractive:

A functioning sequence of living-training environments.
Movement toward criterion-indexing among the living-training progressions.
A shifting of assessment-training activities to small living units and industrial practicum locations.

From an ecological perspective, the interfacing will also require a significant change in our conceptual approach to client assessment and training. Specifically,

Systems-level case management will determine available movement-placement options.
Diagnostic programmers will assess the options as to the behavioral skills necessary to adapt successfully.
Training activities will focus on the required skills and occur in the actual living-work environments.
Assistance or environmental modification will be done by facilitators/enablers, permitting the clients to live and work in more independent-productive environments.

Changes in the Service Delivery System

Current demographics suggest a return to nuclear families. This trend, combined with the political-social changes toward individualism, private sector services, and reduced public monies, will affect the service delivery system in one or more of the following ways:

1. *Changed Residential Services* There will be a general end to currently constituted group homes over the next decade. A number of reasons account for this, including: shifting our focus from normalization to the well-being or quality of life of persons; the expense of group homes (Braddock, 1981); increasing community resistance to the largeness and questionable safety of these residences; the institutional flavor of some of them (Sternlicht, Schalock,

and Harper, 1979); but most importantly, group homes are serving the wrong population. The mildly and moderately handicapped population found in most group homes today can, with adequate training and assistance, function well in semi-independent living arrangements (Schalock, Gadwood, and Brown, 1983; Willer, 1981).

Concurrently, we will see a shift from residential programs that provide short-term training to those that provide long-term care. The vehicle will be Intermediate Care Facilities (15 and under) and Skilled Nursing Facilities developed for the severe, profound, and/or multi-handicapped person. Eight states now finance small, private intermediate care facilities for mentally retarded persons; at least seven more plan to do so by 1984 (Braddock, 1981).

The dissolution of group homes and the changed emphasis in residential programs are consistent with the development of four new residential living-training services. These include:

a. *Transitional home-teacher programs* Home-teachers become employees of the agency and receive a salary, board and room fee, and insurance benefits. The home-teacher approach has been used successfully by ENCOR (Omaha, Nebraska) for the last year, with reported significant savings.
b. *Staffed and/or supervised apartments* These living units are also used for environmentally based training in community living skills. They, along with the person's subsequent semi- or independent living arrangement, will provide more appropriate environments for living and learning the skills necessary for community living and integration.
c. *Respite care* Respite care is currently a popular and growing concept in service provision. It consists of providing temporary day or night relief services to families caring at home for developmentally disabled persons. Since the services enable the disabled person to remain with the family, respite care assures the continuity of normal living patterns for the persons involved. A number of respite care models are now in use, including (Upshur, 1982):

Respite placement agencies that recruit and train community providers (similar to foster parent recruitment) and match client requests with providers. Care is provided in client's or provider's home.

Group day care that provides respite care in the form of group daytime care, where persons are brought to a facility or family day care home to relieve families of constant care.

Community residences, in which some group homes reserve one or two beds for overnight respite, or will take clients in an emergency.

Group care or residential treatment facility, in which programs primarily set up as long- or short-term treatment facilities reserve one or two beds for overnight respite.

Group respite providers, which are group residential programs operated solely as respite care (separate from other types of longer term treatment services).

Pediatric nursing homes/hospitals that primarily serve as long-term nursing facilities or acute care hospitals, but will provide overnight respite in a medical emergency.

Private respite provider that involves nurses and others who provide overnight care in their own homes, but are not affiliated with any agency.

State institutions that provide overnight care when no other alternative exists.

d. *Natural home* This is the best "new" service: A return to living with the natural family—the environment that is the most normal and that should foster a better quality of life for the disabled person. While this alternative is cheaper (Braddock, 1981), it will probably require financial incentives and support services including respite care, sitter services, parent training, and readily available telecommunications.

2. *Smaller Service/Control Networks* Human service programs are increasingly being held accountable for normalization, cost-effectiveness, and acceptance. These demands raise the issue of which service delivery mechanism can best implement appropriate, comprehensive, and cost-efficient habilitative programs. Economic hard times affect not only the availability of resources but the public's and lawmakers' attitudes toward how those resources should be allocated. It has been the author's experience that local control is a predominant issue when one interacts with consumer representatives and agency providers. For example, the man on the street generally cannot distinguish between handicapping conditions, but would proclaim profound knowledge in the area of distributing the resources to serve "the population." In discussing control of local programs, it is important to identify the entire constituency and how its individual components fit into the control equation. In the constituency, everyone, of course, wants to be in control. Fortunately, that is not possible, since with control comes the responsibility of control, which cannot be diffused over a heterogeneous group. Human service organizations, by joining together and organizing ("synergizing") their constituencies, can develop and impart feelings of control and accountability that tend to unify heterogeneous groupings of people. One vehicle to implement this smaller, more responsive service network is to provide services on a regional basis.

Regionalization should not be confused with regionalism, of which we are all guilty; nor should it be confused with state agencies with regional offices. Rather, regionalization involves regional operations designed to actually provide services in geographically designated areas. The timely advantages of regionalization are discussed briefly below.

a. *Responsiveness* One characteristic of large bureaucracies, which most states have become, is a diffusion of responsibility and accountability. The net result is one or more of the following negative or questionable by-products: fragmented services, which preclude a continuum of training facilities, programs, and placement options that promote a person's increased independence and productivity; a sparcity of community-based, less restrictive program options; competition among agencies for control, funds, services provided, and increasingly, "available clients"; client movement based on availability of alternatives and convenience, rather than on demonstrated skill attainments; minimal parental or guardian input; a relative lack of ongoing internal and external monitoring of the quality of services provided; and high costs related to programmatic input (administration, staff, buildings) rather than output (client growth and development).

With regional direction, control, and synergism, however, locally important policies and priorities can be implemented with significant input and stability provided by parents, local governing bodies, and elected officials. It was this type of responsiveness that permitted Nebraska within two years after regionalization to go from a few to a full array of community-based programs.

b. *Equalization of service patterns* Any human service delivery system needs to be sensitive to the entire geographic area served and to provide services whenever needed. This issue becomes critical as programs increasingly face problems related to financial resources, transportation, limited professional generic staff, availability of trained personnel, and limited existing physical facilities. However, the professional, political, and advocacy personnel of an area are best able to determine the needs and service delivery mechanisms required to provide viable, coordinated services. Once established, these services can implement deinstitutionalization and prevent reinstitutionalization.

A second aspect of equalization deals with small "Mom and Pop" operations. Many small programs are myopic and vulnerable because they lack power and resources. If these are a part of a continuum of regionalized programs, and if they encounter problems, then the region can support and improve them. Otherwise, for modest operations in trouble, the only way to go is down. Similarly, equalization can eliminate the negative aspects of provincialism; provide protection from external control; and result in the development of larger programs that are able to maintain their local emphasis.

c. *Responsibility centers* It is an interesting phenomenon that although everyone wants control, few want the responsibility that accompanies it. If accountability is the unifying theme of a heterogeneous constituency, then measurability and reportability are the vehicles that must be employed to satisfy a constituency's needs. Regionalization can provide an excellent mechanism to implement a responsibility center approach to program management, service delivery, and program evaluation.

d. *Innovation and communication* Because of the rapidly changing nature of our human service delivery challenges, supportive services must be provided to innovate, evaluate, and communicate, and thus improve program services. If a program is small, isolated, or, alternatively, so large that change is almost impossible, then isolation or stagnation will automatically result. The key factor, however, is that supportive service programs are truly the community's programs. They are close to the families of the mentally retarded citizens whom they serve; and they are well known to locally elected officials. They are, therefore, subject to more scrutiny, monitoring, and suggestions for change than any state agency could ever be.

e. *Economics* There are three economic advantages to regionalization. First, it spreads money and jobs around, and thereby can be used as a leverage to further the deinstitutionalization process. Second, community placement can be less expensive (Touché-Ross, 1980). Third, a region may be the best vehicle to use in private leveraging to generate funds for community programs.

3. *Interfacing with the Private Sector* The private sector programs outlined in Chapter 4 reflect the increasing interdependency between public and private groups. This holistic approach is reflected in the following future organizational themes (Leavitt, Pinfield, and Webb, 1974):

Organization and environment—organizations do not exist in a vacuum; they can change if they understand internal and external environmental dynamics.

Organizational styles of thought—organizations will need to be flexible and consequently look at new modes of thought, as opposed to previous thought patterns.

Organizational values—organizations will increase interpersonal and community trust, including providing assistance and volunteer services to human service programs on company time.

SCENARIOS OF THE FUTURE

Our journey has just begun as we face the future of services for developmentally disabled persons. Although the times may seem perilous, today's frustrations can become tomorrow's accomplishments if we do a better job at planning, executing, and managing. Throughout this book, there have been a number of recurring themes and suggestions, which when implemented should transform frustration to accomplishment. These themes include:

1. Good programs require good planning, execution, and management.
2. Resources and technology are available that when combined with systems-level management can significantly increase the handicapped person's independence, productivity, and community acceptance.
3. The "mismatch" (that is, dis-ability) between persons and their environments

can be minimized by training appropriate behavioral skills, providing cognitive and perceptual-motor prosthetics, and modifying the environment's physical barriers and psychological attitudes.

4. Programmatic services should be output-rather than process-oriented, focusing on the development of skills and opportunities for increased independence, productivity, and community integration. The techniques involve environmentally-related client assessment, training, and support services.
5. Effective and efficient programs require integrating clients with different environments, interfacing living-training program progressions, and exchanging resources, technology, and staff capabilities between the public and private sectors.
6. Program improvement and survival depend upon good data that serve as a management tool.

This author envisions two possible future scenarios. The first, and obviously preferred one, follows from the above themes. This scenario involves agencies working together to provide living-training progressions, reduce cost, and provide appropriate training and support services. Within this scenario, managers are systems-oriented and competent because their "journey into incompetence" has been replaced by management skills. Similarly, staff are oriented toward a system, rather than an agency. Instructional staff serve both as trainers and facilitator-enablers, working within the clients' natural environment and using the best technology available. The scenario also includes clients who are acquiring relevant behavioral skills, moving within sequential living-training-work environments, and becoming more independent and productive. And finally, the scenario envisions a financial support system that reinforces client growth and development rather than maintenance or stagnation.

The second scenario envisions agencies that are independent and territorial; managers who persist in their journey into incompetence; staff who continue their center-based training and activity programs; and financial support systems that directly or indirectly result in maintenance status and dependency. Within this scenario, clients continue to live in environments that are inappropriate, stagnating, counterproductive, and socially segregated.

As we rapidly approach the 21st century, the type of environment that will be provided developmentally disabled persons is largely dependent upon the commitment and approach we take now. If the essence of handicapism is the lack of individual independence and productivity, our challenge today is to develop those comprehensive, technologically based programs that will maximize a person's independence, productivity, and community integration.

REFERENCE NOTES

1. Information regarding the geriatric developmentally disabled population can be found in the following references:

Carsrud, A.L., Carsrud, K.B., and Standifer, J. 1980. Social variables affecting mental health in geriatric mentally retarded individuals: An exploratory study. Ment. Retard. 18(2):88–90.

DiGiovanni, L. 1978. The elderly retarded: A little-known group. Gerontologist 18:262–266.

Fozard, J.L., and Popkin, S.J. 1978. Optimizing adult development: Ends and means of an applied psychology of aging. Am. Psychol. 78:875–989.

Jones, L.H. 1972. The problems of aging and protective services for the retarded adult. In: D.H. Stedman (ed.), Issues in Mental Retardation and Human Development, pp. 39–45. Office of Mental Retardation Coordination, U.S. Department of Health, Education and Welfare, DHEW Publication #(05) 73–86, Washington, D.C.

Kelban, M., Lawton, H., Powell, M., Brody, E.M. and Moss, M. 1975. Characteristics of mentally impaired aged profiting from individualized treatment. J. Gerontol. 30:90–96.

Kobrynski, B. 1975. The mentally impaired elderly: Whose responsibility? Gerontologist 15:407–411.

Segal, R. 1977. Trends in services for the aged mentally retarded. Ment. Retard. April:25–27.

Talkington, L.W., and Chiovaro, S.J. 1969. An approach to programming for the aged MR. Ment. Retard. 7:29–30.

2. Advances in biotechnology are available from:

   Research Resources Information Center
   1776 East Jefferson St.
   Rockville, MD 20852
   301/881-4150

   Office of Science and Health Reports
   Division of Research Resources
   National Institutes of Health
   Bethesda, MD 20205
   301/496-5545

   National Technical Information Service
   Springfield, VA 22161

   Urban Institute
   Publications Office
   2100 M St., NW
   Washington, DC 20037

   Wisconsin Vocational Studies Center
   University of Wisconsin-Madison
   Madison, WI 53706

3. The guidelines and requirements are issued under 29 U.S.C. 792, section 502 of the Rehabilitation Act of 1973, as amended they are available from: Office

of Technical Services, U.S. Architectural and Transportation Barriers Compliance Board, 330 C St., S.W., Washington, D.C. 20201, 202/472-2700 (voice) or 202/245-1801 (TDD); or Office of Compliance and Enforcement, U.S. Architectural and Transportation Barriers Compliance Board. 202/245-1801 (voice or TDD).

REFERENCES

Achenbach, T., and Zigler, E. 1968. Cue learning and problem learning strategies in normal and retarded children. Child Dev. 3: 827–848.

Adelson, M. 1980. Mental retardation: Toward a different kind of future. In: S. Plog and M. Santamour (eds.), The Year 2000 and Mental Retardation. Plenum Publishing Corp., New York.

Aiken, M., Dewar, R., DeTomaso, N., Hage, J., and Zeitz, G. 1975. Coordinating Human Services. Jossey-Bass, Inc., Pubs., San Francisco.

Aino, E. A., and Loversidge, R. D. (eds.). 1978. Access for All: An Illustrated Handbook for Barrier-Free Design. Special Press, Columbus, OH.

Albright, L., Hasazi, S. E., Phelps, L. A., and Hull, M. E. 1981. Interagency collaboration in providing vocational education for handicapped individuals. Except. Child. 47:584–589.

Alexis, M., and Wilson, C. Z. 1967. Organizational Decision-making. Prentice Hall, Englewood Cliffs, NJ.

Alkin, M. C. 1972. Evaluation theory development. In: C. H. Weiss (ed.), Evaluating Action Programs: Readings in Social Action and Education. Allyn & Bacon, Inc., Boston.

Allein, M. C. 1973. Accountability defined. In: J. E. Roueche and B. R. Herrscher (eds.), Towards Instructional Accountability: A Practical Guide to Educational Change. Westinghouse Learning Corporation, New York.

Allen, R. C. 1968. The retarded offender: Unrecognized in court and untreated in prison. Fed. Probation 32:22–27.

Alpern, G. D., and Boll, T. J. 1972. Developmental Profile. Psychological Development Publications, Indianapolis, IN.

Anderson, O. W. 1975. Blue Cross Since 1929: Accountability and the Public Trust. Ballinger Publications, New York.

Anthony, W. A. 1980. Mental health research plan. Informer 9(3):20–21.

Aram, J. D., and Stratton, W. E. 1974. The development of inter-agency cooperation. Soc. Serv. Rev. 48:412–421.

Attkisson, C. C., and Broskowski, A. 1978. Evaluation and the emerging human service concept. In: C. C. Attkisson, W. A. Hargreaves, M. J. Horowitz, and J. E. Sorensen (eds.), Evaluation of Human Service Programs. Academic Press, Inc., New York.

Attkisson, C. C., Hargreaves, W. A., Horowitz, M. J., and Sorensen, J. E. 1978. Evaluation of Human Service Programs. Academic Press, Inc., New York.

Austin, M. J. 1978. Professionals and Paraprofessionals. Human Sciences Press, New York.

Baer, D. M., Peterson, R. F., and Sherman, J. A. 1967. The development of imitation by reinforcing behavioral similarity to a model. J. Exp. Anal. Behav. 10:405–416.

Baker, B. L., Seltzer, G. B., and Seltzer, M. M. 1977. As Close as Possible: Community Residences for Retarded Adults. Little, Brown, & Co., Boston.

Baller, W. R., Charles, D. C., and Miller, E. L. 1967. Midlife attainment of the mentally retarded: A longitudinal study. Genet. Psychol. Monogr. 75:235–239.

Balthazar, E. E. 1971. Balthazar Scales of Adaptive Behavior. Section I: The Scales of Functional Independence (BSAB-I). Research Press, Champaign, IL.

Bandura, A. 1976. Self-reinforcement: Theoretical and methodological considerations. Behaviorism 4:135–155.

Bandura, A., Adams, N. E., and Beyer, J. 1977. Cognitive processes mediating behavioral change. J. Pers. Soc. Psychol. 35:125–139.

Barnard, C. L. 1971. The Functions of the Executive. Harvard University Press, Cambridge, MA.

Baroff, C. S. 1974. Mental Retardation: Nature, Cause and Management. John Wiley & Sons, New York.

Bassuk, E. L., and Gerson, S. 1978. Deinstitutionalization and mental health services. Sci. Am. 238(1):46–53.

Batsche, C. 1980. Personnel preparation for serving special vocational needs populations. In: G. D. Meers (ed.), Handbook of Special Vocational Needs Education. Aspen Systems Corporation, Rockville, MD.

Baum, B., Flanigan, P., Hoke, G., Parker, R., Rydman, R., and Schalock, R. 1982. A Sourcebook for Developing Consortia and Community Living Alternatives. Governor's Planning Council on Developmental Disabilities, Springfield, IL.

Baumheier, E. C. 1979. Interagency linkages in the field of developmental disabilities. Paper prepared for Interagency Evaluation Conference, American Association on Mental Deficiency Convention, June, 1979. Miami, FL.

Bazelon, D. L. 1973. The judicial process — A tool for reform. In: The Rights of the Mentally Handicapped: Proceedings from a Bi-regional Conference. National Association of Coordinators of State Programs for the Mentally Retarded, Inc., Arlington, VA.

Beams, F. A. 1979. Advanced Accounting. Prentice-Hall, Inc., Englewood Cliffs, NJ.

Beckhard, R., and Harris, R. 1977. Organizational Transitions: Managing Complex Change. Addison-Wesley Publishing Co., Reading, MA.

Beehr, T. A., and Newman, J. E. 1978. Job stress, employee health and organizational effectiveness: A facet analysis, model, and literature review. Personnel Psychol. 31:665–669.

Beer, M. 1980. Organization Change and Development: A Systems View. Goodyear, Santa Monica, CA.

Begab, M. J., Haywood, H. C., and Garber, H. L. 1981. Psychosocial Influences in Retarded Performance, Vol. 2. Strategies for Improving Competence. University Park Press, Baltimore.

Bell, N. J. 1976. IQ as a factor in community lifestyle of previously institutionalized retardates. Ment. Retard. 14(3):29–33.

Bell, P. 1979. I Can Do It! Cookbook for People with Very Special Needs. K and H Publishers, Newport Beach, CA.

Bellamy, G. T. 1976. Habilitation of the severely and profoundly retarded: A review of research on work productivity. In: G. T. Bellamy (ed.), Habilitation of Severely and Profoundly Retarded Adults. Research and Training Center in Mental Retardation, University of Oregon, Eugene, OR.

Bellamy, G. T., and Wilcox, B. 1981. Secondary Education for Severely Handicapped Students: Guidelines for Quality Services. University of Oregon Center on Human Development, Eugene, OR.

Bellamy, G. T., Horner, R. H., and Inman, D. P. 1979. Vocational Habilitation of Severely Retarded Adults: A Direct Service Technology. University Park Press, Baltimore.

Bellamy, G. T., Horner, R. H., Sheehan, M. R., and Boles, S. M. 1980a. Structured Employment and Workshop Reform: Equal Rights for Severely Handicapped Individuals. University of Oregon Center on Human Development, Eugene, OR.

Bellamy, G. T., Sheehan, M. R., Horner, R. H., and Boles, S. M. 1980b. Community programs for severely handicapped adults: An analysis. JASH 5(4):307–324.

Berelson, B., and Steiner, S. 1964. Human Behavior. New York: Harcourt Brace Jovanovich, Inc., New York.

Berkeley Planning Associates. 1977. Evaluation of Child Abuse and Neglect Demonstration Projects, 1974–1977, Vol. 9. Project Management and Worker Burnout. National Technical Information Service, Springfield, VA.

Berkson, G., and Romer, D. 1981. A letter to a service provider. In: H. C. Haywood and J. R. Newbrough (eds.), Living Environments for Developmentally Retarded Persons. University Park Press, Baltimore.

Bialer, I. 1961. Conceptualization of success and failure in mentally retarded and normal children. J. Pers. 31:258–270.

Bilvosky, D., and Matson, J. 1977. Community Colleges and the Developmentally Disabled. American Association of Community and Junior Colleges, Washington, DC.

Blake, R. R., and Manton, J. S. 1971. Reactions to intergroup competition under win-lose conditions. Manag. Sci. 4:4–12.

Blanc, D. 1976. Training Manual: Paraprofessionals, Vocational Strategies and Special Needs Students. Document Reproduction Service, Arlington, VA.

Blatt, B. 1976. Instruments of change: The executive. In: R. B. Kugel (ed.), Changing Patterns in Residential Services for the Mentally Retarded. President's Committee on Mental Retardation, Washington, DC.

Blatt, B., Bogdan, R., Biklen, D., and Taylor, S. 1977. From institution to community: A conversion model. In: E. Sontag (ed.), Educational Programming for the Severely/Profoundly Handicapped. The Council for Exceptional Children, Reston, VA.

Blav, P., and Scott, W. E. 1963. Formal Organizations. Chandler Publishing Co., New York.

Block, J. H. 1971. Mastery Learning: Theory and Practice. Holt, Rinehart & Winston, New York.

Bogen, D., and Aanes, D. 1975. The Adaptive Behavior Scale as a tool in comprehensive MR programming. Ment. Retard. 13(1):38–41.

Boggs, E. M. 1972. Federal legislation: 1966-1971. In: J. Wortis (ed.), Mental Retardation: An Annual Review, Vol. 4. Grune & Stratton, New York.

Bolton, B., and Cook, D. W. 1980. Rehabilitation Client Assessment. University Park Press, Baltimore.

Borst, D., and Montana, P. J. 1977. Managing Nonprofit Organizations. AMACOM, New York.

Botterbusch, K. F. 1980. A Comparison of Commercial Vocational Evaluation Systems. Materials Development Center, Stout Vocational Rehabilitation Institute, Stout, WI.

Boyen, C. 1978. A flexible approach to career development: Balancing vocational training and training for independent living. Educ. Train. Ment. Retard. 13(2)209–215.

Braddock, D. 1981. Deinstitutionalization of the retarded: Trends in public policy. Hosp. Community Psychiatry 32(9):607–615.

Bradley, V. J. 1978. Deinstitutionalization of Developmentally Disabled Persons. University Park Press, Baltimore.

Brebner, A., Hallworth, H. J., and Brown, R. 1977. CAI programs and terminals for the mentally retarded. In: P. Mittler (ed.), Research to Practice in Mental Retardation: Vol. 2. Education and Training. University Park Press, Baltimore.

Brebner, A., Hallworth, H. J., and Brown, R. I. 1981. Computer-assisted learning with the handicapped. In: P. Mittler (ed.), Frontiers of Knowledge in Mental Retardation: Vol. 1. University Park Press, Baltimore.

Brody, R. 1973. MBO goes to work in the public sector. Harvard Bus. Rev. 51:65–74.

Brolin, D. E. 1976. Vocational Preparation for Retarded Citizens. Charles E. Merrill Publishing Company, Columbus, OH.

Brooks, P. H., and Baumeister, A. A. 1977. A plea for consideration of ecological validity in the experimental psychology of mental retardation. A guest editorial. Am. J. Ment. Defic. 81:407–416.

Brown, B., and Courtless, T. 1977. The mentally retarded offender. In: F. Menolascino (ed.), Challenges in Mental Retardation: Progressive Ideology and Services. Human Sciences Press, New York.

Brown, C. C. 1976. Putting the Corporate Board to Work. Macmillan Publishing Company, Inc., New York.

Brown, L., Nietupski, J., and Hamre-Nietupski, S. 1976. The criterion of ultimate functioning. In: M. A. Thomas (ed.), Hey, Don't Forget about Me! CEC Information Center, Reston, VA.

Brown, L., Pumpian, I., Baumgart, D., Vandeventer, P., Ford, A., Nisbet, J., Schroeder, J., and Gruenewald, L. 1981. Longitudinal transition plans in programs for severely handicapped students. Except. Child. 47:624–630.

Brown, M., and Lewis, H. L. 1976. Hospital Management Systems: Multi-unit Organizations and Delivery of Health Care. Aspen Systems Corp., Rockville, MD.

Bruininks, R. H., Hauber, F. A., and Kudla, M. J. 1980. National survey of community residential facilities: A profile of facilities and residents in 1977. Am. J. Ment. Defic. 84:470–478.

Bruininks, R. H., Kudla, M. J., Hauber, F. A., Hill, B. K., and Wieck, C. A. 1981. Recent growth and status of community-based residential alternatives. In: R. H. Bruininks, C. E. Meyers, B. B. Sigford, and K. C. Lakin (eds.), Deinstitutionalization and Community Adjustment of Mentally Retarded Persons. Monograph No. 4. American Association of Mental Deficiency, Washington, DC.

Bruininks, R. H., Meyers, C. E., Sigford, B. B., and Lakin, K. C. (eds.). 1981. Deinstitutionalization and Community Adjustment of Mentally Retarded People. Monograph No. 4. American Association of Mental Deficiency, Washington, DC.

Buddle, J. F. 1979. Measuring Performance in Human Service Systems: Planning, Organization and Control. AMACOM, New York.

Budner, R., Arnold, I., and Goodman, L. 1971. The plan and the reality: Training and utilization of paraprofessionals for service to the retarded. Am. J. Public Health 61(2):297–307.

Burgdorf, R. L. 1980. The Legal Rights of Handicapped Persons. Paul H. Brookes Publishing Co., Baltimore.

Butterfield, E. C. 1981. Instructional techniques that produce generalized improvements in cognition. In: P. Mittler (ed.), Frontiers of Knowledge in Mental Retardation, Vol. 1. Social, Educational, and Behavioral Aspects. University Park Press, Baltimore.

Cain, L., Levine, S., and Elzey, F. 1963. Manual for the Cain-Levine Social Competency Scale. Consulting Psychologists Press, Palo Alto, CA.

Callahan, C. 1979. New math for nonprofits. The Grantsmanship Center News. March – April:25–30.

Callahan, J. J., Jr. 1981. Management and leadership in times of scarcity: It's not possible to fake it any longer. Vital Speeches 47(22):697–700.

Campbell, T., and Stanley, J. C. 1963. Experimental and Quasi-experimental Designs for Research. Rand McNally, New York.

Caporaso, J. A. 1973. Quasi-experimental approaches to social science: Perspective and problems. In: J. A. Caporaso and L. L. Roos (eds.), Quasi-experimental Approaches: Testing Theory and Evaluation Policy. Northwestern University Press, Evanston, IL.

Carlin, E., Nelson, A. S., Richardson, M., Sells, C. J., and West, M. A. 1981. Human Resources Assessment Project. Child Development and Mental Retardation, University of Washington, Seattle.

Carsrud, A. L., Carsrud, K. B., Henderson, D. P., Alisch, C. J., and Fowler, A. V. 1979. Effects of social and environmental change on institutionalized mentally retarded persons: The relocation syndrome reconsidered. Am. J. Ment. Defic. 84:266–272.

Carter, D. C., and George, T. J. 1973. A Manual for Reporting and Analyzing the Costs and Benefits of Social Services. U.S. Department of Health, Education and Welfare, Community Service Administration, Social Rehabilitation Service, Washington, DC.

Carter, D., and Newman, F. 1976. A Client-Oriented System of Mental Health Service Delivery and Program Management: A Workbook and Guide. National Institute of Mental Health, Rockville, MD.

Carter, R. D. 1977. Help! These Kids Are Driving Me Crazy. Research Press, Champaign, IL.

Carver, R. P. 1974. Two dimensions of tests: Psychometric and edumetric. Am. Psychol. 29:572–578.

Chambliss, C., and Murray, E. 1979. Efficacy attribution, locus of control, and weight loss. Cognit. Ther. Res. 5(6):349–353.

Chandler, J., and Ross, S. 1976. Zoning restrictions and the right to live in the community. In: M. Kindred, A. Cohen, D. Penrod, and T. Shaffer (eds.), The Mentally Retarded Citizen and the Law. The Free Press, New York.

Cherniss, C. 1980a. Human service programs as work organizations: Using organizational design to improve staff motivation and effectiveness. In: R. H. Price and P. Polister (eds.), Evaluation and Action in the Social Environment. Academic Press, Inc., New York.

Cherniss, C. 1980b. Professional Burnout in Human Service Organizations. Praeger Publishers, New York.

Cherniss, C. 1981. Staff Burnout: Job Stress in the Human Services. Sage Publications, Beverly Hills, CA.

Cherniss, C., and Egnatios, E. 1978. Participation in decision-making by staff in community mental health programs. Am. J. Community Psychol. 6: 171–190.

Childs, R. E. 1979. A drastic change in curriculum for the educable mentally retarded child. Ment. Retard. 17(6): 299–301.

Ciarlo, J. A. 1977. Monitoring and analysis of mental health program outcome data. In: M. Guttentag and S. Sarr (eds.), Evaluation Studies Review Annual, Vol. 2. Sage Publications, Beverly Hills, CA.

Close, D. W., Irvin, L. K., Prehm, H. J., and Taylor, V. E. 1978. Systematic correction procedures in vocational individuals. Am. J. Ment. Defic. 83(3): 270–275.

Cobb, H., and Gray, M. 1977. Mental Retardation: Past and Present. President's Committee on Mental Retardation, Washington, DC.

Cohen, J. 1961. An analysis of vocational failure of mental retardates placed in the community after a period of institutionalization. Am. J. Ment. Defic. 65: 371–375.

Coleman, S. L., and Sledman, J. M. 1974. Use of a peer model in language training in an echolalic child. J. Behav. Ther. Exp. Psychol. 5: 275–279.

Comptroller General. 1974. Standards for Audit of Governmental Organizations, Programs, Activities and Functions. U.S. Government Printing Office (Stock #200-00110), Washington, DC.

Comptroller General. 1977. Report to the Congress: Returning the Mentally Retarded Disabled to the Community. Government Needs to Do More. (HRD 76-152), U.S. Government Printing Office, Washington, DC.

Congdon, D. M. 1973. The adaptive behavior scales modified for the profoundly retarded. Ment. Retard. 11: 20–21.

Conley, R. W. 1973. The Economics of Mental Retardation. The Johns Hopkins University Press, Baltimore.

Conley, R. W. 1975. Issues in benefit-cost analyses of the vocational rehabilitation program. Am. Rehabil. 1: 19–23.

Conrad, W. R., and Glenn, W. E. 1976. The Effective Voluntary Board of Directors: What It Is and How It Works. The Swallow Press, Chicago.

Conroy, J. W. 1977. Trends in deinstitutionalization of the mentally retarded. Ment. Retard. 15(1): 44–46.

Corcoran, E., and French, R. 1977. Leisure activity for the retarded adult in the community. Ment. Retard. 15: 21–23.

Cotler, S. B., and Guerra, J. J. 1976. Assertion Training: A Humanistic-Behavioral Guide to Self-Dignity. Research Press. Champaign, IL.

Coulter, W. A., and Morrow, H. W. (eds.). 1978. Adaptive Behavior: Concepts and Measurements. Grune & Stratton, New York.

Craighead, W. E., Kazdin, A. E. and Mahoney, M. J. 1981. Behavior Modification: Principles, Issues and Application (2nd Ed.). Houghton Mifflin, Co., Boston.

Crawford, J. L., Aiello, J. R., and Thompson, D. E. 1979. Deinstitutionalization and community placement: Clinical and environmental factors. Ment. Retard. 17(2): 59–65.

Cronbach, L. J., and Furby, L. 1970. How we should measure "change"—or should we? Psychol. Bull. 74: 68–80.

Crosby, K. G. 1976. Essentials of active programming. Ment. Retard. 14: 3–9.

Crnic, K. A., and Pym, H. A. 1979. Training mentally retarded adults in independent living skills. Ment. Retard. 17(1): 13–16.

Cuff, G. N. 1977. A strategy for evaluating a short course on behavior modification. Ment. Retard. 15(6): 48–50.

Curran, J. P. 1981. Social-skills and assertion training. In: W. E. Craighead, A. E. Kazdin, and M. J. Mahoney (eds.), Behavior Modification: Principles, Issues and Application. Houghton Mifflin Co., Boston.

Dalton, L., and Perloff, R. 1979. Improving Evaluations. Sage Publications, Beverly Hills, CA.

DeJong, G. 1978. The movement for independent living: Origins, ideology and implications for disability research. Paper presented at the annual meeting of the American Congress of Rehabilitation Medicine, November 17, New Orleans, LA.

Dekaban, A. S., and Lehman, E. J. B. 1975. Effects of different dosages of anticonvulsant drugs on mental performances in patients with chronic epilepsy. Acta Neurol. Scand. 52: 319–330.

Delberq, A., Van De Ven, A., and Gustafson, D. 1975. Group Techniques for Program

Planning: A Guide to Nominal Group and Delphi Processes. Scott, Foresman & Company, Glenville, IL.

Denny, M. R. 1966. A theoretical analysis and its application to training the mentally retarded. In: N. R. Ellis (ed.), International Review of Research in Mental Retardation: Vol. 2. Academic Press, Inc., New York.

Dickerson, M. W. 1977. Fostering Children with Mental Retardation. Eastern Michigan University, Foster Parent Training Project, Ypsilanti, MI.

Dokecki, P. 1977. The liaison perspective on the enhancement for human development: Theoretical, historical and experiential background. Community Psychol. 5: 13–17.

Doll, E. A. 1964. Measurement of Social Competence: A Manual for the Vineland Social Maturity Scale. American Guidance Service. Circle Pines, MN.

Douchette, J. 1979. Identifying appropriate instrument for use in evaluating programs for the developmentally disabled. In: P. Sanofsky (ed.), Evaluating Program Effectiveness: The Administrator's Dilemma. SPS Communications, Watertown, MA.

Drucker, P. 1977. People and Performance. Harper's College Press, New York.

Dyer, C. A. 1972. Preparing for Computer Assisted Instruction. Educational Technology Publications, Englewood Cliffs, NJ.

Ebert, R. S. 1979. A training program for community residence staff. Ment. Retard. 17(5): 257–259.

Edelwich, J., and Brodsky, A. 1980. Burn-out: Stages of Disillusionment in the Helping Professions. Human Sciences Press, New York.

Edgerton, R. B. 1975. Issues relating to the quality of life among mentally retarded persons. In: M. J. Begab and S. A. Richardson (eds.), The Mentally Retarded and Society: A Social Science Perspective. University Park Press, Baltimore.

Edgerton, R. B. 1981. Crime, divorce and normalization: Reconsidered. In: R. H. Bruininks, C. E. Meyers, B. B. Sigford, and K. C. Lakin (eds.), Deinstitutionalization and Community Adjustment of Mentally Retarded People. Monograph No. 4. American Association on Mental Deficiency. Washington, DC.

Edgerton, R. B., and Bercovici, S. M. 1976. The cloak of competence: Years later. Am. J. Ment. Defic. 80:485–497.

Egan, G., and Cowan, M.A. 1979. People in Systems: A Model for Development in the Human-Service Professions and Education. Wadsworth. Belmont, CA.

Eisler, R. M., Miller, P. M., and Hersen, M. 1973. Components of assertive behavior. J. Clin. Psychol. 29:295–299.

Elder, J. A., and Magrab, P. R. 1980. Coordinating Services to Handicapped Children: A Handbook for Interagency Collaborates. Paul H. Brookes Publishing Co., Baltimore.

Ellis, N. R. (ed.). 1979. Handbook of Mental Deficiency: Psychological Theory and Research, (2nd Ed.). Lawrence Erlbaum Assoc., Hillsdale.

Epstein, I., and Tripodi, T. 1977. Research Techniques for Program Planning, Monitoring and Evaluation. Columbia University Press, New York.

Eyman, R. K., and Call, T. 1979. Maladaptive behavior and community placement of mentally retarded persons. Am. J. Ment. Defic. 82(2):137–144.

Eyman, R. K., DeMaine, G. C., and Lei, T. 1979. Relationship between community environments and resident changes in adaptive behavior: A path model. Am. J. Ment. Defic. 83(4):330–338.

Faison, K. 1980. Introduction to Team Planning. Meyer's Children's Rehabilitation Institute, Omaha, Neb.

Feurenstein, R., Rand, Y., Hoffman, M. B., and Miller, R. 1980. Instrumental Enrichment: An Intervention Program for Cognitive Modifiability. University Park Press, Baltimore.

Fiedler, D., and Beach, L. R. 1978. On the decision to be assertive. J. Consult. Clin. Psychol. 46:537–546.

Finarelli, H. 1979. The design for a model statewide evaluation system. In: P. Sanofsky (ed.), Evaluating Program Effectiveness: The Administrator's Dilemma. SPS Communications, Watertown, MA.

Flynn, R. J., and Heal, L. W. 1980. Psychometric properties: Program analysis of service systems (Pass-3) and other measures of the cost-effectiveness analysis of residential alternatives. Paper presented at Gatlinburg Conference on Research in MR/DD, March, 1980, Gatlinburg, Tenn.

Flynn, R. J. 1981. National studies of the effectiveness of conventional vocational education: A research view. In: K. P. Lynch, W. E. Kiernan, and J. A. Stark (eds.), Prevocational and Vocational Education for Special Needs Youth: A Blueprint for the 80's. Paul H. Brookes Publishing Co., Baltimore.

Foss, G., and Peterson, S. L. 1981. Social-interpersonal skills relevant to job tenure for mentally retarded adults. Ment. Retard. 19(3)103–106.

Foxx, R., and Arzin, N. 1976. Toilet Training the Retarded. Research Press, Champaign, IL.

Fredericks, H. B., Anderson, R. B., Baldwin, V. L., Grove, D., Moore, W. G., Moore, M., and Beaird, J. H. 1977. The Identification of Competencies of Teachers of the Severely Handicapped. Oregon Teaching Research Division, Monmouth, OR.

Freidman, R. B. 1973. A computer program for simulating the patient-physician encounter. J. Med. Educ. 48:92–97.

French, W. 1974. The Personnel Management Process: Human Resources Administration. 3rd Ed. Houghton Mifflin Co., Boston.

French, W., and Bell, C. 1973. Organization Development: Behavioral Science Interventions for Organizational Improvements. Prentice-Hall, Englewood Cliffs, NJ.

Friedman, P. H. 1968. The effects of modeling and role playing on assertive behavior. Unpublished doctoral dissertation, University of Wisconsin, Madison, Wis.

Friedman, P. H. 1977. Human and legal rights of mentally retarded persons. Int. J. Ment. Health 6(1):50–72.

Freudenberger, H. J., and Richelsen, G. 1980. Burnout: The High Cost of High Achievement. Anchor Press/Doubleday, New York.

Gadow, K. D. 1981. Prevalence of drug treatment for hyperactivity and other childhood behavior disorders. In: K. D. Gadow and J. Loney (eds.), Psychosocial Aspects of Drug Treatment for Hyperactivity. Westview Press, Boulder, CO.

Gadow, K. D., and Kalachnik, J. 1981. Prevalence and pattern of drug treatment for behavior and seizure disorders of TMR students. Am. J. Ment. Defic. 85(6):588–595.

Gann, M. L. 1966. The role of personality factors and job characteristics in burnout: A study of social service workers. Dissertation Abstracts International 40:3366.

Gann, M. L. 1979. The role of personality factors and job characteristics in burnout: A study of social service workers. Doctoral dissertation, University of California, Berkeley.

Gappert, G. 1979. Post Affluent America: The Social Economy of the Future. New Viewpoints, Division of Franklin Watts, New York.

Gardner, J. M. 1972. Teaching behavior modification to non-professionals. J. Appl. Behav. Anal. 5:517–521.

Gardner, W. I., and Cole, C. L. 1980. Behavioral Treatment of Aggression in the Mentally Retarded: What Happened to Behavioral Assessment? Rehabilitation Research and Training Center in Mental Retardation, Madison, Wis.

Gardner, W. I., and Cole, C. L. 1981a. Use of behavior therapy with the mentally retarded in community settings. In: F. Menolascino (ed.), Mental Retardation and Mental Health: Bridging the Gap. McGraw-Hill Book Co., New York.

Gardner, W. I., and Cole, C. L. 1981b. Meeting the mental health needs of the mentally retarded. Community Serv. Bull. 1(3):1–3.

Gartner, A. 1979. Career Ladders and a Training Model for the (Re)Training of Direct Service Workers in Community Based Programs for the DD. The Graduate School and University Center of City University of New York, Center for Advanced Study in Education (New Careers Training Lab), New York.

Gatty, B. 1981. Business finds profit in hiring the disabled. Nation's Business, 30(August): 30–35.

General Accounting Office. 1980. Better Reevaluations of Handicapped Persons in Sheltered Workshops Could Increase Their Opportunities for Competitive Employment. General Accounting Office, Washington, DC.

George, M. J., and Baumeister, A. A. 1981. Employee withdrawal and job satisfaction in community residential facilities for mentally retarded persons. Am. J. Ment. Defic. 85(6):639–647.

Gettings, R. M. 1977. Hidden impediments to deinstitutionalization. State Government 50:214–219.

Gibson, R. W., Lawrence, P. S., and Nelson, R. O. 1976. Comparison of three training procedures for teaching social responses to developmentally disabled adults. Am. J. Ment. Defic. 81:379–387.

Glaser, R. 1971. A criterion-referenced test. In: J. W. Popham (ed.), Criterion-Referenced Measurement. Educational Technology Publications, Englewood Cliffs, NJ.

Gleim, I. N. 1977. CPA Examination and Review. Convention Press, Jacksonville, FL.

Gold, M. W. 1973. Research on the vocational habilitation of the retarded: The present, the future. In: N. R. Ellis (ed.), International Review of Research in Mental Retardation, Vol. 6. Academic Press, Inc., New York.

Gold, M. W. 1976. Task analysis of a complex assembly task by the retarded blind. Except. Child. 43:78–84.

Goldsmith, J. B., and McFall, R. M. 1975. Development and evaluation of an interpersonal-skill training program for psychiatric inpatients. J. Abnorm. Psychol. 84:51–58.

Goldstein, A. 1978. Prescriptions for Child Mental Health and Education. Pergamon Press, New York.

Golin, A. K. and Ducanis, A. J. 1981. The Interdisciplinary Team: A Handbook for the Education of Exceptional Children. Aspen Systems Corp., Rockville, MD.

Gollay, E. 1981. Some conceptual and methodological issues in studying the community adjustment of deinstitutionalized mentally retarded people. In: R. H. Bruininks, C. E. Meyers, B. B. Sigford, and K. C. Lakin (eds.), Deinstitutionalization and Community Adjustment of Mentally Retarded Persons. Monograph No. 4. American Association on Mental Deficiency, Washington, DC.

Gollay, E., Freedman, R., Wyngaarden, M., and Kurtz, N. R. 1978. Coming Back: The Community Experience of Deinstitutionalized Mentally Retarded People. Abt Associates, Cambridge, MA.

Gottman, J. M., and Glass, G. V. 1978. Analysis of interrupted time-series experiment. In: T. R. Kratochovill (ed.), Single-Subject Research: Strategies for Evaluating Change. Academic Press, Inc., New York.

Gray, S. W., Klaus, R. A., and Ramsey, B. K. 1981. Participants in the Early Training Project: 1962–1977. In: M. J. Begab, H. C. Haywood, and H. L. Garber (eds.), Psychosocial Influences in Retarded Performance, Vol. 2. Strategies for Improving Competence. University Park Press, Baltimore.

Green, W. 1977a. Basic Skills and Activities Compendium. Teaching Resource Center, New York.

Green, W. 1977b. Paraprofessional Training Manual: An Inservice Approach for Training Staff Working with the Severely-to-Profoundly Handicapped. Teaching Resource Center, New York.

Greenberg, S. F., and Valletutti, P. J. 1979. Stress and the Helping Professions. Paul H. Brookes Publishing Co., Baltimore.

Greenwald, C. S. 1977. Group Power: Lobbying and Public Policy. Praeger Publishers, New York.

Greiner, L. E. 1967. Patterns of organization change. Harvard Bus. Rev. 62(3):119–128.

Gross, J., and Skopin, J. 1977. Deinstitutionalization Consortium Final Report. Ohio State University, Nisonger Center, Columbus, OH.

Grossman, H. J. (ed.). 1977. Manual on Terminology and Classification in Mental Retardation. American Association on Mental Deficiency (Special Publication No. 2), Washington, DC.

Grupe, F. H. 1974. Consortia and academic change. In: C. Dwyer and L. D. Patterson (eds.), Interinstitutional Interface: Making the Right Connection. American Association for Higher Education, Washington, DC.

Gustafson, D., Sheekla, R., Delbcrq, A., and Walster, W. 1973. A comparative study of differences or subjective likelihood estimates made by individuals, interacting groups, delphi groups, and nominal groups. Organiz. Behav. Human Perform. 9:280–291.

Gutride, M. E., Goldstein, A. P., and Hunter, G. F. 1973. The use of modeling and role playing to increase social interaction among asocial psychiatric patients. J. Consult. Clin. Psychol. 40:408–415.

Hale, G. 1979. The Sourcebook for the Disabled. Paddington Press, New York.

Hallworth, H. J., and Brebner, A. 1978. Computer assisted instruction and the mentally handicapped: Some recent developments. In: Proceedings of the 16th Annual Convention—Association for Educational Data Systems. Association for Educational Data Systems, Washington, DC.

Halpern, J., Sackett, K., Binner, P., and Mohr, C. 1980. The Myths of Deinstitutionalization: Policies for the Mentally Disabled. Westview Press, Boulder, CO.

Hamilton, J., and Segal, R. (eds.). 1975. Proceedings of the Conference on the Gerontological Aspects of Mental Retardation. University of Michigan, Ann Arbor.

Hampton, D. R., Summer, C. E., and Webber, R. A. 1973. Organizational Behavior and the Practice of Management. Scott, Foresman, & Company. Glenview, IL.

Hanley-Maxwell, C., and Heal, L. W. 1980. Legislative constraints and facilitations for community integration. In: A. R. Novak and L. W. Heal (eds.), Integration of Developmentally Disabled Individuals into the Community. Paul H. Brookes Publishing Co., Baltimore.

Hargreaves, W. A., and Attkisson, C. C. 1978. Evaluating program outcomes. In: C. C. Attkisson, W. A. Hargreaves, M. J. Horowitz, and J. E. Sorensen (eds.), Evaluation of Human Service Programs. Academic Press, Inc., New York.

Hargrett, N. 1981. Potential behavioral consequences of attributions of locus of control. J. Appl. Psychol. 82(1):63–68.
Harper, R. S. 1979. Resources for MR/DD programs in rural settings. In: R. L. Schalock (ed.), MR/DD Services in Rural America, It Is Time. Institute for Comprehensive Planning, Washington, DC.
Hart, E. 1978. How retarded children can be helped. In: Readings in Mental Retardation. Special Learning Corporation, Guilford, CT.
Hart, V. 1978. Beginning with the Handicapped. Charles C Thomas, Springfield, IL.
Hasenfeld, Y., and English, R. A. (eds.). 1974. Human Service Organizations: A Book of Readings. University of Michigan Press, Ann Arbor, MI.
Hawkins, C. 1978. Individual Program Plan: A Model System for Community Facilities. University of Iowa Division of Developmental Disabilities, Iowa City.
Haywood, H. C. 1977. Alternatives to normative assessment. In: P. Mittler (ed.), Research to Practice in Mental Retardation, Vol. 2. University Park Press, Baltimore.
Haywood, H. C. 1981. Reducing social vulnerability is the challenge of the eighties. Ment. Retard. 19(4):190–195.
Haywood, H. C., and Newbrough, J. R. 1981. Living Environments for Developmentally Retarded Persons. University Park Press, Baltimore.
Haywood, H. C., and Wachs, T. D. 1981. Intelligence, cognition and individual differences. In: M. J. Begab, H. C. Haywood, and H. L. Garver (eds.), Psychosocial Influences in Retarded Performance, Vol. 1. Issues and Theories in Development. University Park Press, Baltimore.
Heal, L. W., Novak, A. R., Sigelman, C. K., and Switzler, H. N. 1980. Characteristics of community residential facilities. In: A. R. Novak and L. W. Heal (eds.), Integration of Developmentally Disabled Individuals into the Community. Paul H. Brookes Publishing Co., Baltimore.
Heal, L. W., Sigelman, C. K., and Switzky, H. N. 1978. Research on community residential alternatives for the mentally retarded. In: N. R. Ellis (ed.), International Review of Research in Mental Retardation, Vol. 9. Academic Press, Inc., New York.
Heitman, R. J., and Justin, J. E. 1980. Locus of control and social reinforcement in the motor performance of educable mentally retarded students. Educ. Train. Ment. Ret. 12(3):204–208.
Henshel, A. 1972. The Forgotten Ones. A Sociological Study of Anglo and Chicano Retardates. University of Texas Press, Austin.
Herzberg, F., Mausner, B., and Snyderman, B. 1959. The Motivation to Work. 2nd Ed. John Wiley & Sons, Inc., New York.
Hickey, A. E. 1976. Computer-assisted and computer-managed instruction. In: R. L. Craig (ed.), Training and Development Handbook: A Guide to Human Resource Development. McGraw-Hill Book Company, New York.
Hirshoren, A., and Burton, T. A. 1979. Teaching academic skills to trainable mentally retarded children: A study in tautology. Ment. Retard. 17(4):177–179.
Hobbs, N. 1975. The Future of Children. Jossey-Bass, Inc., Pubs., San Francisco.
Hoffman, B. 1962. The Tyranny of Testing. Collier Books, New York.
Hopperton, R. 1975. Zoning for Community Homes: Handbook for Local Legislative Change. Law Reform Project, Ohio State University, Columbus, OH.
Horjesi, C. 1979. Service delivery in rural areas: Context, problems, and issues. In: R. Wiegerink and J. W. Pelosi (eds.), Developmental Disabilities: The DD Movement. Paul H. Brookes Publishing Co., Baltimore.
Horner, R. H., Wuerch, B. B., and Boomer, J. D. 1981. Performance of three severely

mentally retarded adults on vocational response chains during extinction. Am. J. Ment. Defic. 86(1):97–103.

Houts, P., and Scott, R. 1975. Goal Planning with Developmentally Disabled Persons. Pennsylvania State University College of Medicine, Hershey, PA.

Houts, P., and Scott, R. 1976. Goal Planning Strategies for Difficult Client Behaviors. Pennsylvania State University College of Medicine, Hershey, PA.

Hull, J. T., and Thompson, J. C. 1980. Predicting adaptive functioning of mentally retarded persons in community settings. Am. J. Ment. Defic. 85:253–261.

Humble, J. W. (ed.). 1970. Management by Objectives in Action. McGraw-Hill Book Co., New York.

Janicki, M. P. 1981. Personal growth and community readiness environments. In: H. C. Haywood and J. R. Newbrough (eds.), Living Environments for Developmentally Retarded Persons. University Park Press, Baltimore.

Jenkins, P. 1977. Guide to Accounting for Nonprofits. The Grantsmanship Center, Los Angeles.

Jenkins, S., Stephens, B., and Sternberg, L. 1980. The use of parents as parent trainers of handicapped children. Educ. Train. Ment. Retard. 15(4):256–263.

Johnson, R. B., and Magrab, P. R. 1976. Developmental Disorders: Assessment, Treatment, and Education. University Park Press, Baltimore.

Joint Commission on Accreditation of Hospitals. 1979. Principles for Accreditation of Community Mental Health Service Programs. Joint Commission on Accreditation of Hospitals, Chicago.

Jones, K. J., and Jones, P. P. 1976a. The Measurement of Community Placement Success and Its Associated Costs. Interim Report 2. Florence Heller School for Advanced Studies in Social Welfare, Brandeis University, Medford, MA.

Jones, P. P., and Jones, K. J. 1976b. Costs of Ideal Services to the Developmentally Disabled Under Varying Levels of Adequacy. Interim Report Number 4. (HEW Contract OS-74-278). Florence Heller School for Advanced Studies in Social Welfare, Brandeis University, Medford, MA.

Justice, R. S., Bradley, J., and O'Connor, G. 1971. Foster family care for the retarded: Management concerns for the caretaker. Ment. Retard. 9(4):12–15.

Justice, R. S., and Close, D. W. 1980. Community resources: Their utilization. Paper presented at American Academy on Mental Retardation, May, 1980, San Francisco.

JWK International Corporation. 1980. Wage Earnings of Handicapped Individuals in Sheltered Employment. JWK International Corporation, Annandale, VA.

Kamhi, A. G. 1981. Developmental vs. difference theories of mental retardation: A new look. Am. J. Ment. Defic. 86(1):1–7.

Karan, O. C. 1976. Contemporary views on vocational evaluation practices with the mentally retarded. In: O. C. Karan, P. Wehman, A. Renzaglia, and R. Schutz (eds.), Habilitation Practices with the Severely Developmentally Disabled, Vol. 1. University of Wisconsin, Madison, WI.

Karan, O. C. 1981. From the classroom into the community. In: K. P. Lynch, W. E. Kiernan, and J. A. Stark (eds.), Prevocational and Vocational Education for Special Needs Youth. Paul H. Brookes Publishing Co., Baltimore.

Karan, O. C., and Schalock, R. L. 1983. An ecological approach to assessing vocational and community living skills. In: C. O'Connell-Mason (ed.), Vocational Habilitation. Charles E. Merrill Publishing Co., Columbus, OH.

Kastner, L. S., Reppucci, N. D., and Pezzoli, J. J. 1979. Assessing community attitudes toward mentally retarded persons. Am. J. Ment. Defic. 84(2):137–144.

Katz, S., and Yekutiel, E. 1974. Leisure time problems of mentally retarded graduates of training programs. Ment. Retard. 12(3):54–57.

Kaufman, K. R., and Katz-Garris, L. 1979. Epilepsy, mental retardation, and anticonvulsant therapy. Am. J. Ment. Defic. 84:256–259.

Kazdin, A. E. 1975. Covert modeling, imagery assessment, and assertive behavior. J. Consult. Clin. Psychol. 43:716–724.

Keith, K. D. 1979. Computer assisted dental simulations. Paper presented at annual convention of the Association for the Development of Computer-Based Instructional Systems, February, San Diego, CA.

Keith, K. D., Lipson, L. F., and Jones, G. L. 1980. Dimensions of a scoring system for evaluation of clinical simulations. Paper presented at the Annual Conference for the Association for the Development of Computer-Based Instructional Systems, April, Washington, DC.

Kimble, G., Garmezy, N., and Zigler, E. 1980. Principles of General Psychology. John Wiley & Sons, Inc., New York.

Kiresuk, T. J. 1973. Goal attainment scaling at a county mental health service. Evaluation. Monograph No. 1:15–30.

Kiresuk, T. J. 1979. The role of evaluation in managing human service programs. In: P. Sanofsky (ed.), Evaluating Program Effectiveness: The Administrator's Dilemma. SPS Communications, Watertown, MA.

Kiresuk, T. J., and Sherman, R. E. 1968. Goal attainment scaling: A general method for evaluating comprehensive community mental health programs. Community Ment. Health J. 4:443–453.

Kittrie, N. 1971. The Right to Be Different. Deviance and Enforced Therapy. The Johns Hopkins University Press, Baltimore.

Kolstoe, O. P. 1961. An examination of some characteristics which discriminate between employed and nonemployed retarded males. Am. J. Ment. Defic. 66:472–482.

Kolstoe, O. P. 1972. Mental Retardation, an Educational Viewpoint. Holt, Rinehart & Winston, New York.

Kraus, R. 1978. Therapeutic Recreation Service: Principles and Practices. W. B. Saunders Company, Philadelphia.

Kugel, R., and Shearer, A., 1976. Changing Patterns in Residential Services for the Mentally Retarded. President's Committee on Mental Retardation, Washington, DC.

Kurtz, R. A. 1975. Advocacy for the mentally retarded: The development of a new social role. In: M. J. Begab and S. A. Richardson (eds.), The Mentally Retarded and Society: A Social Science Perspective. University Park Press, Baltimore.

Lackey, L. D., and Burke, B. J. 1980. Training program for residential staff of community living arrangements. Paper presented at the annual meeting of the American Association on Mental Deficiency, May 11–16, San Francisco.

Lambert, M. M., and Nicoll, R. E. 1976. Dimensions of adaptive behavior of retarded and non-retarded public school children. Am. J. Ment. Defic. 81(2):135–146.

Landesman-Dwyer, S., Berkson, G., and Romer, D. 1979. Affiliation and friendship of mentally retarded residents in group homes. Am. J. Ment. Defic. 83:571–580.

Landesman-Dwyer, S., Sackett, G. P., and Kleinman, J. S. 1980. Relationships of size to resident and staff behavior in small community residences. Am. J. Ment. Defic. 85(1):6–17.

Landesman-Dwyer, S., Stein, J. G., and Sackett, G. P. 1978. A behavioral and ecological study of group homes. In: G. P. Sackett (ed.), Observing Behavior, Vol. 1. Theory and Applications in Mental Retardation. University Park Press, Baltimore.

Lane, M. J. 1980. Handbook for Nonprofit Organizations. AMACOM, New York.

Larsen, L. A. 1977. Community services necessary to program effectively for the severely/profoundly handicapped. In: E. Sontag, J. Smith, and N. Certo (eds.), Educational Programming for the Severely and Profoundly Handicapped. The Council for Exceptional Children, Division on Mental Retardation, Reston, VA.

Laski, F. J. 1977. Legal strategies to secure entitlement to services for severely handicapped persons. In: G. T. Bellamy, G. O'Connor, and O. C. Karan (eds.), Vocational Rehabilitation of Severely Handicapped Persons: Contemporary Service Strategies. University Park Press, Baltimore.

Laski, F. J., and Spitalnik, D. M. 1980. A review of Pennhurst implementation. Community Serv. Forum 1(1):1–8.

Lauber, D., and Bangs, F. S. 1974. Zoning for Family and Group Care Facilities: Planning Advisory Service Report No. 300. American Society of Planning Officials, Chicago.

Lawler, E. E. 1973. Motivation in Work Organizations. Brooks Cole, Monterey, CA.

Lawler, E. E., and Lyman, W. P. 1967. The effect of performance on job satisfaction. Indust. Rel. 7:20–28.

Lawler, E. E., and Rhode, J. G. 1976. Information and Control in Organizations. Goodyear, Santa Monica, CA.

Lawrence, P. R., and Lorch, J. W. 1962. Organization and environment. Harvard Business School, Division of Research, Cambridge, MA.

Lawrence, P. R., and Lorch, J. W. 1969. Developing Organizations: Diagnosis and Action. Addison-Wesley Publishing Co., Reading, MA.

Lazar, I., Snipper, A. S., Royce, J., and Darlington, R. B. 1981. Policy implications for preschool intervention research. In: M. J. Begab, H. C. Haywood, and H. L. Garber (eds.), Psychosocial Influences in Retarded Performance, Vol. 1. Issues and Theories in Development. University Park Press, Baltimore.

Leavitt, H. 1972. Managerial Psychology. 3rd Ed. University of Chicago Press, Chicago.

Leavitt, H., Pinfield, L., and Webb, E. 1974. Organizations of the Future: Interaction with the External Environment. Praeger Publishers, New York.

Leggett, J., and Archer, R. 1979. Locus of control and depression among psychiatric inpatients. Psychol. Rep., December:835–838.

Levin, H. M. 1975. Cost-effectiveness analysis in evaluation research. In: M. Guttentag and E. L. Struening (eds.), Handbook of Evaluation Research, Vol. 2. Sage Publications, Beverly Hills, CA.

LeVine, S., and Zubrack, F. 1975. Five models of inservice programs. In: H. Stone and J. Hunzeker (eds.), Education for Foster Family Care: Models and Methods for Foster Parents and Social Workers. Child Welfare League of America, New York.

Levinson, H. 1970. Management by whose objective? Harvard Bus. Rev. 48:128–129.

Levitt, E. E. 1963. Psychotherapy with children: A further evaluation. Behav. Res. and Ther. 1:45–51.

Linstone, H. A. 1980. The postindustrial society and mental retardation. In: S. Plog and M. Santamour (eds.), The Year 2000 and Mental Retardation. Plenum Publishing Corp., New York.

Linvill, W. K. 1980. The impact of technological advances on the lives of mentally retarded persons in the year 2000. In: S. Plog and M. Santamour (eds.), The Year 2000 and Mental Retardation. Plenum Publishing Corp., New York.

Lippman, L. 1979. Independent Living for Disabled Persons. Public Affairs Pamphlets, #504, #522, #540, #557, Center for Independent Living, New York.

Lira, E. T., Nay, R., McCullough, J. P., and Etkin, M. W. 1975. Relative effects of modeling and role playing in the treatment of avoidance behaviors. J. Consult. Clin. Psychol 43:608–618.

Lombardo, V. 1980. Paraprofessionals in special education. Charles C Thomas, Springfield, IL.

Lord, F. M. 1963. Elementary models for measuring change. In: C. W. Harris (ed.), Problems in Measuring Change. University of Wisconsin Press, Madison, WI.

Luborsky, L., and Backrach, H. M. 1974. Factors influencing clinicians' judgments of mental health: Experiences with the health-sickness rating scale. Arch. Gen. Psych. 31:292–299.

Luckey, R. E., and Newman, R. S. 1975. President's Panel recommendations today. Ment. Retard. 13(4):32–35.

Lund, S., and Kiresuk, T. J. 1979. Individualized goal attainment as a method of program evaluation in mental health. In: E. J. Posavac (ed.), Impacts of Program Evaluation on Mental Health Care. Westview Press, Boulder, CO.

Lynch, K. P., Kiernan, W. E., and Stark, J. A. 1981. Sociological, educational and behavioral/biomedical advances and their future implications for special needs youth. In: K. P. Lynch, W. E. Kiernan, and J. A. Stark (eds.), Prevocational and Vocational Education for Special Needs Youth. Paul H. Brookes Publishing Co., Baltimore.

McCarver, R. B., and Craig, E. M. 1974. Placement of the retarded in the community: Prognosis and outcome. In: N. R. Ellis (ed.), International Review of Research in Mental Retardation, Vol. 7. Academic Press, Inc., New York.

McClelland, D. C. 1973. Testing for competence rather than for intelligence. Am. Psychol. 28:1–14.

McClure, R. F. 1968. Reinforcement of verbal social behavior in moderately retarded children. Psychol. Rep. 23:371–376.

McCormick, E. J. 1979. Job Analysis: Methods and Applications. AMACOM, New York.

McCray, P. 1980. Suggested Guidelines for Evaluating Work Samples. Stout Vocational Rehabilitation Institute, University of Wisconsin, Menomonie, WI.

McDevitt, S. C., Smith, P. M., Schmidt, D. W., and Rosen, M. 1978. The deinstitutionalized citizen: Adjustment and quality of life. Ment. Retard. 16(1):22–24.

MacDonald, M. L., Linquist, C. U., Kramer, J. A., McGrath, R. A., and Rhyne, L. D. 1975. Social skills training: Behavioral rehearsal in groups and dating skills. J. Counsel. Psychol. 22:224–230.

McFall, R. M., and Marston, A. R. 1970. An experimental investigation of behavior rehearsal in assertive training. J. Abnorm. Psychol. 76:295–303.

McGregor, D. 1957. An uneasy look at performance appraisal. Harvard Bus. Rev. 35:89–95.

McGregor, D. 1960. The Human Side of Enterprise. McGraw-Hill Book Co., New York.

McGuire, C., Solomon, L. M., and Bashook, P. G. 1976. Construction and Use of Written Simulations. The Psychological Corp., New York.

McHale, J. 1980. Mental retardation and the future: A conceptual approach. In: S. Plog and M. Santamour (eds.), The Year 2000 and Mental Retardation. Plenum Publishing Corp., New York.

McInerney, M., and Karan, O. C. 1981. Federal legislation and the integration of special education and vocational rehabilitation. Ment. Retard. 19(1)21–23.

McIntire, J. 1954. Causes of turnover in personnel. Am. J. Ment. Defic. 58(3):2–12.

McLain, R. E., Silverstein, A. B., Brownlee, L., and Hubbell, M. 1979. Attitudinal versus ecological approaches to the characterization of institutional treatment environments. Am. J. Community Psychol. 7:159–165.

McMahan, R. S. 1979. An economist looks at the business of rehabilitation. J. Rehabil. Admin. 3(4):161–169.

Mager, R. F. 1962. Preparing Instructional Objectives. Fearon Publishing Comp., Belmont, CA.

Magrab, P. R., and Elder, J. O. (eds.). 1979. Planning for Services to Handicapped Persons: Community, Education, Health. Paul H. Brookes Publishing Co., Baltimore.

Mahoney, M. J. 1978. Experimental methods and outcome evaluation. J. Consult. Clin. Psychol. 46(4):600–672.

Makower, J. 1981. Computers '81: Planning your next system. Eastern Airlines Rev. May:93–95.

Malick, K. 1979. Job accommodation through job restructuring and environment modification. In: D. Vandergoat and J. Worrell (eds.), Placement in Rehabilitation. University Park Press, Baltimore.

Mamula, R. A., and Newman, N. 1973. Training programs for care providers. In: R. A. Mamula, and N. Newman (eds.), Community Placement of the Mentally Retarded: A Handbook for Community Agencies and Social Work Practitioners. Charles C Thomas, Springfield, IL.

Marks, H. E., and Wade, R. 1981. A device for reducing object destruction among institutionalized mentally retarded persons. Ment. Retard 19(4):181–182.

Mars, L. 1978. Caseload activity in state vocational rehabilitation agencies. Am. Rehabil. 9:23–31.

Martuza, V. R. 1977. Applying Norm-Referenced and Criterion-Referenced Measurement in Education. Allyn and Bacon, Boston.

Maslow, A. H. 1962. Toward a Psychology of Being. Van Nostrand Reinhold Company, Newark.

Maslow, A. H. 1970. Motivation and Personality. 2nd Ed. Harper & Brothers, New York.

Mason, S. E. 1979. Multihospital Arrangements: Public Policy Implications. American Hospital Association, Chicago.

Matson, J. L. 1979. Decreasing inappropriate verbalizations of a moderately retarded adult by a staff assisted self-control program. Aust. J. Mentl. Retard. 5:242–245.

Matson, J. L., and Adkins, J. 1980. A self-instructional social skills training program for mentally retarded persons. Ment. Retard. 18(5):245–248.

Matson, J. L., and Stephens, R. M. 1978. Increasing appropriate behavior of explosive chronic psychiatric patients with a social skills training package. Behav. Modif. 2:61–65.

Matson, J. L., and Zeiss, R. A. 1978. Group training of social skills in chronically explosive severely disturbed psychiatric patients. Behav. Engin. 5:41–50.

Matson, J. L., and Zeiss, R. A. 1979. The buddy system: A method of generalized reduction of inappropriate interpersonal behavior of retarded psychotic patients. Br. J. Soc. Clin. Psychol. 18:401–405.

Mayeda, T. 1979. The use of client data in program planning and analysis. In: P. Sanofsky (ed.), Evaluating Program Effectiveness: The Administrators Dilemma. SPS Communications, Inc., Watertown, MA.

Mayeda, T., and Lindberg, G. 1980. Performance Measures of Skill and Adaptive Competencies. Lanterman State Hospital and Developmental Center, Pomona, CA.

Mechner, F. 1965. Science education and behavioral technology. In: R. Glaser (ed.), Teaching Machines and Programmed Learning, Vol. 2. National Education Association, Washington, DC.

Meers, G. D. (ed.), 1980. Handbook of Special Vocational Needs Education. Aspen Systems Corporation, Rockville, MD.

Menolascino, F. J. 1977. Challenges in Mental Retardation: Progressive Ideology and Services. Human Sciences Press, New York.

Menolascino, F. J. 1983. Mental Retardation and Mental Health: Bridging the Gap. University Park Press, Baltimore.

Menolascino, F. J., Schalock, R. L., and Harper, R. S. 1980. Regionalization and the 1980s. Community Serv. Forum, 1(2):1–5.

Mercer, C. D., and Snell, M. E. 1977. Learning Theory Research in Mental Retardation: Implications for Teaching. Charles E. Merrill Publishing Co., Columbus, OH.

Meredith, R. L., Saxon, S., Doleys, D. M., and Kyzer, B. 1979. Social skills training with mildly retarded young adults. J. Clin. Psychol. 35:396–402.

Metcalf, R. W., and Titard, P. L. 1976. Principles of Accounting. W. B. Saunders Co., Philadelphia.

Meyer, J. 1980. An exploratory nationwide survey of child care workers. Child Care Q. 9:17–25.

Meyers, C. E., Nihira, K., and Zetlin, A. 1979. The measurement of adaptive behavior. In: N. R. Ellis (ed.), Handbook of Mental Deficiency: Psychological Theory and Research. Erlbaum, Hillsdale, NJ.

Meyer's Children's Rehabilitation Institute. 1980. Value Based Training (Value-Based Skills Training Curriculum for Community-Based Mental Retardation Programs). Meyer's Children's Rehabilitation Institute, University of Nebraska Medical Center, Omaha, NE.

Miller, R. V. 1959. Merit rating in industry: A survey of current practices and problems. ICR Res. 5:14–25.

Mintzberg, H. 1973. The Nature of Managerial Work. Harper & Row, New York.

Mithaug, D. E., and Hagmeier, L. D. 1978. The development of procedures to assess prevocational competencies for severely handicapped young adults. AAESPH Rev. 3:94–114.

Moise, L. 1980. As We Grew with Barbara. Dillon Press, Inc., Minneapolis, MN.

Moos, R. H. 1974a. Evaluating Treatment Environments: A Social-Ecological Approach. John Wiley & Sons, New York.

Moos, R. H. 1974b. The Social Climate Scales: An Overview. Consulting Psychologists Press, Palo Alto, CA.

Mori, A. A. and Masters, L. F. 1980. Teaching the Severely Mentally Retarded: Adaptive Skills Training. Aspen Systems Corp., Rockville, MD.

Morrison, J. H. 1976. Determining training needs. In: R. L. Craig (ed.), Training and Development Handbook: A Guide to Human Resource Development. McGraw-Hill Book Co., New York.

Morrissey, P. A. 1981. Training the hard-to-train: The politics of the next decade. In: K. P. Lynch, W. E. Kiernan, and J. A. Stark (eds.), Prevocational and Vocational Education for Special Needs Youth: A Blueprint for the 80's. Paul H. Brookes Publishing Co., Baltimore.

Murphy, G. 1975. Foster Care of the Developmentally Disabled: A Basic Course for Foster Parents and Foster Care Workers. Boston University School of Social Work, Boston.

Nadler, D. A. 1977. Feedback and Organizational Development: Using Data Based Methods. Addison-Wesley Publishing Co., Reading, MA.

Nanus, B. 1980. Living and working in the year 2000. In: S. Plog and M. Santamour (eds.), The Year 2000 and Mental Retardation. Plenum Publishing Corp., New York.

National Institute on Mental Retardation. April, 1971. A National MR Manpower Model:

A Comprehensive Planning and Organization Programme for Training Personnel in the Field of MR. National Institute on Mental Retardation, Toronto, Canada.

Nelsen, W. C. 1972. Entrepreneurship and innovation in consortia. J. Higher Educ. 43:544–551.

Nelson, R. O., Gibson, F., and Cutting, D.S. 1973. Videotaped modeling: The development of three appropriate social responses in a mildly retarded child. Ment. Retard. 11(6):24–28.

Newbrough, J. R. 1977. Liaison services in the community context. J. Community Psychol. 5:24–27.

Newman, H. G., and Doby, J. T. 1973. Correlates of social competence among trainable mentally retarded children. Am. J. Ment. Defic. 77:722–732.

Nihira, K., Foster, R., Shellhaas, M., and Leland, H. 1975. Adaptive Behavior Scales Manual. American Association on Mental Deficiency, Washington, DC.

Nihira, L., and Nihira, K. 1975. Jeopardy in community placement. Am. J. Ment. Defic. 79:538–544.

Nirje, B. 1969. The normalization principle and its human management implications. In: R. Kugel and W. Wolfensberger (eds.), Changing Patterns in Residential Services for the Mentally Retarded. President's Committee on Mental Retardation, Washington, DC.

Noble, J. H. 1977. The limits of cost-benefit analysis as a guide to priority-setting in rehabilitation. Evaluation Q. 1:347–480.

Novak, A. R., and Heal, L. W. 1980. Integration of Developmentally Disabled Individuals into the Community. Paul H. Brookes Publishing Co., Baltimore.

Nunnally, J. C., and Durham, R. 1975. Validity, reliability and special problems in evaluation research. In: E. L. Struening and M. Guttentag (eds.) Handbook of Evaluation Research Vol. 1. Sage Publications, Beverly Hills, CA.

Oberg, W. 1972. Make performance appraisal relevant. Harvard Bus. Rev. 50:61–67.

O'Brien, F., and Azrin, N. H. 1972. Developing proper mealtime behaviors of the institutionalized retarded. J. Appl. Behav. Anal. 5:389–399.

O'Connor, G. 1976. Home Is a Good Place: A National Perspective of Community Residential Facilities for Developmentally Disabled Persons: Monograph No. 2. American Association on Mental Deficiency, Washington, DC.

O'Leary, K. D., and Kent, R. N. 1973. Behavior modification for social action: Research tactics and problems. In: C. L. Hamerlynck et al. (eds.), Critical Issues in Research and Practice. Research Press, Champaign, IL.

O'Leary, K. D., and Wilson, G. T. 1975. Behavior Therapy: Application and Outcome. Prentice Hall, Inc., Englewood Cliffs, NJ.

Ordiorne, G. S. 1965. Management Decisions by Objectives. Prentice-Hall, Inc., Englewood Cliffs, NJ.

Ordiorne, G. S. 1976. Management by objectives. In: R. L. Craig (ed.), Training and Development Handbook: A Guide to Human Resource Development. McGraw-Hill Book Co., New York.

O'Toole, R. 1972. The Cleveland Rehabilitation Complex: A Study of Interagency Coordination. Vocational Guidance & Rehabilitation Services, Cleveland, OH.

Ouchi, W. 1981. Theory Z: How American Business Can Meet the Japanese Challenge. Addison-Wesley, Reading, MA.

Page, T. J., Christian, J. B., Iwata, B. A., Reid, D. H., Crow, R. E., and Dorsey, M. F. 1981. Evaluating and training interdisciplinary teams in writing IPP goals and objectives. Ment. Retard. 19(1):12–19.

Palmer, F. H., and Anderson, L. W. 1981. Early intervention treatments that have been tried, documented and assessed. In: M. J. Begab, H. C. Haywood, and H. L. Garber (eds.), Psychosocial Influences in Retarded Performance. Vol. 2. Strategies for Improving Competence. University Park Press, Baltimore.

Panyan, M. C., and Patterson, E. T. 1974. Teaching attendants the applied aspects of behavior modification. Ment. Retard. 12:30–32.

Park, L. D. 1975. Barriers to normality for the handicapped adult in the United States. Rehabil. Lit. 36:4–10.

Parry, S. B., and Ribbing, J. R. 1976. Using outside training consultants. In: R. L. Craig (ed.), Training and Development Handbook: A Guide to Human Resource Development. McGraw-Hill Book Co., New York.

Perlman, L. G. (ed.). 1975. Legal Barriers and Stigma as it Affects Employment of Persons with Epilepsy. U.S. Department of Education Rehabilitation Services Conference, Washington, DC.

Perrow, C. 1970. Members as resources in voluntary organizations. In: W.R. Rosengren, and M. Lefton (eds.), Organizations and Clients: Essays in the Sociology of Service. Charles E. Merrill Publishing Co., Columbus, OH.

Peters, T. J. 1978. Symbols, patterns and settings: An optimistic case for getting things done. Organiz. Dynam. 7(2):34–47.

Peterson, R. O., and Duffany, B. H. 1976. Job enrichment and job design. In: R. L. Craig (ed.), Training and Development Handbook: A Guide to Human Resource Development. McGraw-Hill Book Co., New York.

Phelps, L. A. 1975. Instructional Development for Special Needs Learners: An Inservice Resource Guide. University of Illinois Press, Urbana, IL.

Pines, A., and Maslack, C. 1978. Characteristics of staff burnout in mental health settings. Hosp. Community Psychiatry 29(4):12–20.

Plog, S. 1980. The year 2000 and mental retardation: An interpretation and critique. In: S. Plog and M. Santamour (eds.), The Year 2000 and Mental Retardation. Plenum Publishing Corp., New York.

Plog, S., and Santamour, M. (eds.). 1980. The Year 2000 and Mental Retardation. Plenum Publishing Corp., New York.

Pomerantz, D. J., Barclay, C. R., Gleckel, W. L., Windell, I., and Reiter, G. K. 1981. Training a self-monitoring skill to mentally retarded children at the primary educational level: Initial results and curricular implications. In: P. Mittler (ed.), Frontiers of Knowledge in Mental Retardation, Vol. 1. University Park Press, Baltimore.

Pomerantz, D. J., and Marholin, D. 1977. Vocational habilitation: A time for change. In: E. Sontag (ed.), Educational Programming for the Severely and Profoundly Handicapped. The Council for Exceptional Children, Reston, VA.

Popovich, D. 1981. Effective Educational and Behavioral Programming for Severely and Profoundly Handicapped Students: A Manual for Teachers and Aides. Paul H. Brookes Publishing Company, Baltimore.

Popovich, D., and Laham, S. L. 1982. The Adaptive Behavior Curriculum, Vols. 1 and 2. Paul H. Brookes Publishing Company, Baltimore.

Posavac, E. J., and Carey, R. G. 1980. Program Evaluation: Methods and Case Studies. Prentice-Hall, Inc., Englewood Cliffs, NJ.

President's Committee on Employment of the Handicapped. September, 1977. Pathways to Employment. President's Committee on Employment of the Handicapped, Washington, DC.

President's Committee on Mental Retardation. 1976. A Plan for Deinstitutionalization of Mentally Retarded Persons. President's Committee on Mental Retardation. Washington, DC.

Price, R. H. 1979. The social ecology of treatment gains. In: A. Goldstein and F. Kanfer (eds.), Maximizing Treatment Gains. Academic Press, Inc., New York.

Provencal, G., and Evans, D. 1977. Resident Manager Education: A Curriculum Model for Educating Foster Parents and Group Home Personnel. Macomb-Oakland Regional Center, Mt. Clemens, MI.

Rappaport, J. 1977. Community Psychology: Values, Research and Action. Holt, Rinehart & Winston, Inc., New York.

Reilly, R. 1976. Life Manager Training Programs. John F. Kennedy Institute, Baltimore.

Reiter, S., and Levi, A. M. 1980. Factors affecting social integration of non-institutionalized mentally retarded adults. Am. J. Ment. Defic. 85:25–30.

Reynolds, M. 1975. Trends in special education: Implications for measurement. In: M. Reynolds and W. Hively (eds.), Domain-Referenced Testing in Special Education. University of Minnesota Leadership Training Institute/Special Education, Minneapolis, MN.

Richardson, S. A. 1978. Careers of mentally retarded young persons: Services, jobs, and interpersonal relations. Am. J. Ment. Defic. 82:349–358.

Richardson, S. A. 1981. Living environments: An ecological perspective. In: H. C. Haywood and J. R. Newbrough (eds.), Living Environments for Developmentally Retarded Persons. University Park Press, Baltimore.

Rimm, D., and Masters, J. 1979. Behavior Therapy. Academic Press, Inc., New York.

Risley, T. R., and Wolf, M. M. 1967. Establishing functional speech in echolalic children. Behavior Res. Ther. 5:73–88.

Rivett, P. 1968. An Introduction to Operating Research. Basic Books. New York.

Rivinus, T. M. 1980. Psychopharmacology and the mentally retarded patient. In: L. S. Szymanski and P. E. Tanguay (eds.), Emotional Disorders of Mentally Retarded Persons. University Park Press, Baltimore.

Roberts, E. V. 1977. Forward. In: S. Stoddard Pfleuger (ed.), Independent Living: Emerging Issues in Rehabilitation. Institute for Research Utilization, Washington, DC.

Robinson, N. M., and Robinson, H. B. 1976. The Mentally Retarded Child: A Psychological Approach. 2nd Ed. McGraw-Hill Book Co., New York.

Rockart, J. F. 1979. Chief executives define their own data needs. Harvard Bus. Rev. 79(3):81–93.

Roeber, R. J. C. 1973. The Organization in a Changing Environment. Addison-Wesley Publishing Co., Reading, MA.

Romer, D., and Berkson, G. 1980a. Social ecology of supervised communal facilities for mentally disabled adults: II. Predictors of affiliation. Am. J. Ment. Defic. 85:229–242.

Romer, D., and Berkson, G. 1980b. Social ecology of supervised communal facilities for mentally disabled adults: III. Predictors of social choice. Am. J. Ment. Defic. 85:243–252.

Roos, P., McCann, B., and Addison, M. (eds.). 1980. Shaping the Future: Community-Based Residential Services and Facilities for Mentally Retarded People. University Park Press, Baltimore.

Rosen, M., Clark, G. R., and Kivitz, M. S. 1977. Habilitation of the Handicapped. University Park Press, Baltimore.

Ross, E. C. 1980. Developing public policy for persons with disabilities: The case for a categorical approach. Ment. Retard. 18(4):159–163.

Ross, R. T., Boroskin, A., and Giampiccolo, Jr., J. S. 1974. Fairview Behavior Evaluation Battery for the Mentally Retarded. Fairview State Hospital, Research Department, Costa Mesa, CA.

Ross, D. M., Ross, S. A., and Evans, T. A. 1971. The modification of extreme social withdrawal by modeling with guided participation. J. Behav. Ther. Exp. Psych. 2:273–279.

Rossi, P. 1979. Evaluation: A Systematic Approach. Sage Publications, Beverly Hills, CA.

Rossi, P. H., and Wright, S. R. 1977. Evaluation resource: An assessment of theory, practice, and politics. Evaluation Q. 1:5–52.

Rotatori, A., Switzky, H. N., and Fox, R. 1981. Behavioral weight reduction procedures for obese mentally retarded individuals: A review. Ment. Retard. 19(4):157–161.

Rothenberg, J. 1975. Cost-benefit analysis: A methodological exposition. In: M. Guttenberg and E. L. Struenings (eds.), Handbook of Evaluation Research, Vol. 2. Sage Publications, Beverly Hills, CA.

Rotter, J. B. 1975. Some problems and misconceptions related to the construct of internal control of reinforcement. J. Consult. Clin. Psychol. 43:56–67.

Rowitz, L. 1979. The importance of client/program impact measures in evaluation design. In: P. Sanofsky (ed.), Evaluating Program Effectiveness: The Administrator's Dilemma. SPS Communications, Inc., Watertown, MA.

Rusch, F. R., and Mithaug, D. E. 1980. Vocational Training for Mentally Retarded Adults. Research Press, Champaign, IL.

Rutter, L. 1981. Strategies for the essential community: Local government in the year 2000. Futurist 5(4):19–28.

Ryan, K. R. 1979. Establishing an effective human service agency cost accounting system. In: R. L. Schalock (ed.), MR/DD Services in Rural America. . . It is Time. Institute for Comprehensive Planning, Washington, DC.

Sali, J., and Amir, M. 1971. Personal factors influencing the retarded person's success at work: A report from Israel. Am. J. Ment. Defic. 76:42–47.

Salzberg, C. L., and Langford, C. A. 1981. Community integration of mentally retarded adults through leisure activity. Ment. Retard. 19(3):127–131.

Sarason, S. B. 1972. The Creation of Settings and the Future Societies. Jossey-Bass, Inc., Pubs., San Francisco.

Sarata, B. P. V. 1975. Employee satisfactions in agencies serving retarded persons. Am. J. Ment. Defic. 79:435–442.

Sarata, B. P. V., and Jeppesen, J. C. 1977. Job design and staff satisfaction in human service settings. Am. J. Community Psychol. 5:229–236.

Savino, M., Sterns, P., Merwin, E., and Kennedy, R. 1973. The lack of services to the retarded through community mental health programs. Community Ment. Health J. 9:158–168.

Schalock, R. L. 1981. What do you do with them after they are educated? The need to interface school and community based programs. In: K. P. Lynch, W. E. Kiernan, and J. A. Stark (eds.). Prevocational and Vocational Education for Special Needs Youth: A Blueprint for the 80's. Paul H. Brookes Publishing Co., Baltimore.

Schalock, R. L., and Drake, H. 1980. Vocational rehabilitation and the significantly handicapped: The Mid-Nebraska Model. In: P. Wehman (ed.), Competitive Employment. Paul H. Brookes Publishing Co., Baltimore.

Schalock, R. L., and Gadwood, L. S. 1979. Program Handbook. Mid-Nebraska Mental Retardation Services, Hastings, NB.

Schalock, R. L., and Gadwood, L. S. 1980. Community Living Skills Screening Test: Remediation and Standardization Manuals. Mid-Nebraska Mental Retardation Services, Hastings, NB.

Schalock, R. L., Gadwood, L. S., and Brown, P. S. 1983. Effects of different training environments on acquisition of community living skills. Appl. Res. Ment. Retard.

Schalock, R. L., and Harper, R. S. 1978. Placement from community-based mental retardation programs: How well do clients do? Am. J. Ment. Defic. 83:240–247.

Schalock, R. L., and Harper, R. S. 1979a. Kittens and cats in rural America. Paper presented at the Convention of the American Association on Mental Deficiency, May 29, Miami Beach, FL.

Schalock, R. L., and Harper, R. S. 1979b. Training in independent living can be done. J. Rehabil. Admin. 3(3):128–132.

Schalock, R. L., and Harper, R. S. 1981a. A systems approach to community living skills training. In: R. H. Bruininks, C. E. Meyers, B. B. Sigford, and K. C. Lakin (eds.), Deinstitutionalization and Community Adjustment of Mentally Retarded People. Monograph No 4. American Association on Mental Deficiency, Washington, DC.

Schalock, R. L., and Harper, R. S. 1981b. Independent living and the disabled: A systematic approach to independent living training. In: P. Mittler (ed.), Frontiers of Knowledge in Mental Retardation, Vol. 1: Social, Educational and Behavioral Aspects. University Park Press, Baltimore.

Schalock, R. L., and Harper, R. S. 1982. Skill acquisition and client movement indices: Implementing cost-effectiveness analysis in rehabilitation programs. Evaluation Prog. Plan. 5:223–231.

Schalock, R. L., and Harper, R. S. 1983. Untying some Gordian knots in program evaluation. J. Rehabil. Admin. 7(1):12–20.

Schalock, R. L., Harper, R. S., and Carver, G. 1981. Independent living placement: Five years later. Am. J. Ment. Defic. 86(2):170–177.

Schalock, R. L., Harper, R. S., and Genung, T. 1981. Community integration of mentally retarded adults: Community placement and program success. Am. J. Ment. Defic. 85(5):478–488.

Schalock, R. L., and Karan, O. C. 1979. Relevant assessment: The interaction between evaluation and training. In: T. G. Bellamy, G. O'Connor, and O. C. Karan (eds.), Vocational Rehabilitation of Severely Handicapped Persons. University Park Press, Baltimore.

Schalock, R. L., Karan, O. C., and Harper, R. S. 1980. An evaluation-remediation model for serving people with significant handicaps. Ment. Retard. 18:231–233.

Schalock, R. L., Ross, B. E., and Ross, I. 1976. Basic Skills Screening Test and Remediation Manual. Mid-Nebraska Mental Retardation Services, Hastings, NB.

Schalock, R. L., and Spearman, S. 1981. Environmental demands and the mentally retarded. In: K. Kiernan, R. B. Edgerton, and M. Begab (eds.), Impact of Specific Settings on Behavior and Development. University Park Press, Baltimore.

Scheerenberger, R. C. 1975. Managing Residential Facilities for the Developmentally Disabled. Charles C Thomas, Springfield, IL.

Scheerenberger, R. C. 1976. Deinstitutionalization and Institutional Reform. Charles C Thomas, Springfield, IL.

Scheerenberger, R. C. 1981. Deinstitutionalization: Trends and difficulties. In: R. H. Bruininks, C. E. Meyers, B. B. Sigford, and K. C. Lakin (eds.), Deinstitutionalization and Community Adjustment of Mentally Retarded Persons. Monograph No. 4. American Association on Mental Deficiency, Washington, DC.

Scheerenberger, R. C., and Felsenthal, D. 1977. Community settings for MR persons: Satisfaction and activities. Ment. Retard. 15(4):3–7.

Schein, E. H. 1970. Organizational Psychology. 2nd Ed. Prentice-Hall, Inc., Englewood Cliffs, NJ.

Schinke, S. P., and Landesman-Dwyer, S. 1981. Training staff in group homes serving mentally retarded persons. In: P. Mittler (ed.), Frontiers of Knowledge in Mental Retardation, Vol. 1: Social, Educational and Behavioral Aspects. University Park Press, Baltimore.

Schulman, E. D. 1980. Focus on the Retarded Adult: Programs and Services. C. V. Mosby Company, St. Louis.

Schutz, R. P., and Rusch, F. R. 1981. Competitive employment: Toward employment integration for mentally retarded persons. In: K. P. Lynch, W. E. Kiernan, and J. A. Stark (eds.), Prevocational and Vocational Education for Special Needs Youth: A Blueprint for the 80's. Paul H. Brookes Publishing Co., Baltimore.

Schwenkmeyer, B., and Goodman, M. E. 1972. Putting Cooperation to Work. Management Division, Academy for Educational Development, New York.

Seitz, V., Apfel, N. H., and Rosenbaum, L. K. 1981. Project Head Start and Follow Through: A longitudinal evaluation of adolescents. In: M. J. Begab, H. C. Haywood, and H. L. Garber (eds.), Psychosocial Influences in Retarded Performance. Vol. 2. Strategies for Improving Competence. University Park Press, Baltimore.

Sheldon, A., Barrett, D., and Gupta, A. 1978. Managing multi-institutional collaboration. Faculty discussion paper in Health Policy Management, Harvard School of Public Health, March 1978, Cambridge, MA.

Sherif, M. 1958. Superordinate goals in the reduction of intergroup conflict. Am. J. Sociol. 63:4–15.

Sigelman, C. K. 1976. A Machiavelli for planners: Community attitudes and selection of a group home site. Ment. Retard. 14(1):26–29.

Sink, J. M. 1981. Transfer of vocational skills. Paper presented at a Conference on Model Vocational Programs: New approaches for the 80's. Atlanta Association for Retarded Citizens, June 3, Atlanta, GA.

Sitkei, E. G. 1980. After group home living — what alternatives? Results of a two year mobility follow-up study. Ment. Retard. 18(1):9–13.

Skarnulis, S. 1976. Least restrictive alternatives in residential alternatives in residential services. Am. Assoc. Educ. Severely Profoundly Handicap. Rev. 1:1–20.

Smeets, P. M. 1981. Developing a calculator to enable retarded adults to make financial transactions. In: P. Mittler (ed.), Frontiers of Knowledge in Mental Retardation, Vol. 1. University Park Press, Baltimore.

Smith, C. B., and Cooney, L. L. 1979. Illinois Case Management Study, Vols. 1–3. Illinois Governor's Planning Council for Developmental Disabilities, Springfield, IL.

Smith, D. 1979. In Our Own Interest: A Handbook for the Citizen Lobbyist in State Legislatures. Madrona Publ., Seattle.

Smith, J. D., and Polloway, E. A. 1979. The dimension of adaptive behavior in mental retardation research: An analysis of recent practices. Am. J. Ment. Defic. 84:203–206.

Sorensen, J. E., and Grove, H. D. 1977. Cost-outcome and cost-effectiveness analysis: Emerging nonprofit performance evaluation techniques. Account. Rev. 52(3):658–675.

Sorensen, J. E., and Phipps, D. W. 1972. Cost finding: A tool for managing your community mental health center. Admin. Ment. Health 1(1):68–73.

Soyka, P. 1977. Thursday's Child Has Far to Go: Help at Home for Handicapped Children and Their Families. National Council for Homemaker-Home Health Aide Services, New York.

Spaniol, L. 1977. A program evaluation model for rehabilitation agencies and facilities. J. Rehabil. Admin. 1(2):4–15.

Sprague, R. L., and Baxley, G. B. 1978. Drugs for behavior management with comments on some legal aspects. In: J. Wortis (ed.), Mental Retardation and Developmental Disabilities, Vol. 5. Brunner/Mazel, Inc., New York.

Staats, A. W. and Butterfield, W. H. 1965. Treatment of non-reading in a culturally deprived juvenile delinquent: An application of reinforcement principles. Child Dev. 36:925–942.

Stacy, D., Doleys, D. M., and Malcolm, R. 1979. Effects of social-skills training in a community-based program. Am. J. Ment. Defic. 84(2):152–158.

Stark, J. A. 1978. A systems approach to barrier analysis. In: R. L. Schalock (ed.), A Model Comprehensive Service Delivery System for Persons with Developmental Disabilities. Illinois Governor's Planning Council on Developmental Disabilities, Springfield, IL.

State of Indiana, Division of Mental Retardation and Other Developmental Disabilities. July 1, 1979. Community Living Arrangements for Persons with Special Developmental Needs (Section 3). Indianapolis, IN.

State of Massachusetts Department of Mental Health. 1979. Resources for Programs Meeting Universal Needs, Pilot Application of Active Criteria for Program Services. Department of Mental Health, Boston.

State Office of Mental Retardation and Developmental Disabilities. 1980. A Compilation of Standards for Various Treatment and Residential Facilities. State of New York, State Office of Mental Retardation and Developmental Disabilities, Albany, NY.

Steinberg, H. I., Miller, J. R., and Menzel, T. E. 1981. The single audit in government. J. Accountancy, 32(June):56–66.

Sternlicht, M. 1977. Issues in counseling and psychotherapy with mentally retarded individuals. In: I. Bialer and M. Sternlicht (eds.), The Psychology of Mental Retardation: Issues and Approaches. Psychological Dimensions, New York.

Sternlicht, M., Schalock, R. L., and Harper, R. S. 1979. The viability of group living homes: The implications of semi-institutional living. Paper presented at the American Association on Mental Deficiency 103rd Annual Meeting, May 27–June 2, Miami Beach, FL.

Stern-Otago, K. L. 1980. Curriculum modification and instructional practices. In: G. D. Merrs (ed.), Handbook of Special Vocational Needs Education. Aspen Systems Corp., Rockville, MD.

Stoddard, S. 1978. Independent Living: Concept and programs. Am. Rehabil. 3(6):2–4.

Stores, G. 1975. Behavioral effects of antiepileptic drugs. Dev. Med. Child Neurol. 17:647–658.

Stromsdorfer, E. W. 1972. Review and Synthesis of Cost-Effectiveness Studies of Vocational and Technical Education. Ohio State University Press, Columbus, OH.

Struthers, R. D. 1977. A benefit/cost model developed in a state vocational rehabilitation agency. J. Rehabil. Admin. 1(2):26–39.
Stucky, P. E., and Newbrough, J. R. 1981. Mental health of mentally retarded persons. In: H. C. Haywood and J. R. Newbrough (eds.), Living Environments for Developmentally Retarded Persons. University Park Press, Baltimore.
Suchman, E. A. 1967. Evaluative Research: Principles and Practice in Public Service and Social Action Programs. Russell Sage Foundation, New York.
Suchman, E. A. 1972. Action for what? A critique of evaluative research. In: C. H. Weiss (ed.), Evaluating Action Programs: Readings in Social Action and Education. Allyn & Bacon, Inc., Boston.
Sutherland, J. W. 1977. Managing Social Service Systems. Petrocelli Books, New York.
Sutton, G. W., Michael, J. G., and Wanner, J. A. 1981. The least restrictive living alternative: Toward behavioral criteria for appropriate placement of mentally retarded persons. Paper presented at the American Association on Mental Deficiency Annual Convention, May 26, Detroit.
Swanson, B., and Willis, D. 1979. Understanding Exceptional Children and Youth. Rand McNally College Publishing Co., Chicago.
Switzky, H., Rotatori, A. F., Miller, T., and Freagon, S. 1979. The developmental model and its implications for assessment and instruction for severely/profoundly handicapped. Ment. Retard. 17(4):167–170.
Szymanski, L. S., and Tanguay, P. E. (eds.). 1980. Emotional Disorders of Mentally Retarded Persons. University Park Press, Baltimore.
Teffin, I. 1959. Six merit rating systems. Personnel J. 37:288–295.
Thompson, T. 1977. History of treatment and misconceptions concerning the mentally retarded. In: T. Thompson and J. Grabowski (eds.), Behavior Modification of the Mentally Retarded, 2nd Ed. Oxford University Press, New York.
Throne, J. M., Hand, R. J., Hupka, M. L., Lankford, C. W., Luther, K. M., McLennan, S. L., and Watson, J. B. 1977. Unified programming procedures for the mentally retarded. Ment. Retard. 15:14–17.
Toffler, A. 1980. The Third Wave. Bantam Books, New York.
Touché-Ross Report. 1980. Cost study of the community based mental retardation regions and the Beatrice State Developmental Center. Report submitted to Nebraska Department of Public Institutions, Lincoln, NB.
Tripodi, T., Fellin, P., and Epstein, I. 1978. Differential Social Program Evaluation. F. E. Peacock, Itasca.
Tripodi, T., and Harrington, J. 1979. Uses of time-series designs for formative program evaluation. J. Soc. Serv. Res. 3(1):67–78.
Tu, J. B. 1979. A survey of psychotropic medication in mental retardation facilities. J. Clin. Psychiatry 40:125–128.
Turner, R. 1969. The public perception of protest. Am. Socio. Rev. 34:815–831.
Turoff, M. 1970. The design of a policy delphi. Technol. Forecasting Soc. Change 2:15–21.
Tynan, D. D. 1980. Paraprofessionals in experiential training. Paper presented at the annual meeting of the American Association on Mental Deficiency, May 11–16, San Francisco.
Ulrey, G., and Schnell, R. 1981. A program for developing professional services at a residential institution. Ment. Retard. 19(4):163–167.
Underhill, W., and Newman, F. L. 1974. Developing a Unit of Service Cost Reporting System. Eastern Pennsylvania Psychiatric Institute, Philadelphia.

United Way of America. March 15, 1981. Management needs and the 1980's. p. 19. New York Times.

Upshur, C. C. 1982. Respite for mentally retarded and other disabled populations: Program models and family needs. Ment. Retard. 20(1):2–6.

Urban Institute. 1979. Report of the Comprehensive Service Needs Study. Urban Institute, Washington, DC.

U.S. Department of Health and Human Services, 1979. Training and Employment Services Policy Analysis. First year progress report. U.S. Department of Health and Human Services, Washington, DC.

U.S. Department of Labor. 1977. Dictionary of Occupational Titles. 4th Ed. U.S. Department of Labor, Washington, DC.

U.S. Departent of Labor, 1979. A Study of Wage Payments to Handicapped Clients in Sheltered Workshops Certified under the Fair Labor Standards Act. U.S. Department of Labor, Washington, DC.

U.S. Department of the Treasury, Internal Revenue Service. 1979. Publication 557: How to Apply for Recognition of Exemption. Washington, DC.

Valletutti, P. J., and Christopolis, F. 1977. Interdisciplinary Approaches to Human Services. University Park Press, Baltimore.

Vash, C. L. 1975. The psychology of disability. Report of the State of the Art Conference. Center for Independent Living, Berkeley, CA.

Waisman Center on Mental Retardation and Human Development, University of Wisconsin. 1976. Living in a Family Environment (LIFE): A Training Program for Group Home Parents. Stanfield House, Los Angeles.

The Wall Street Journal. America's Sheltered Workshops. October 17, 1979.

Walls, R. T., and Tseng, M. S. 1976. Measurement of client outcomes in rehabilitation. In: B. Bolton (ed.), Handbook of Measurement and Evaluation in Rehabilitation. University Park Press, Baltimore.

Walls, R. T., and Werner, T. J. 1977. Vocational behavior checklists. Ment. Retard. 15:30–35.

Walton, R. E., and Dutton, J. M. 1969. The management of interdepartmental conflict: A model and review. Admin. Sci. 14:522–542.

Watson, L. S. 1970. Behavior modification of residents and personnel in institutions for the mentally retarded. In: A. A. Baumeister and E. C. Butterfield (eds.), Residential Facilities for the Mentally Retarded. Aldine Publishing Company, Chicago.

Wehman, P. 1981. Competitive Employment: New Horizons for Severely Disabled Individuals. Paul H. Brookes Publishing Co., Baltimore.

Wehman, P., and McLaughlin, P. J. 1980. Vocational Curriculum for Developmentally Disabled Persons. University Park Press, Baltimore.

Wehman, P., Schleien, S., and Kiernan, J. 1980. Age appropriate recreation programs for severely handicapped youth and adults. JASH 5(4):395–407.

Weisgerber, R. A., Dahl, P. R.,, and Appleby, J. A. 1980. Training the Handicapped for Productive Employment. Aspen Systems Corp., Rockville, MD.

Weisman, D. C. 1982. A Practical Approach to Adapted Physical Education. Addison-Wesley Publishing Co., Reading, MA.

Weiss, C. H. (ed.). 1972. Evaluating Action Programs: Readings in Social Action and Education. Allyn & Bacon, Inc., Boston.

Weissman, H. H. 1973. Overcoming Mismanagement in the Human Service Professions. Jossey-Bass, San Francisco.

Weissman-Frisch, N., Crowell, F. A., and Inman, D. P. 1980. In-servicing vocational trainers: A multiple perspective evaluation approach. JASH 5(2):158–173.

Whitehead, C. W. 1979. Sheltered workshops in the decade ahead: Work and wages or welfare. In: T. Bellamy, G. O'Connor, and O. Karan (eds.), Vocational Rehabilitation for Developmentally Disabled Persons: Contemporary Service Strategies. University Park Press, Baltimore.

Whitehead, C. W. 1981. Final report: Training and employment services for handicapped individuals in sheltered workshops. U. S. Department of Health and Human Services, Office of the Assistant Secretary for Planning and Evaluation, Washington, DC.

Wicker, A. W. 1979. Ecological psychology: Some recent and prospective developments. Am. Psychol. 34(9):755–765.

Wiegerink, R., and Pelosi, J. W. (eds.). 1979. Developmental Disabilities: The DD Movement. Paul H. Brookes Publishing Co., Baltimore.

Wildavsky, A. 1972. The self-evaluating organization. Soc. Admin. 32:520–527.

Willer, B. 1978. Post-institutional adjustment of the retarded returned to the natural families. Paper presented at the annual convention of the American Association on Mental Deficiency, May, 1978, Denver, CO.

Willer, B. 1981. The future residential services for mentally retarded persons. Community Serv. Forum 1(4):1–4.

Willer, B., Scheerenberger, R. C., and Intagliata, J. 1978. Deinstitutionalization and mentally retarded persons. Community Ment. Health Rev. 3(4):1–12.

Willer, B., Scheerenberger, R. C., and Intagliata, J. 1980. Deinstitutionalization and mentally retarded persons. In: A. R. Novak and L. W. Heal (eds.), Integration of Developmentally Disabled Individuals into the Community. Paul H. Brookes Publishing Co., Baltimore.

Willms, J. D. 1981. Neighborhood attitudes toward group homes for mentally retarded adults. In: P. Mittler (ed.), Frontiers of Knowledge in Mental Retardation, Vol. 1. Social, Educational, and Behavioral Aspects. University Park Press, Baltimore.

Windle, C. 1962. Prognosis of mental subnormals. Am. J. Ment. Defic.: Monogr. Suppl. 66(5).

Wolfensberger, W. 1980. A call to wake up to the beginning of a new wave of "euthanasia" of severely impaired people. Educ. Train. Ment. Retard. 15(3):171–173.

Wolfensberger, W., Nirje, B., Olshansky, S., Perske, R., and Roos, P. 1972. The Principle of Normalization in Human Services. National Institute on Mental Retardation, University of York, Toronto, Canada.

Wolpert, J. August, 1978. Group homes for the mentally retarded: An investigation of neighborhood property impacts. Study prepared for the New York State Office of Mental Retardation and Developmental Disabilities, Albany, NY.

Wyatt, J. W., and Wyatt, M. B. 1971. Business Law: Principles and Cases. 4th Ed. McGraw-Hill Book Co., New York.

Yager, V. 1978. OT/PT at Whitmore. Tucson Unified School District Training Films, Tucson, AZ.

Yaron, A., and Walker, M. 1979. Do individualized habilitation plans preclude measurement of client change across agencies? In: J. Adams, C. B. Smith, and C. Travis (eds.), Readings on Interagency Evaluation. The Nisonger Center, Columbus, OH.

Ysseldyke, J. E., and Salvia, J. A. 1974. Diagnostic-prescriptive teaching: Two models. Except. Child. 41:181–186.

Zaharia, E. S., and Baumeister, A. A. 1978a. Estimated position replacement costs for technician personnel in a state's public facilities. Ment. Retard. 16:131–134.

Zaharia, E. S., and Baumeister, A. A. 1978b. Technician turnover and absenteeism in public residential facilities. Am. J. Ment. Defic. 82:580–593.

Zaharia, E. S., and Baumeister, A. A. 1979. Cross-organizational job satisfaction of technician-level staff members. Am. J. Ment. Defic. 84:36–39.

Zaleznik, A. 1966. Human Dilemmas of Leadership. Harper & Row, New York.

Zaleznik, A. 1970. Power and politics in organizational life. Harvard Bus. Rev. 70(4):47–60.

Zigler, E. 1966. Research on personality structure in the retardate. In: N. R. Ellis (ed.), International Review of Research in Mental Retardation, Vol. 2. Academic Press, Inc., New York.

Zigler, E., and Balla, D. A. 1977. Impact of institutional experience on the behavior and development of retarded persons. Am. J. Ment. Defic. 82(1):1–11.

Zigler, E., and Trickett, P. K. 1978. IQ, social competence, and evaluation of early childhood intervention programs. Am. Psychol. 33:789–798.

Zisfein, L., and Rosen, M. 1973. Personal adjustment training: A group counseling program for institutionalized mentally retarded persons. Ment. Retard. 11(4):16–20.

Zisfein, L., and Rosen, M. 1974. Effects of a personal adjustment training group counseling program. Ment. Retard. 12(3):50–53.

Zuckerman, H. S. 1979. Multi-institutional Hospital Systems. Hospital Research and Educational Trust, Chicago.

Zusman, J., and Wurster, C. R. 1975. Program Evaluation. D. C. Heath & Co., New York.

INDEX